Fatally Cricket

Fatally Cricket

Alan Haselhurst

The Professional and Higher Partnership Ltd

ISBN 978-1-907076-75-6
First published 2013 by The Professional and Higher Partnership Ltd
Registered address: Suite 7 Lyndon House, 8 King's Court, Willie Snaith Road,
Newmarket, Suffolk, CB8 7SG, UK
http://pandhp.com

Credits
Cartoons: Hoby (www.hobycartoons.com)
Text design and typesetting:
The Running Head Limited (www.therunninghead.com)
Cover design: Richard Carr, Carrdesignstudio (www.carrstudio.co.uk)
Printing and binding: Berforts Information Press (www.berforts.co.uk)

Contents

For Annabel, my first grandchild

With love – and in case anyone else omits
to dedicate a book to her.

Acknowledgements

THE FACT THAT THIS BOOK appears owes much to the encouragement of my publisher, Anthony Haynes. In the autumn of 2011 he gave me lunch in the course of which he politely enquired if I had done any more writing. In fact I had. Four pages compiled about a year earlier. Then my new parliamentary responsibilities took over to such an extent that pen and paper (yes, I write in longhand) had to be put aside. Still I took it as encouragement that Anthony's enquiry was made. During the Christmas break I retrieved the four pages and added another thirty.

Wanting to incorporate a sort of whodunit into the activities of the Outcasts Cricket Club, I continued to doubt my capacity. I am a devotee of detective fiction. All Agatha Christie's work was absorbed in my early life, but I know I am not in the same class. Nor have I the time to research forensic details as mastered by modern writers of crime novels. But, heck, my books are meant to be light-hearted. So spurred on by the body count, I kept going. I hope I have broken no golden rules of the genre whilst at the same time perpetrating a little mild deception. Any fault is down to me – unless you want to blame Anthony for tickling my vanity.

I am seriously grateful to him for his continuing support. I would like to thank David Williams of The Running Head for his professional enhancements. My wife, Angela, has meticulously and tirelessly (?) transferred all my words to disc. My son, David (www.hobycartoons.com), has once again produced some amusing illustrations. He, his brother Mark, brother-in-law Gavin and his sister Emma have all vetted the script: I have appreciated their advice and comments. The supportive words of Michael Dobbs and Ed Smith are extremely welcome.

More than anything else an author needs readers. So, if you have got this far, I owe you my warmest thanks. I hope your sense of humour coincides with mine – and you don't need a degree in cricket to get some pleasure from this book.

Are there to be any more? I rather fancy the idea of the Outcasts playing the Lords and Commons Cricket Club. I'm even twenty pages into it. So, Anthony Haynes willing, *Politically Cricket* might see the light of day.

Now, Annabel, it's time for your bedtime story. Let's see, where have we got to? Have we had the third death yet?

Members of the Outcasts Cricket Club

Rashid Ali
Colin Banks
Alan Birch
Ray Burrill
Phil Cole
Charlie Colson
Dean Faulds
John Furness
Richard Furness
Tim Jackson
Winston Jenkins
Toby Lederwood
Kevin Newton
Harry Northwood
Jon Palmer
David Pelham
Nigel Redman
Tom Redman
Greg Roberts
Basil Smith
Stewart Thorogood
Simon Crossley (Scorer)
Syd Breakwell (Umpire)

A SHOT RANG OUT. It was a harsh intrusion into the peaceful setting of a village cricket match. In the countryside gunshots are not unusual. Farmers are not averse to potting rabbits or scaring birds off their crops. In those circumstances more than one shot would be expected. It might have been a car backfiring. It was the fact that some people thought they had heard a scream that tended to rule out these explanations. However, no further disturbance occurred. Spectators' attention gradually drifted back to the action being played out in front of them.

Three members of the Outcasts Cricket Club – the visiting team – were in no position to offer an opinion on what might and might not have happened to upset the even tenor of events. Having not been picked to play, Tom Redman, Kevin Newton and John Furness were ostensibly part of the support contingent. At this particular time they were closeted in the Snug bar of The Cow's Corner, an excellent establishment always equipped with the finest real ales – quite simply the kind of hostelry which every cricket ground should have in close attendance. Since the landlord had added his new dining area the Snug had become especially well insulated from the sounds of outdoor activity. The only noise to rise above the level of conversation was the regular whoosh as the pumps dispensed another foaming pint. Tom, Kevin and John still had two varieties to sample before stepping out to engage with what was happening in (and around) the match.

The shot, with or without the scream, had not made any severe impression on proceedings in the field of play beyond the batsman from the home team choosing to take a fresh guard. As always in this fixture it was a hard-fought contest. The Outcasts had yet to record a victory on this ground. The bowler, Stewart Thorogood, glanced heavenwards as though seeking divine inspiration. He hitched his trousers. Three balls in the over remained. Stewart ran in to deliver another medium-paced ball which passed off stump. The batsman offered no stroke. A healthy-sized crowd continued to ponder the outcome of the game.

Some patrons strolled to and from The Cow's Corner. The sun shone. A light breeze rippled across the ground. The batsman dabbed Stewart's next ball to third man and walked a comfortable single. The neatness of the shot earned him a smattering of polite applause. The hapless mis-field of a day-dreaming Richard Furness earned a louder response as it gifted the batsman three extra runs. For the devoted lover of cricket the scene was idyllic. Even the most disinterested casual observer might have given a nod of approval on coming upon this tableau of traditional English village life. The countryside at its best. Unspoiled. A joyous day. Carefree it might be said.

There was just one little snag. In a house neighbouring the ground a man lay dead. He was the eighth to die.

Introduction

IT HAD BEGUN SOME YEARS EARLIER in a bar, as often things do. January. St Albans. Charlie Colson, passable all-rounder with the Outcasts Cricket Club, was doing his day job. He was attending a Paint Seminar. Once the serious business was out of the way delegates drifted to the bar in the hotel and conference centre, which was St Albans' newest attraction. Charlie was feeling very pleased with himself. He had made several useful contacts and taken, by way of bonus, a few orders. No harm he thought in one or two drinks and a little more networking before the end-of-seminar dinner. For a while bonhomie prevailed. A few rounds were consumed. Then numbers thinned. Some people left to get ready for dinner. Others just left. It made Charlie question what had persuaded him to stay. It was Friday night. Fellow Outcasts would be gathering at their favourite watering hole. A quick call or two and he was certain he would be able to link up with his mates. Then again he had splashed out £40 by reserving a place for dinner.

His musing was interrupted by a voice coming from over his shoulder. 'It looks like it's just you and me now. How about buying a girl a drink?' So he was not alone. The lady in question must have been powdering her nose. He had thought from earlier that she had had her eye on him. He hoped that her scrutiny meant no second thoughts about the 1000 gallon order for vinyl emulsion which he had prised out of her just after lunch. 'Sure,' he said smilingly, 'same again?' He ordered a white wine spritzer and another pint of Gilder's Special, a brew which had been new to him three pints ago. They touched glasses. She gave him what he thought was a cheeky grin. It made her look younger, Charlie thought, and really quite attractive for someone who might have been anything up to twice his age.

The following morning Charlie was in reflective mood as he tucked into a second helping at the breakfast buffet. He was hungry and attracted a few comments about the two empty places at last night's dinner. Charlie had been otherwise engaged. No salesman could have done more to consolidate an order. They had talked paint, both matt and gloss, but not for long. They had gossiped about some of their fellow delegates before straying into other subjects of mutual interest. It was unusual, Charlie thought, to discover a woman with so much enthusiasm for cars. The works of Gilbert and Sullivan kept them absorbed at intervals. It was only shortly before lights out that cricket was mentioned. Charlie's companion said she knew someone who was a very keen cricketer. He played for a club in a village somewhere in Essex. Middle Daychurch it was called. Charlie had never heard of it. Before he fell asleep though he must have mentioned his own involvement with cricket. When he woke, he really was alone. No-one was powdering their nose in the bathroom. One souvenir of the encounter remained: a folded sheet of hotel writing paper. It contained a brief message: 'For cricket in M.D. ring Roy (03333 876543) and mention my name'. She had signed herself Helen with an X.

Charlie chewed his way through another portion of Cumberland sausage as he struggled to recall those parts of his night which were less obvious than others. What was the connection between Helen, whom he had only known in her capacity as a manager of a hardware retail company in the West Country, and a cricket club in Essex? What had they discussed? Had he told her about the Outcasts? Had he unwittingly made some sort of commitment on behalf of his club? Who was Roy? Should he ring him? Two rounds of toast and three black coffees put Charlie in better shape to be able to take a more balanced view of his experience. It had certainly been unexpected reward for a 1000 gallon order of vinyl emulsion. He could only wonder what premium gloss might have led to.

Charlie had been reluctant to mention this episode to any of his fellow Outcasts. This was untypical, because in laddish style he was wont to be exuberant about his exploits. Never more so than when he was fuelled by drink. However, something happened which caused him to be discreet. A week after the business gathering in St Albans he was at a wedding. It was a company colleague who was getting hitched. The emphasis was more on colleague than an actual mate. Charlie suspected that the guy was short of real pals. So he thought he was doing a good deed by agreeing to be an usher. Once sucked into the arrangements he fairly quickly regretted his impulsiveness.

The organisation of the wedding was understandably in the hands of the bride's parents. They proved to be uninterested in input from any other

quarter, least of all their daughter's fiancé. It was decreed that the principals were to be dressed in period costume. Charlie could see that not even the groom was comfortable with this arrangement. However, the groom did not protest. He was either utterly spineless or too much in love. Charlie hated the whole idea, quite sure in his own mind and especially when in front of a mirror that he looked a buffoon. The Outcasts must never be allowed to see a photograph. Worse was to come. The extravagance behind the costume was not matched in the wedding breakfast. The meal was of the rubber chicken variety. The supply of sparkling white wine was inadequate and no barrel of beer was available to lighten Charlie's mood. The speeches had been long and unfunny. He positioned himself as far from the dance floor as possible whilst assessing his chances of making an early exit. Suddenly there was an arm around his waist. It arrived with a question. 'Are you as pissed off with this as I think you are?' That was how he met Liz Allason. It was a life-changing event.

Another factor reinforced his determination to put events at St Albans firmly behind him. Out of good professional practice he had made a post-sales call to Helen's company. He was told that she no longer worked there, but Charlie would be pleased to know that the paint was selling well. Subject to competitive pricing and assured delivery he might expect repeat orders. Such good news dissuaded Charlie from probing Helen's whereabouts. His company's interests, not to mention his end-of-year bonus, were foremost. He put the lady and with her Middle Daychurch Cricket Club out of his mind. His thoughts now concentrated on Liz, who had readily agreed a first date and then a second. As far as he was concerned a chapter had been closed and Charlie did not expect it to reopen. And so it seemed as an enjoyable cricket season passed whilst his relationship with Liz flourished.

First encounter

COME WINTER THE OUTCASTS had to make plans for the following season. They did not have a settled list of matches. Their fixture list was more a work in progress. Opponents came and went. Not every club found the Outcasts to their taste. It might be a complete mismatch of cricketing prowess which caused a fixture to be discontinued. Alternatively the Outcasts may have turned up late or short of numbers or drunk or in any combination of these circumstances. It was therefore slow progress to build up a programme which would keep them occupied most of the summer weekends.

Their unofficial headquarters was The Sink and Plumber. Situated in south-west London it was a haven for the real ale connoisseur, but not for the smart set. The landlord tolerated a measure of riotous behaviour. Correspondingly his clientele were not looking for fancy furnishings and fittings. The mutual satisfaction lay in the amount of beer which the establishment shifted. Members of the Outcasts were the prime shifters. It had not taken the landlord long to recognise that the pattern of his sales reflected the presence or otherwise of the Outcasts. In full attendance on a regular basis in the winter months takings soared to such an extent that the landlord would start to contemplate how luxurious a holiday he might be able to afford in the summer.

When the Outcasts met there to discuss their prospects for that self-same summer, a cloud of gloom descended. There had been an appreciable fallout from the fixture list of the previous season. Recriminations were inevitable. The Outcasts generally thought it better to admit their failings or indiscretions. Few of them could claim an unblemished record. On this occasion there was early recognition that they should never have gone to Badmore Hill. It would have been far better even at short notice to have pulled out of the match claiming illness or whatever. The day of the match, a Sunday, followed two successive parties to which Tim Jackson, who looked after their social interests, had gained them access. The second party was held in a private house of some elegance. The owners might have wished that the Outcasts had pulled out of this as well, because the property and its landscaped garden had lost much of its elegance by the time that the last Outcast had been carried out. The eight who managed to present themselves at Badmore Hill did their club no favour. The iciness of their reception had clearly not melted by the time the attempt to renew the fixture was made.

Colin Banks was the Outcasts' Mr Charm, at once their fastest bowler and fastest mover. He was the one to put his hand up when the case of Trimhorne Green Cricket Club was raised. 'It was a mistake anyone could have made.' Colin looked around for any signs of sympathy. All he got were some nervous smiles and from David Pelham a wink although equal penitence was due. On arrival at the ground Colin had taken an immediate shine to a bubbly redhead. Having eased through his chat-up lines, he learned that she was the sister of one of the opposing players and would be loyally watching the match. With the Outcasts fielding first Colin had done some mild bragging about his bowling and looked forward to chatting (and in his mind something more) during and after the tea interval.

David Pelham's exact role in the team had not been defined. His own estimation was a batsman who bowled. His record to date persuaded his friends to see him more as a bowler, who batted. It remained a close call. But on that day judgement was not to be advanced as he was cast in the role of twelfth man. His eye had also fallen on the bubbly redhead – too late as Colin had all too swiftly moved in. There was honour amongst Outcasts and so David moved on. A twelfth man in a village cricket match is not always kept busy. So David had scope to wander about, in and out of the pavilion, keeping half an eye on the cricket. An hour had passed when there was a scurry of new arrivals, principally it seemed of ladies to prepare the tea. David had been called out to supply a pair of replacement gloves to Kevin Newton, who was deputising behind the stumps for the Outcasts' first-choice keeper, Rashid Ali. Re-entering the pavilion David had nodded in friendly fashion to the bubbly redhead, who seemed to be dividing her attention between the field of play and a fashion magazine. Inside he did a double-take, for there buttering bread was a dead ringer for the girl outside. He felt compelled to check. Yes, there were two of them. Not twins he judged, but sufficiently alike to stimulate his interest. 'Hi, I'm David, can I help?'

The seeds had been sown; the bitter harvest was gathered when the Outcasts were an unpromising 67–4 chasing 223. David had sought to ingratiate himself further by drying the teacups and plates. 'How about a stroll?' might have been thought an inoffensive gambit, but David had managed to load it with sufficient innuendo that the response was distinctly icy. 'I think not.' David, sensing trouble, backpedalled. 'I mean it's nice outside and, er, we might catch up with your sister.' 'My sister?' The initial scowl gave way to puzzlement before enlightenment took over. 'Oh, you mean . . . no, you foolish man, she's my daughter.' David felt a cold hand clutch his innards. The grip tightened when out of the rear window he saw the daughter stumble out of the adjoining copse followed a second later by Colin Banks with green stains on his trousers that had nothing to do with his bowling stint. The girl's hair and top seemed to have suffered collateral damage. She had not presented a happy sight. The match had ended in considerable discord.

More admissions had followed at The Sink and Plumber. The air was cleared. Catharsis was complete. With another round purchased thoughts turned to how the gaps in the fixture list could be plugged. Stewart Thorogood, a genuine Outcasts all-rounder, had shown some administrative initiative by bringing with him a list of club sides in Essex and Hertfordshire. This was the Outcasts' favourite area of operation. Stewart distributed copies to his colleagues. As they went through the sheets of paper there were various cries and comments: 'Oh Christ, we can't go back there'; 'Well, they're out, especially since you started that fire, Phil' (this was directed at Phil Cole, very much a bits and pieces cricketer, and provoked immediate retaliation: 'Isn't Loveridge Masway where you were as sick as a dog all over the bar, John?') And so it went on, punctuated by one or two positive suggestions and yet another round of the pub's guest bitter, Bayliss's Guardian Ale.

'Hang on a minute, there's one here that rings a bell.' This was Charlie Colson. 'Middle Daychurch. Have we tried them?' 'Not really,' chipped in Alan Birch, the Outcasts' most successful batsman and pretentious gourmand. 'It's a bit of a funny set-up actually,' Alan continued, 'dominated by one family and difficult to break into. Mind you, there's a very good restaurant in the village'. 'But have we made any contact recently?' persisted Charlie. Alan looked towards Stewart and then to Winston Jenkins. They both shook their heads. No-one else piped up. 'Well then,' said Charlie, 'I may be able to help'. He struggled to extract his wallet from the front pocket of his slim-fit jeans which he had bought in defiance of Liz's suggestion that easy-fit might have been a better match for his beer consumption. Finally he produced a crumpled piece of paper. 'This is it. I've got a contact. It's a guy called Roy. From memory I think he's one of their team. There's a number here.' Charlie spent the rest of the evening fending off questions as to how he had come by the information. What he could not fend off was responsibility for making the call.

By the time they staggered out of The Sink and Plumber a shortlist of prospective club opponents had been put together. Stewart Thorogood had undertaken to find out contact details for the various fixture secretaries, but insisted that the chore of making the actual contacts be shared out. The second accomplishment of the gathering had been the recruitment of two new members. They were at the time sixteen in number. In a discussion at the end of the previous season it had been recognised that, even assuming fitness (tested in the Outcasts' case usually more by their social habits than by sporting injury), a membership of sixteen was insufficient guarantee that every fixture could be fulfilled with eleven players and a twelfth man.

The twins, Tom and Nigel Redman, were in the retail book trade and had the additional tie of a demanding mother who lived with hypochondria. Alan Birch was a retail pharmacist and could not guarantee his availability for every Saturday match. John Furness worked at his family's garden centre. Jon Palmer sold luxury cars and Colin Banks houses; both could find themselves on duty at weekends, however sympathetic their employers. Stewart Thorogood nursed political ambitions and was sometimes diverted from cricket to meetings at which he could advance his interests. That left nine players whose occupations were less likely to intrude on weekends, but that was not the same thing as assuring their presence in a fit and proper state to play. So it was good news when Dean Faulds announced that when giving blood he had found himself on a recuperation bed next to a young guy called Ray Burrill, who was training to be a vet. This was the first time that his fellow Outcasts were made aware that Dean gave blood. Much ribaldry followed. 'They're taking it 40% proof now are they, Dean?' It took a while to establish that Ray had moved recently into the area and professed to have played regularly when at school and 'wouldn't mind a game'.

Colin Banks was next to contribute. 'I've just got a new flatmate.' Before he could say any more the rejoinders quickly came. 'Who is she?' 'Blonde or brunette?' 'Settling down, are you?' And there was more before Colin could explain that he had decided to rent his spare room. His mother had called him a few weeks ago to say that the son of a friend of hers was moving to

London to work for a bank. Could Colin as an estate agent fix him up with a flat? In truth Colin's lifestyle was increasing his expenditure whilst his commission was not keeping pace. He gave his mother a guarded response and agreed to meet the individual in question. Colin had to admit that he took an immediate liking to Greg Roberts. He was pleased to see that he had a taste for good ale if not a capacity equal to that of Colin. It was more with a view to his personal enrichment than thoughts of the Outcasts which brought Colin to the point of offering a flat-share to Greg. It was beyond this point that the subject of cricket was first mentioned. Greg alluded to the England team's upcoming overseas tour. Colin immediately proposed another round overcoming slight protest from his companion. A lively discussion followed in which Colin found that he and Greg were entirely of the same mind about the composition of the touring party. Colin mentally adjusted downwards the level of rent he intended to propose before getting round to asking whether Greg actually played cricket. 'Well, I like to, but I'm honestly not much cop.' That was enough for Colin. Modesty became the Outcasts. 'I'll be in touch,' he said as they parted.

No-one was admitted to membership of the Outcasts simply on the say-so of his proposer. There was nothing like a formal interview. The candidates were invited to one of the Outcasts' regular social gatherings at The Sink and Plumber. It was a matter then of congeniality. The only test was the candidate's appreciation of real ale. Capacity for it was also taken into account. The landlord customarily had three varieties on sale. Each had to be sampled and assessed. It was only after both Ray and Greg had been judged to have satisfied the examiners in that respect that any questions relating to their cricket prowess were raised. Of the two Ray appeared to have more to offer in terms of playing ability. Greg probably shaded it in the consumption stakes. His sharing a flat with Colin would be likely to bring him on well. Ray was visibly failing during the sixth round, but this was not held against him. Fortunately his new comrades would never learn how violently sick he had been when he had got back to his digs. It would prove to be only a temporary handicap.

And so ahead of the new season the Outcasts' strength had been increased, at least in a numerical sense. They could boast in addition their own umpire in the person of ex-policeman, Syd Breakwell, who had a comprehensive knowledge of the laws of cricket albeit with no comprehensive skill in applying them in real-time situations. The Outcasts were also lucky to have a regular scorer, who had not so far missed a match. Simon Crossley's value was boosted by his single-minded interest in scoring. He had no ambition to play. He kept immaculate score sheets. His interest in cricket bordered on the obsessive. Shy and retiring by nature, he had not to date been infected by the somewhat brash joie-de-vivre exhibited by the players whose exploits he chronicled. He was Mr Accuracy and Mr Reliability combined.

A great deal of work had had to be done to reconstruct the fixture list. All the Outcasts had gone about their assigned tasks with diligence and in many instances great persistence. Charlie Colson's experience was the most vivid. It perplexed him as well. The first move was to ring the number which Helen had left with a view to speaking to the man called Roy. Charlie tried several times, but the number just rang out. There was no connection to an answer machine. He was starting to think he had been the victim of a hoax when one morning after letting the phone ring for more than a minute someone answered. For want of any better opening Charlie said, 'Is that Roy?' 'Roy who?' 'I don't know.' 'Well, how am I expected to know?' On a different tack, 'Is that Middle Daychurch Cricket Club?' 'No, it ain't.' At that Charlie was about to give up and replace the receiver, but the voice at the other end said, 'This is Middle Daychurch Sports Club.' Charlie could not stop himself responding with, 'Can I speak to Roy then?' 'Look mate,' came the reply, 'I've already told you I don't know no Roy. I'm just the meter man doing my round and I'm now getting behind my schedule chatting to you like this.' 'You couldn't possibly tell me who the bill gets sent to when you've done your very valuable job?' 'I don't know about that, mate, because that kind of information is confidential.' 'Please.' 'It's more than my job's worth, mate, but hang on a minute there's a note on the board here saying all enquiries to Roy Groves.' 'I thought you said you didn't know anyone called Roy.' 'I don't, mate, I've never met him.' It showed much for Charlie's resilience that he maintained his composure to make a last effort forlorn though it might be. 'Is there a phone number with the name? There was silence at the other end and then some muttering. 'I don't know whether I should.' Pause. 'But it's been nice talking to you. I can tell you're an educated man. Play cricket, do you?' Pause. 'Oh, maybe it won't do harm.' Pause. '876421. But don't tell anyone I told you. I've got to go now.' The phone was put down before Charlie had time to say thanks. He hoped the dialling code was the same as the one given by Helen.

Seemingly it was, but that did not help to advance matters. The answer phone message which met Charlie Colson's first call was, unlike many he had heard, a model of clarity. Nothing fancy. No accompanying jingle. No incomprehensible jabber. Just a straightforward statement: 'You have reached the home of Roy and Jeanette Groves. There's no-one here to take your call at the moment. Please leave a message stating your name and number and we'll get back to you as soon as possible. Thank you for calling. Goodbye.' Charlie's satisfaction lasted three days during which no return call had been made. Maybe his message had not been received. There could have been a fault on the Groves' answering machine. So he tried again. Still no luck. Still the automated response. Within a fortnight Charlie had grown heartily fed-up with the smoothly modulated voice of, he presumed, Roy Groves.

More than two weeks having passed Charlie was gearing himself up to report failure to his fellow Outcasts. He realised that not every village cricket club had got as far as setting up its own website. Any other means of trying to get a fix on Middle Daychurch Cricket (or Sports) Club would involve more research time than Charlie was minded to give. In any case other Club members had been having better luck and so the Outcasts were not going to have too much of an idle season after all. So Charlie had pretty well given up on Middle Daychurch when Liz greeted him on his return home (they had become more intimate by then) with the news that a Mr Groves had called. There would come a time when Charlie would wish he had not.

Roy Groves had left his office number. When Charlie called it the next day he was not expecting to be confronted by a multiple choice menu which included the advice that his call might be monitored for training purposes. Having digested that he was connected to a firm called Turnbury, Lomax and Smith (no mention of Groves) who seemed to be involved in tax matters and financial advice, Charlie (not knowing the extension of the person to whom he wished to speak) finally got through to the operator and asked for Mr Groves. 'May I ask who's calling?' Charlie obliged. 'May I ask what it is in connection with?' 'It's a little difficult to explain,' said Charlie realising that he had given no prior indication to Roy Groves why he wanted to speak to him. As he had got his name from the notice-board of the Middle Daychurch Sports Club he had blithely assumed that the nature of his call would have been obvious to Mr Groves. 'I'm returning his call.' 'You're not a tax inspector, are you?' Charlie assured her that whatever else he was he was not a tax inspector. 'I'll see if he's free. Please hold.' Some seconds passed. 'I'm putting you through.' There was a click and then the line went dead. Charlie gave vent to his feelings before steeling himself to repeat the process. Again there would come a time when he would look back on that decision with regret.

Charlie's mood softened when Roy Groves was profuse with apology. Charlie's first call must have come just as the Groves had departed on their annual skiing holiday. A fortnight in Zermatt had been extended by an accident incurred by his wife. ('Yes, she's well on the road to recovery now, thank you.') They had returned home to a power outage ('It has been a severe cold snap, hasn't it? I hope you weren't affected') and he'd had difficulty retrieving messages. He was so sorry that he had not thought to give Charlie his direct line number. Finally Charlie got the chance to explain his business. Roy Groves had listened without interruption until Charlie had completed his somewhat convoluted story. Then he said, 'I don't have much to do with the cricket side of things at the club. I'm simply their accountant, but I also help them with the business and administrative running of the club. There's someone else you'll have to talk to if it's a cricket matter'. Charlie was starting to speak again when Roy Groves cut in. 'On second thoughts before you make any approach it might be a good idea if I told you a bit about the club. It's, ah, shall we say, a little unusual. Look, why don't we have lunch? Could you spare the time? Perhaps a Saturday? There's a very good local restaurant.' Charlie thought he had heard some of this before. It was interesting that Alan Birch's remarks were being confirmed. He could so easily have concluded that pursuit of Middle Daychurch was not worth any further bother. Yet he could not help feeling intrigued. He accepted the invitation and a date was set. A date with destiny indeed.

It was nothing much to look at. A converted village hall with an extension scarcely evoked an image justifying the high-blown name which it had been accorded. Without any traditional or cultural link with the Essex village in which it stood Le Rêve Royal had nevertheless established a burgeoning reputation. It was rumoured that a Michelin inspector had already called. As to the fare on offer the restaurant's name did not mislead. It was very French. The same could not be said of the proprietors although their constant front-of-house exchanges in French gave a more than passable impression of Parisian roots. They were in fact Essex boys through and through although they had met in France, trained there and it was there too they had fallen in love.

Inside, the impression gained did much to compensate for the exterior. It was immaculate in an understated way. It was also packed. 'I'm surprised it does lunches on a Saturday,' remarked Charlie when he and Roy Groves had been seated. Within a few minutes he had revised upwards his view of the accountant who seemed altogether a jollier character than his office persona had conveyed. He nevertheless wore a suit which contrasted sharply with Charlie's rugby shirt and worn jeans and with how most of the clientele were dressed. 'They're booked out in the evenings,' said Roy Groves. 'If you want to come for dinner, you have to make a reservation months ahead. At lunch times during the week they get a lot of business trade. So as a sop to the locals they began Saturday lunchtime opening.' He added with a smile, 'And they offer a discount to anyone living within a ten mile radius. I just qualify! Anyway let's eat and then I'll tell you about the village sports club.'

Charlie Colson received a thorough background briefing. There were three Daychurch villages as Charlie had already ascertained. Near Daychurch and Far Daychurch were no more than hamlets. Middle Daychurch was the largest settlement and the most picturesque. It was helped by having a recognisable village centre which was enhanced on one side by the cricket ground and on the other by a large pond surrounded by willows on green banks from which a profusion of daffodils was already visible. The population was about four hundred. In numerical terms there was a dominant family which came from farming stock, but had spread over the years into a range of other activities. Control of the cricket club had been in its hands for three generations.

The family was called Carter. Its present head, Edwin Carter, had played cricket for Middle Daychurch for sixty-five years. He was now in his eighty-second year. Until three years ago he had been wicketkeeper, but when the extras per innings which he had conceded had begun to mount to serious proportions he was finally relieved of the gloves. He had then seized the umpire's coat from Bill Pledger, who had stood for the Middle Daychurch Club for fifteen years and was better sighted than his usurper. Edwin Carter had taken less than three months to establish himself as the most partisan umpire on the circuit. It was a reputation which he relished. Naturally he was the club chairman. He made it his principal duty to select the team. It was with the greatest distaste that he had been forced to abandon the traditional rule that only someone born in Middle Daychurch could join the club. The rule had been relaxed only to cover the two other Daychurch villages. Even with this change it was rare for members of the Carter family to account for less than half the team. 'It's a tyrannical set-up,' concluded Roy Groves, 'and you need to know that they are always highly competitive.'

'So why do other clubs continue to play them?' Charlie thought that was a reasonable first question. Roy Groves spread his hands expansively. 'You've got to understand that there are many sides that relish the challenge. They like being tested.' Mindful of the club which he represented, Charlie's follow-up was quick. 'And the others?' Roy Groves smiled. 'You see it's a lovely village, it's a good ground, for all its idiosyncrasies the club prides itself on good hospitality and there's a fantastic pub. Have you had a chance to see it?' Charlie had to admit that he hadn't and a surreptitious glance at his watch told him he would be pushed to make it if they closed the doors at 3 p.m. in winter.

'Is it generally a strong team?' 'Yes and no,' came the reply. 'It's all a question of how far family loyalty or prejudice affects team selection. When the old man was playing towards the end they were gifting runs to their opponents. I don't know a lot about cricket, but it must have been like ten players taking on twelve. That began to cause unrest in family circles. Don't mistake me, the club has some good players even if some of them are called Carter.'

'Do you think they'd give the Outcasts a game?' Roy Groves scratched his head. 'I've really no idea, but I don't see why not – if you're still interested after what I've told you. I don't think their fixture list is overloaded. In recent years some clubs have lost patience with them.' Charlie laughed. 'You don't exactly sound like a recruiting sergeant.' 'Well, that isn't any part of my portfolio. I don't really have anything to do with the cricket.' His saying that triggered a thought in Charlie's mind. 'I notice the club is actually called the Middle Daychurch Sports Club. Is there any significance in its being a sports club? What else do they play?' 'Nothing,' came the reply. Seeing the expression on Charlie's face, Roy Groves quickly added, 'There's a story to that as well'. His guest convincingly avoided a sigh whilst realising that the prospect of an investigatory visit to the pub was fading.

It seemed that a rumour had circulated a couple of years ago that a group of people wanted to establish a football club in the village. There was only one parcel of vacant land designated or indeed suitable for recreational purposes. It was owned by an elderly widow of comfortable means and meagre financial acumen. She had kept hold of the land as insurance cover for her social care needs. Edwin Carter had not been slow to react. Himself a widower of no more than three weeks' standing at the time, he had proposed marriage to the widow, Ethel Daniels, and been accepted. This was sufficient to give him de facto control of the land. He pushed through a constitutional amendment converting Middle Daychurch Cricket Club into a sports club and announced that he would inaugurate a football club once he had any necessary permissions. To date, apart from the change to the club's rules, nothing else had occurred. The board outside the ground still read Middle Daychurch Cricket Club. All this had left many people disappointed, not least, it was assumed, Mrs Daniels. Edwin Carter had professed his belief in a long engagement.

'So no football yet then,' concluded Charlie. 'Will it happen, do you think?' 'Oh, I think so, eventually, but, as you will have gathered from what I've said, it was a predatory move on the old man's part. He didn't want anyone else muscling in on sports activities in the village. I think his sons will have a more relaxed attitude.' The accountant hesitated. 'Or his grandsons. And, of course, if he doesn't tie the knot, Mrs Daniels' brother might want a say in the matter.' Putting aside that last thought, Colin had to ask, 'Just how many Carters are there?' 'Put it this way. On a numbers basis they could field a full side, but some of them don't play and from time to time some of the others are not available. That's particularly the case with the ones at school or college.'

'This patriarch,' said Charlie 'seems something of a handful. Do you mind my asking why you are happy to do work for him?' Roy Groves took the question in good part. 'Well, he pays me. I suppose that helps. What I do is not very demanding. It's all background stuff. I don't have too much direct contact with him, but I've always got on with him when we do see each other. He's a rogue, I suppose, but in a funny sort of way I quite like him. There's a lot that don't and that's for sure. Take the former umpire I mentioned, Bill Pledger. He took off very threateningly. Didn't say anything, but if looks could kill.' 'Is he still around?' 'We don't see much of him these days unless we have need to go to the garage he keeps on the other side of Near Daychurch. Have you had a chance to see the ground yet?' It was probably a bit late for the pub, but Charlie reckoned that he would not have completed his task unless he had set foot inside the Middle Daychurch ground. 'No, let's do it,' he said, 'if you're sure you have time.'

They got up from the table. Charlie started to ask whether he could go halves on the bill although he had not seen one presented. 'Don't worry,' said Roy Groves, 'it's on my account.' Charlie hoped his expression of gratitude hid any feeling of relief. Even Saturday prices were well above his own budget. The joint owners, Marcel and Pierre (Marty and Pete to their close friends), obviously used to seeing Roy Groves, bade them an effusive farewell. At his host's suggestion they walked to the ground. 'Probably do us good straight after lunch,' he had said. It was a fine day and it took not much more than five minutes to reach the club's ground. Through long experience Charlie's eyes found The Cow's Corner first. If they did not deceive him, it seemed it might still be open. Before he could be sure his attention was drawn to the pavilion.

Middle Daychurch's cricket pavilion was an imposing building. In design it was reminiscent on a smaller scale of the pavilion which graced Lord's Cricket Ground. There was a flight of steps to the entrance door. Charlie discovered inside a foreshortened Long Room across which ran a balcony reached by stairs at either end and leading to separate dressing rooms for the players. At the back were a kitchen and a meeting room. Charlie glanced enquiringly at Roy Groves, who nodded and confirmed that this was all the work of Edwin Carter and his now deceased brother. However, he went on to explain that it was not the original building. The old pavilion had been pulled down after control of the club had been wrested by Edwin's father from the hands of the Hamilton family who had been previous benefactors. There had been a bitter struggle and although it had happened half a century ago there was still lingering resentment in some quarters.

They were about to part company when Charlie remembered to ask, 'How's Helen?' Roy Groves looked at him blankly. 'Helen who, I don't think I . . .,' but Charlie cut him off. 'You know, Helen Morrison, she's in hardware.' 'I don't know any Helen, I'm afraid, in or out of hardware.' Perplexed but persistent Charlie went on, 'But she's the lady who gave me your name and telephone number. You could say she's the reason I'm here.' 'Well, it's been good to see you, but I just don't know this Helen Morrison who pointed you in my direction.' And Roy Groves indicated that he had nothing more to add. He left Charlie rooted to the spot. Puzzled that mention of the name had caught his suave host off-guard Charlie propelled himself towards The Cow's Corner.

Far from being closed the pub was doing a good trade. Charlie had to concede that its reputation must have spread far. As someone who knew his real ale he soon saw why. There were some excellent brews on offer and when he had located the Snug bar he found some rare delights. Of the people he spoke to during the next two happy hours there were few who could add anything significant to what he had learned from Roy Groves. As the taxi took him back to the nearest station he resolved that he would give a balanced report at the next meeting with his teammates, but he was sure in his own mind that what he would have to say about The Cow's Corner would seal the deal. Thanks to Roy Groves he could include in his report which member of the Carter family acted as the Middle Daychurch fixtures secretary and his contact details.

Whether it was from conviction that Middle Daychurch was a fixture worth having or on account of Charlie Colson's efforts to secure the opening the Outcasts gave it their stamp of approval. So late in the evening was the decision made that some of them could not recall making it. However, it took only one phone call for the whole thing to be fixed up. Charlie had taken responsibility for seeing the deal through. He had found himself speaking to Michael Carter, one of Edwin's grandchildren. The request was accepted with such alacrity that Charlie supposed that Michael had been forewarned that the call would come. From what he had heard Charlie could not imagine a new fixture being agreed without the approval of the chairman. The only date on offer was in early September which meant after the Gigton weekend (*Occasionally Cricket* 1999). That was not a problem for the Outcasts, but it was the beginning of one.

It was not until mid-season that they picked up more information about what to expect when they played Middle Daychurch. They had travelled to North Hertfordshire for a game against Bagworth. The Outcasts and the Bagworth team were well matched in their playing skills and social tastes. The match on this occasion was a stop-start affair caused by sudden, short, but frequent showers. This had provided more opportunity than usual for chat. Awareness of the short-lived nature of the rain interruptions forbade recourse to the local pub and so the players lounged around the pavilion. The recently refurbished building boasted an up-to-date television set which enabled those interested to keep an eye on England's progress in a one-day international match being played a hundred miles away in brilliant sunshine. Once England and county prospects had been exhausted as topics, conversation turned to the two clubs' own performance. The comments were typically frank and laced with deprecatory humour.

At one point the humour died. It coincided with Alan Birch asking if Bagworth had played Middle Daychurch. Episodically between passages of play the Bagworth captain gave the Outcasts the benefit of his team's experience of encounters with Middle Daychurch. 'You've got to understand that they're a tight-knit unit, family dominated. They're not a fun team to play. They play hard and they very much play to win. I don't really know what drives them. But I know who drives them.' 'Edwin Carter?' prompted Charlie Colson. 'Yeah, the old man, right enough. And he's not beyond bending the rules. We've not beaten them yet, though we came close once.'

How they came close once could not be explained until the players had completed another six overs. 'Well, it was last year when we had Bill's son turning out for us once or twice. Got his blue as a fresher and you may know how he's been getting on since.' One or two of the Outcasts were able to nod in sudden realisation. 'He took the Daychurch bowlers to the cleaners. We got to within twenty of their score before they got him or rather the umpire got him.' 'The old man, I suppose,' Charlie chipped in. 'Yeah, with a vengeance. It pitched outside leg stump and kept going straight. Of course he should never have padded it away with that umpire just waiting for his chance. Mind you, if looks could kill.'

The question had to be asked. 'So why do you carry on with the fixture?' It was Jon Palmer, who had leant across. The Bagworth skipper smiled. 'I suppose we see it as a sort of extra challenge – a match where we try a bit harder. We put ourselves to the test when we play Daychurch. Anyway I don't want to put you off. There are compensations. The facilities are good. It's usually a bloody good tea. And you won't find many better pubs than The Cow's Corner.' At the mention of this name there was an emphatic nod from Charlie Colson. The skipper went on: 'Once some of the older ones have gone home the younger guys come along to the pub. They're then perfectly good company.' There was a shout: 'It's stopped raining.'

It was only later in post-match festivities in The Bosie Arms that one more important fact was revealed. The captain of the defeated Bagworth team tapped his raised glass (probably his fourth by then) and said, 'You mustn't go to Daychurch having had a few jars. If the old man smells alcohol on your breath, he'll disqualify you.' The Outcasts exchanged glances and then they turned to fix their gaze on the retreating back of Charlie Colson, who had suddenly realised that he needed the gents.

There had been a reappraisal in light of what they had heard at Bagworth, but curiosity coupled with the attractions of The Cow's Corner prevailed. No other gossip they picked up on their travels deflected them. As the season moved on there was heightened team anticipation about the visit to Middle Daychurch. Curiosity affected one member in particular. Charlie Colson continued to wrestle with the mystery of Helen and the nature of her connection with the village. During his 'research' visit to The Cow's Corner he had made a few fruitless enquiries before concentrating on the serious evaluation of the ales on offer. At a later date he had contacted her old firm again to ask if she had left any forwarding details. He was first met with a recital of company policy of not revealing such information to third parties on grounds of data confidentiality. He managed by sheer persistence to penetrate this barrier, but finally after he had spun a somewhat emotional pretence to the head of personnel he got the facts. Helen had left no contact information of any kind. The information which they had previously held was no longer available. Her file was missing.

The Outcasts had stumbled into a relationship with Executive Sporting Coachways. To be precise the stumbling had been done by Phil Cole. He had been out one night with some of his workmates on the pull. The word on the street suggested the recently opened Bluebird Club and so after a few rounds to get them in the mood that was where they looked for the action. At the end of a noisy, sweaty evening Phil heard himself asking Lorraine for a date. Phone numbers were exchanged and a date it duly became. A mid-priced Italian restaurant, two glasses of Prosecco, a bottle of Barolo, cappuccino, a liqueur, the walk home – all accompanied by lively conversation – and Phil Cole was thinking that it was a sure-fire preliminary to a perfect evening. But the ending came on the second step leading to the front door of Lorraine's flat and there was no more in it than a peck on the cheek and the final words, 'I'll ring you'.

Depression set in and was intensified when it struck Phil that he had no idea where he was. He had expected to be leaving in daylight. Having had other things on his mind as they strolled from restaurant to flat, he had made no mental note of the way they had come. Confused he walked back towards a junction, guessed a right turn and then a left. He was still lost. Perhaps it should have been a left and then a right. He retraced his steps and tried that. He arrived at a crossroads which did not look at all familiar. However, something else did. He was sure he could make out to his left a sign which offered comfort to the lonely wayfarer: Pullinger's Power Ales. As he approached he saw they were available in diminutive premises announcing themselves as The Goat and Cheese. With relief he strode into the bar.

Several pints later he emerged with his appreciation of Pullinger's Power Ales enlarged. The same could not be said of his knowledge of the local geography. He had gone half a mile before realising that he was no closer to getting home. Not a sign of a taxi. There were no passers-by. He vaguely noticed that houses had given way to commercial premises. He felt tired, his spirits sagging and his legs weakening. He saw a gate and a doorway. He sat down to clear his head and that was where he was found in the morning by Bill Blimp, the proprietor of Executive Sporting Coachways.

This was in effect the Outcasts' introduction to a coach service which had established a somewhat extraordinary niche in the market. Bill Blimp's vehicles bore graphic testimony to the character of his clientele. Physical disrepair coupled with an unfriendly odour made for a challenging onboard atmosphere. But Bill Blimp's prices were low and his level of tolerance of the behaviour of his passengers high. So the Outcasts had begun to use this travel option on an on/off basis. Even they from time to time wanted relief from what they christened the puke wagon. They had nevertheless contracted Executive Sporting Coachways for the visit to Middle

Daychurch – probably with the prospect of an extended stay in The Cow's Corner in mind.

Despite the fascinating scenario which had been painted for them there was not an overwhelming response when Charlie Colson, the obvious choice for captain and match manager, asked for availability. No more than thirteen of the Outcasts registered to play. This was the bare minimum, because for once they were without their regular scorer. Simon Crossley was on extended honeymoon. The thirteenth man was the involuntary scorer. It did not bode well for the wellbeing of Simon's meticulously pre-served scorebook. In the end it was not seriously disturbed.

The day began murkily, more February than September. The Blimp coach passed through one shower on the way to Middle Daychurch. The journey was otherwise unremarkable. The usual trademarks of Executive Sporting Coachways – mechanical breakdowns and getting lost – were absent. They sailed into the cricket club car park ahead of time and completely sober. A reception party came down the steps of the pavilion. It was obvious who was in charge. For all his years Edwin Carter was an erect stern-looking man. His greeting to Charlie Colson was polite, but distant. Those who followed him to shake hands with the rest of the team were pleasant enough, but hardly effusive. The Outcasts felt that they were under close scrutiny. No time was wasted. They were encouraged to get ready. The toss took place. It was won by the home team. The Outcasts were invited to bat first.

A taste of what could lie ahead came in the third over when Stewart Thorogood was adjudged to be caught behind the wicket off a ball that his bat had missed by several inches. Arthritic or not Edwin Carter's finger rose like a rocket. Stewart's mood was not helped by hearing the bowler say to the umpire, 'Thanks, Granddad,' as, trailing his bat, he trudged back to the pavilion. Six more overs passed without incident before the rain came. In this time the Outcasts saw only two bowlers, both grandsons of Edwin. The wicket-taker was Richard Love; from the other end the opening bowler, rather older and less quick, was Philip Carter. Once the players had returned to the shelter of the pavilion there was no mixing. The home team went into their changing room and the door closed behind them. The Outcasts took their cue from that and also retreated. Bringing up the rear the two not out batsmen, Jon Palmer and Rashid Ali, were able to make out the voice of Edwin Carter who was obviously barking out instructions to his players. The rain got worse and there was no further play before tea.

By comparison with what had gone before, the tea interval was a cordial affair. The quality of the fare provided was excellent and the continuing rain meant there was more time to enjoy it. Members of the home team entered into conversation with the Outcasts, but it was a little stilted. If any of the visitors asked a question about who was who in the home team, the answer seemed very guarded. The old man sat apart, a small table having been set up for him in the corner. The Outcasts felt that they were under observation. Two of their opponents were placed at the end of the main table. They seemed to speak only to each other. The Outcasts discovered later that they were from Near Daychurch and were (definitely) not family.

Tea had lasted three quarters of an hour when the weather gave a hint of brightening. All the players got up to ready themselves for a resumption. Edwin Carter accompanied by Syd Breakwell stepped out to examine ground conditions. The rain had petered out and the view of the umpires was that, if they didn't start then, they never would. The Daychurch captain was Joseph Carter. As Edwin's eldest son that was naturally the case, although he was no young man himself. He approached Charlie Colson to suggest reducing the match to twenty overs a side. That was agreed. The ball was tossed to David Carter, a grandson of Edwin's deceased brother, and Rashid Ali found himself tested by some accurate off spin. The players had barely changed ends before there was a gust of wind, the light worsened and the rain came down again. As they rushed back to escape it Jon Palmer heard Joseph Carter say, 'It's probably only a short, sharp shower.' He was to hear it three more times after a succession of false starts, not one of which lasted longer than eight deliveries.

Stiff but polite farewells were exchanged after the rain-wrecked match. The Outcasts boarded the coach for the start of the return journey. Bill Blimp drove them from the car park of the cricket club all the way to the car park of The Cow's Corner where the landlord already appeared to be doing good trade. With thirteen Outcasts on the premises it was about to experience a major boost. Not having had a drop all day without even the compensation of playing cricket the Outcasts were thirsty men. Syd Breakwell was content to find a table in the corner, settle down with a Scotch and water and hope for someone with whom he could have a good yarn. He had been instructed by Stewart Thorogood to have a good listen as well.

Almost an hour had passed before the first member of the home team showed up. 'Sorry, you must think us very rude,' said David Carter, 'but we couldn't move until the chairman had given his pep talk. He insists on waiting till we've showered and changed. Once he's left we can go our own way. Christ, I could do with a pint.' One was swiftly pushed into his hand and the first bond between Middle Daychurch Cricket Club and the

Outcasts was forged. David's brother, Andrew, was the next to appear and he was quickly followed by Michael, the fixtures secretary, Richard Love and Charles Bell. Last to arrive were the two players from Near Daychurch, Martin Norwell and Brian Stagden. It was immediately noticeable that in the atmosphere of The Cow's Corner there seemed no longer any sign of distance between the Carter and non-Carter team members. Rashid Ali quietly noted that the only absentees were the oldest and youngest Carters. Nor was there any sign of Richard Love's mother, Maisie, who was the scorer for Middle Daychurch. 'If she came through the door,' said Richard, 'I don't know which of us would be the more surprised.'

The day ended much better than it had been earlier endured. Yet even with a core of good company and a collection of an excellent range of bitters the Outcasts decided it was wise policy not to overstay on their first visit. But no-one left the village in any doubt about their wish to return. Charlie Colson had shaken hands with Michael Carter to seal the deal. The sense of satisfaction born that night would not have indefinite duration.

The visit to Middle Daychurch proved to be the last cricket activity for the Outcasts in that season. Heavy rain blanketed much of southern England for several days. What should have been their best fixture was called off at twenty-four hours' notice. The secretary of Weasden CC rang Winston Jenkins with the news that their pitch was waterlogged. 'We're really sorry about that. We were thirsting for revenge after last year and I bet you lot were thirsty for more of our local ale.' (Weasden had its own niche brewery.) Winston freely admitted that great disappointment would be felt, but said that he fully understood. They exchanged a few words of disgust about the weather with Winston mentioning that the previous week's match had been ruined. 'Oh yes,' said the Weasden man, 'I'd heard you'd been to Middle Daychurch. We played them six weeks ago. That's a strange set-up, isn't it?' But before the set-up could be subjected to further comment the voice at the other end said, 'Sorry, must go, I've got a customer.' Winston was left to speculate about what sort of strangeness the Weasden team had discovered. And he idly wondered what it was his opposite number was trying to sell.

With the enforced week off the Outcasts did not meet again in strength until the end of the month. An evening at The Sink and Plumber was devoted to a review of the season. There were performance awards for feats both on and off the cricket field. The Outcasts' record had contained its usual ups and inevitably some very colourful downs. Only once these had been cheerfully and sometimes embarrassingly recollected did the name of Middle Daychurch crop up. Charlie Colson was only a short way into his report when he was interrupted by Basil Smith, the club's off spinning accountant. Fumbling with his wallet – the evening was fairly well advanced – he produced a newspaper cutting which he then had difficulty unfolding. 'It was in today's *Times*,' he explained as the piece of paper continued to put up its resistance. 'An obituary notice.' Glances were exchanged. Basil was probably the only man present who would bother to read the obituary column in the *Times* or any other newspaper. Finally he managed to recite it:

CARTER – EDWIN ARCHIBALD on 28th September.
The dearly beloved husband of the late Mary,
much loved and respected father of Joseph, Maisie, Douglas and Paul
and grandfather and great-grandfather to their families.
Chairman of Middle Daychurch Cricket Club.
Will be sadly missed. Funeral Service to be held
at Warbrick Crematorium on 5th October at
12 noon. All enquiries to Bell and Son,
The Mount, Ringingham

Initial surprise gave way to speculation. As Basil pointed out on glancing at the cutting again it did not say 'peacefully at home', 'peacefully' or even 'suddenly'. 'He looked well enough when we saw him,' said Tim Jackson, who was unofficially the Outcasts' social secretary, being better at fixing parties than batting at No. 11. (He was also the last person who would be asked to bowl.) 'Might have been a stroke,' said Charlie Colson. 'Or a heart attack,' Dean Faulds, middle-order bat, suggested. 'Yes,' said Basil, but it doesn't say anything about donations to the Stroke Association or the Heart Foundation.' 'Could've been just old age,' offered Jon Palmer, 'after all he was in his eighties.' Various other causes of death were rehearsed, but they still ended none the wiser. Ribaldry crept in. 'Sadly missed,' snorted David Pelham looking towards Stewart Thorogood, 'like he missed your never coming anywhere near hitting that ball when he gave you out caught behind.' 'There are probably a few more on the circuit feeling like that,' responded Stewart, 'but I wonder how Middle Daychurch will get on now he's out of the way.' 'And I wonder which of them'll take over the reins or do I mean the whip?' asked John Furness. 'Bound to be one of the family,' said Charlie. This was followed by Nigel Redman (medium-fast bowler) saying with a smirk, 'I think we can safely say it won't be Maisie.' General laughter ensued and discussion turned to other topics.

Charlie Colson might have contained his curiosity about the death of Edwin Carter until such time as it was necessary to renew the fixture for the following year. However, after Winston Jenkins had forwarded an email sent to him and several other fixture secretaries by Carlton Abbots Cricket Club, he felt stirred to action. The text of the email was far blacker in its attempted humour than any comments which had been passed between the Outcasts. It was Charlie's opinion that it had crossed a line, however much the club in question had felt wronged in the past by Edwin Carter. He made the impulsive decision to attend the funeral.

On the appointed day he had arrived at the crematorium in good time. The turnout, he thought, was thin. The Carter family itself constituted a substantial presence. Others he could not identify might have been locals, but there were no faces familiar to him to suggest that other cricket clubs had sent a representative. Perhaps the content of the unpleasant email reflected too wide a feeling about the deceased. Charlie was still looking around him when someone placed a hand on his arm. He recognised the voice more readily than the appearance, because when he had last seen Michael Carter he had been in cricket whites rather than the dark grey suit in which he was now dressed. 'It's very good of you to come.' 'Well, having met him so recently I thought it only right to pay respects.' 'Not many others it seems,' said Michael ruefully. 'I think I can understand why. Granddad took no prisoners.' Charlie was about to ask the burning question as to granddad's cause of death when Michael said, 'Look, I must dash. We're having drinks and snacks afterwards back at our village pub. You'll be very welcome.' Charlie did not need a second invitation.

The floral tributes lined the pathway to the crematorium entrance. Charlie deliberately held back until he was sure that family members would have chosen their preferred seats. So he had time to cast an eye over wreaths and other arrangements. After the service he again held back until the main body of the congregation had filed out. Only because the image had been recently in his mind he thought there was something different in respect of the flowers. He suddenly realised what it was. An extra wreath had been placed on the left-hand side of the path. Yet he was sure that no-one had come into the building after him. He bent to examine it. There was a card headed simply 'In Memoriam'. The sender was not identified other than by what could have been a monogram. Charlie thought he could make out the letter 'K', but it was obscured by what looked like a squiggle or a snake half imposed on it. There was also a misshaped cross which he supposed was a kiss, although viewed another way it could be taken for a dagger.

Arriving in Middle Daychurch, a pensive Charlie Colson found a large notice displayed outside The Cow's Corner: 'Closed for Family Function'. Inside, the guests seemed to be divided into two groups. As far as Charlie could make out the younger members of the Carter family had occupied the Snug leaving the elders in the main bar area. As on previous evidence the young Carters were more inclined to chat, Charlie hoped that he would be able to return home with some answers. He did not know whether to be pleased or sorry that the only drinks on offer were those prescribed by the hosts. He was better able to limit his input than might have been possible if the beer pumps had not been covered. He reintroduced himself to Andrew and David Carter who were the sons of the deceased's nephew. Now in their late twenties they had been in their teens when their grandfather, Edwin's brother, Donald, had died. They betrayed no special grief for their great-uncle.

Edwin Carter, ever stubborn about continuing to drive his own car despite the pleadings of his immediate family, had seemingly lost control of the vehicle. It had smashed into a tree with appalling consequences. Examination of the body confirmed that he had suffered a heart attack. His own doctor confirmed that in recent years Edwin had been on medication. On assurance from his family that Edwin had been meticulous in keeping his car well maintained the case was closed. A piece of information known to only one member of the family was withheld. Edwin had refused to believe that he was a less good driver in old age than he had been earlier in life. He loved speed. Even without being aware of that Charlie could see all too clearly what must have happened. He tentatively tried another question. 'Who's likely to take charge of the club now?' Andrew gave a funny sort of smile. 'I reckon my dad will fight his cousins for that privilege.' Charlie saw the disapproving look on his brother's face. Time to go, he reckoned. Saying his farewell to Michael as he moved towards the exit, he noticed two older men engaged in what had the appearance of an animated discussion. He knew that one of them was the eldest son, Joseph, and from memory the other might have been the next eldest, Douglas. Charlie got the impression that the fight for the succession might already have begun. Before he got into his car he turned to look wistfully at the excellent ale house he was leaving. He said to himself almost out loud, 'It'll be a year before I see this place again'. But although he could not then have known it he would be back rather sooner than that.

Second encounter

IN THE WINTER THE OUTCASTS would meet collectively on a few occasions to transact any necessary business. Then there might be parties which Tim Jackson was expert in locating and accessing. They also maintained social links on an ad hoc basis. It was a time to research new and unfamiliar ales being trialled at pubs within reasonable distance. Fixtures for the forthcoming season were reviewed at The Sink and Plumber and the news was encouraging. It was noted that Middle Daychurch had willingly re-engaged, suggesting a slot in August. 'There'll be quite a bit to talk about there,' observed David Pelham. Within a couple of weeks that became a distinct understatement.

Saturday morning after a severely heavy night. The flat shared by Colin Banks and Greg Roberts looked a complete tip. Greg had been the first to rise. Greg was always the first to rise. Colin not infrequently enjoyed female company overnight and his Saturdays rarely started early. That was not the reason for his non-appearance on this occasion. If both men had had a skinful the night before, Colin had outdone his companion. Greg put the coffee machine to work, swallowed a couple of pills, cleared a space on the settee and switched the television to a sports channel in search of cricket somewhere in the world. A silent curse. American football, snooker, curling, wrestling, golf and downhill slalom, but no cricket. He turned to a rolling news channel and went to the kitchen to check if the coffee was ready. Returning he caught the newscaster's last two words 'cricketing curse'. The on-screen picture faded with Greg thinking that the building shown was vaguely familiar. But he soon had something more immediate to think about.

Slumped on the settee Greg withdrew his attention from the latest hunt for a mystery mammal frightening people in Rotherham and turned it instead to the mess around him. He contemplated a pair of jeans on the rug in front of him. He did not remember stripping off in the sitting room before going to bed. Pause for thought. Wait a minute, he had not been wearing his denims last night. He had chosen his flash new track suit bottoms. Where were they? He stretched out his leg to poke the jeans to one side with his big toe. That did not reveal what he had expected. He sat up sharply. A bra. What was that doing there? He looked towards Colin's bedroom door. But it was his which opened.

Greg realised a little later that the expression on his face must have been something extraordinary to behold. The girl who had appeared was worth his gaze, but it would have been better for Greg if his mouth had not fallen open in shock. He was hit by a rush of thoughts. She must have been in his bed. He had got out of it without even noticing she was there. Had he really brought her home? Perhaps this was all down to Colin. No, Colin would have kept to himself anyone as attractive as the girl who stood before him. Or perhaps Colin had another girl with him now. But surely he would have remembered if they had come back with two girls. These questions darted through his brain and gave way to a quite different feeling. Had he thought her attractive? No, she was stunning. Being only partly clad may have added to the impression. His head was sore, his throat was dry, no caffeine had yet entered his system and it was too soon for the pills to have had any effect. But lust returned and then he started to remember.

'Hi, Greg, either give me back my clothes or come back to bed.' Greg had made his first move before another voice stopped him in his tracks. 'Police were called last night to Middle Daychurch Cricket Club in Essex where a man had been found dead. No details have been released, but a police spokeswoman said that no third party involvement was suspected although they were keeping an open mind until they had completed their enquiries. This is the second tragedy to have hit the Middle Daychurch club within a short space of time. The club chairman was killed in a road accident shortly after the end of the cricket season.' A picture of the club pavilion filled the screen. The voice-over added, 'Perhaps all connected with the club may be thinking it has been visited by a cricketing curse. And now to other news . . .'

The news may not have been personal, but it killed any passion which might have been welling up inside him. The girl had remained silent whilst Greg had been so evidently transfixed by the news on television. Finally he stammered, 'Hi,' realised he could not recall her name and rushed on, 'I'm terribly sorry, that was some bad news – Can I get you some coffee and . . . maybe your clothes?' She laughed, 'Both, I think. Can I use the shower?' Greg could not think what state the bathroom might be in, but he felt this was no time for niceties. 'Sure. I'll leave the coffee for a few minutes. Toast, cereal, juice?' As she went into the bathroom she replied, 'No worries. I'll sort it when I'm dressed.' The bathroom door closed. Greg could hear the shower. He shot into his bedroom checking first the drawer in the bedside table. He saw to his relief that he had not forgotten everything that night. He threw on a jumper and some jeans before returning to the kitchen. At the sink he splashed some water on his face, took a comb from a conveniently placed empty jam jar and tried to restore some order to his dishevelled hair.

He stationed himself discreetly close to the kitchen entrance so that he could glimpse her perhaps in no more than a towel over the short distance between bathroom and bedroom. He knew he would like to see her again. Next time he would want to be more conscious of the experience. However, on this occasion he had come to the conclusion that he would feel better if she had left before Colin had woken and joined them. He was in no mood for what he imagined Colin's banter would be. In any case he was keen to get on the phone to Charlie Colson to see if he knew any more about what had happened in Middle Daychurch. No impolite rush was necessary. His guest said that she would be off home later that day. 'I'll give you a call,' said Greg hopefully. 'Sure,' she said, 'this is my number. That'll be great.' She handed him a piece of paper which he stuffed in his pocket. He gave her a hug and a kiss and she was gone.

'He's at the pub,' said Liz Allason when Greg rang Charlie. 'David slept on the floor here last night and it's now a case of the hair of the dog. They said they'd be back if I promised a full English. The deadline expires in twenty minutes. After that I don't care if it's all congealed.' In fact Greg's phone rang after five minutes. It was Charlie from the pub unprompted by Liz. 'Hey, Greg, have you seen the news about Middle Daychurch? It looks as though Douglas Carter has topped himself. They found him hanging from the balustrade in the pavilion.' 'That's a lot more than I got from the TV news.' 'Ah well, it's obvious, mate, that you don't read the titillating tabloids.' 'I'm surprised you do,' retorted Greg. 'There just happened to be one on the bar counter.' 'Open at which page, I wonder?' 'It's gotta to be true,' said Charlie, avoiding that crack, 'I'll ring Michael Carter early next week.' 'Enjoy your full English,' said Greg. Before ending the call he heard Charlie say, 'Oh Christ, is that the time? Get that pint down you, Dave.'

As the call ended the door of Colin's bedroom opened. 'What the hell's been going on here? Can't a guy get any sleep? I'm surprised you're up and dressed after your performance last night.' It was quickly obvious that

Colin, who had not had overnight female company, was keen to talk about Greg's adventure. The latter was not sure how much he wanted to have the detail supplied. He preferred to impart his information to Colin, but his flatmate, not yet having had direct experience of Middle Daychurch, was far more interested in the situation closer to home. Greg's private life had not shown itself as being as remotely colourful as Colin's. The scene on this particular morning was role reversal and Colin was keen to make the most of it. The most reaction Greg got from Colin was to the effect that funny things happen in some of these remote villages. After a further bout of teasing Greg's patience snapped: 'So, OK, I had a bloody good time. You're just jealous, because you were on your own for once.' Colin laughed. 'Condition you were in, I doubt if you'd have known how to have a good time.' 'Well, she seems keen to see me again. She left me her number.' For effect he extracted the piece of paper from his pocket. She had indeed left her number, but unfortunately not her name. The number told him only one thing. It began 0061. She was Australian. Maybe not that keen after all.

Monday's newspapers covered the Middle Daychurch story either soberly or in a couple of cases sensationally. The basic facts were confirmed. By Tuesday police interest had evaporated. Charlie left it until Wednesday before ringing Michael Carter. 'We're in shock here,' he was told. 'There was never any sign of anything wrong with Uncle Douglas. No illness or anything like that. He always seemed cheerful enough. Why would he do it?' Michael ended plaintively. Charlie learned that the funeral would be held on the following Saturday. Charlie hesitated before asking whether it would be all right to attend the funeral. Michael said with seeming gratitude that his presence would be appreciated. No other cricket club on the circuit had shown any interest, nor sympathy for that matter.

Much sooner than he would have anticipated, Charlie Colson was back in Middle Daychurch, this time at the parish church. He came by train and taxi. He felt his devotion to duty deserved the reward of an hour or two in The Cow's Corner once the wake was over. He remembered to look carefully at the flowers laid out in the churchyard. There it was, ahead of the service unlike at the crematorium. Again the card accompanying the lilies was hardly affectionate. It said simply 'Goodbye' and was signed with the odd-looking symbol accompanied by what he was sure now was a dagger. Going inside the church Charlie resolved to subject the congregation to close scrutiny. Which one of them was 'K'? He was no wiser by the end of the service. There were just too many faces to which he could not attach a name.

43

It did not take long to walk from the church to the pub. As Charlie did not join family members at the graveside he and a few others reached The Cow's Corner ahead of the main party. Charlie was pleased to note that, unlike the last occasion, the pub was open for business with just the main bar cordoned off for the private function. The Snug bar, which had direct access from the car park, was dispensing drink to a small number of customers. One or two others who had kept pace with Charlie obviously concurred with his decision to get a quick pint in ahead of the formal gathering. Introductions were made and gossip was exchanged. 'Poor devil,' said a portly, red-faced man, who had chosen Scotch rather than beer, 'not getting the top job must have set him back something terrible.' 'What,' exclaimed Charlie, 'you're not saying that Douglas Carter killed himself because he wasn't going to be the club chairman?' 'No, I'm not saying that,' said the red-faced man, 'all I'm saying is he was very disappointed.' 'And with good reason, if you ask me,' said another equally red-faced, but younger man, who Charlie noted with appreciation was on his second pint. 'Dougie, if you ask me,' he continued with some emphasis, 'is, er, was the backbone of that club and' – there was a slight pause to allow him another swig of his ale – 'a better cricketer. That Joseph's too old already, but, if you ask me, he'll hold on as long as Edwin did.'

Charlie was not sure he wanted to ask the man any more. Seeing the main body of the Carter family arrive in the main bar, he slipped through to join them. Michael came up to him, thanked him for the respect he was showing and made a few introductions. Charlie got into conversation with Barbara Love, daughter of Maisie, and got another angle on the Carter family. 'They're all – well, nearly all – cricket crazy. If you've played here already, you'll have probably got that message. But it's the family-first

44

thing which tends to get in the way. I can't believe that Uncle Doug could have been so upset by it all.' She took out a tissue as a tear slipped out of the corner of her eye. Charlie hesitated before saying, 'But you surely don't think that his brother becoming captain could have driven your Uncle Doug to such despair as to . . .' His voice trailed away as he could see more tears coming. When she had recovered Barbara said, 'Well, no I don't really. It's all too stupid. I just wouldn't have thought he was that kind of man. But look what's happened. He must have been and none of us realised it.' At that she could hold tears back no longer. People looked in their direction making Charlie feel uncomfortable. Not wanting it thought that he was harassing the young woman, Charlie muttered, 'Sorry,' and moved away.

By the window there was a group of young men looking uncomfortable in, mostly, ill-fitting suits which Charlie reckoned they were unaccustomed to wearing. He thought he recognised a face. 'You were playing for the village when my club, the Outcasts, came here last year, weren't you?' Lee Lingrove answered cautiously, giving every indication that he had not remembered him from the ruined match. There were four of them and they all seemed ill at ease. Charlie could not be sure of their ages, but he wagered they would have been more cheerful with pints in their hands than the anaemic cordials enforced by the observation of their elders. Charlie soon discovered his error. After a stilted conversation during which Lee had volunteered no introductions, the youngest of his companions thrust his half-full glass in Charlie's direction and whispered hoarsely, 'Get us a vodka to stick in that, mate, will you?' Charlie might have reacted to the lack of civility in the approach, but noticed that a £10 note was accompanying the glass. Another voice. 'Cheers, mate.' Another glass. Charlie could see the perils of hesitation or argument. He put his own glass on an adjacent table. With the command, 'Mind that for me, mate,' he made for the Snug. When he returned with mission accomplished two more depleted glasses and a banknote awaited him. A few minutes later some rudimentary conversation began and Charlie acquired the names of his new friends.

'If we parked ourselves nearer the doorway to the Snug, won't it be easier for you to get another round in?' This was Tom, like Lee a grandson of Joseph. Charlie could see a £20 note in his palm. He looked around. Everyone else in the bar seemed preoccupied in conversation. Weighing the odds, he reckoned loosened tongues might yield information which could be useful ahead of the Outcasts' next visit. He thought he performed the manoeuvre slickly and was rewarded by a nod from Lee. 'Thanks, Charlie, have the next one on us.' Bonding, thought Charlie, wondering how long the session might last. He hoped it would end without one of the youthful quartet throwing up in the corner. He underestimated their resilience for all were still standing seemingly unaffected when the bell rang. There followed a clearing of the throat before the voice of Joseph Carter thanked people for coming, meaning that it was then time for them to go. The solemnity of his words was dented by two loud hiccups from a source close to Charlie, but when eyes turned in that direction he had slid covertly into the Snug from which he had originated.

On his journey home Charlie made an effort to summarise what he thought he had learned from his encounter with the younger and possibly wilder section of the Carter family. He had assumed to begin with that they were all cousins. It was a surprise when after the fourth or fifth vodka (by then they were doubles) Lee had mockingly addressed one of the others as 'Uncle James'. It turned out that whilst Lee and Tom, both grandsons of Joseph, were cousins Brian and James Carter were sons of Joseph's younger brother, Philip. So despite being of similar age Brian and James were uncles to Lee and Tom. All four were keen cricketers and competed for places in the village team. Nevertheless Charlie had sensed tensions. They did not think they were getting sufficient of the action. It was not just that their elders were picked ahead of them. Their cousins from the other side of the family (Donald Carter's grandchildren) were favoured ahead of them. Brian and James complained that being Paul Carter's children seemed to put them at a disadvantage. Their father did not 'get on' with brother Joseph and had been closer to the recently deceased Douglas. To all this Tom Carter had pointed out that even as Joseph's grandson he had not had much of a look-in. He had at that point prodded his cousin, Lee Lingrove, in the chest and said, 'Curly here seems to be the favourite. I can't think why.' Charlie had not needed an explanation for the nickname as Lee's head was closely cropped. However, he had noticed how his uncles had guffawed over Tom's remark.

Charlie had probed the grumbles he had heard, pointing out the presence of two Near Daychurch players in the team against the Outcasts. That had led to a lively argument, with Tom and Lee contending that Martin Norwell and Brian Stagden were 'You've got to admit it, the two best f****** batsmen in the side'. The emphasis of the f-word had caused some frowning heads to turn in their direction. Brian and James had rebutted the assertion in the same strength of language, but at much lower volume. Having not had the opportunity of seeing Martin, Brian or any other team member bat, Charlie could contribute nothing to the heated, vodka-charged exchange. Whatever their reputation the Carters were perhaps not such a happy family. Something said by James stuck in Charlie's mind. Lee had said that at least James had been twelfth man once or twice. This had produced a snort from James. 'Big deal, running round all day while the old guys come off for a rest. Maybe the only way I'm going to get a proper go this season is if someone gets their 'ead bashed in.' It was probably just the vodka talking.

As the summer progressed these events receded into the background. The Outcasts had donned their cricket boots and their drinking boots in equal measure. Their performance had embraced one or two exhilarating highs and several notorious lows. The visits to Rockcliffe School and Willingfold-in-the-Myre have been chronicled elsewhere (*Eventually Cricket* 2001). They had been obliged to get by without the services of Executive Sporting Coachways although the firm would rise again from the scrap yard. A new recruit had been fortuitously acquired in the person of Harry Northwood, a hesitating student, but unhesitating in his appetite for real ale. As with most fixtures in this season there had needed to be a preliminary debate about transport. Ahead of the visit to Middle Daychurch it had been mercifully short. Tom Redman had bounded into The Sink and Plumber with good news. Earlier in the week a man had come into the bookshop run by Tom and Nigel with a request to place an advertisement in the window. On the neat card which he asked to display was the description of a twenty-seater coach which was available for hire (except Wednesdays and Sundays). The hire fee to which fuel costs had to be added was more than the level charged by Bill Blimp, but it nevertheless stimulated Tom's interest. He asked whether there was scope for negotiation and explained the purpose behind the question. The eyes of the man with the coach lit up. 'Cricket,' he said, 'that's a good enough cause for me. You display my notice and I'll cut you a deal on the coach hire.' After some polite discussion a deal was arrived at which Tom was confident would be approved by his fellow Outcasts. To get over the fact that none of the Outcasts were qualified to drive a coach its owner volunteered his own services declaring that a trip into the countryside to watch a village cricket match was his idea of heaven. Tom, based on what he had been told by Middle Daychurch, had not wanted to disillusion Stephen Marshall.

The Outcasts' practice of rotating the captaincy meant that Jon Palmer was the man in charge for the trip to Middle Daychurch. Availability had dealt him a team weighted more towards batting than bowling. It also contained a strong party-going contingent after Tim Jackson had revealed his acquaintance with a Cynthia Lovelock who knew Maria Turton who had a friend who was holding a party at Fenworth, a manorial pile close to the Daychurch villages. This add-on to the cricket match had to be negotiated with Stephen Marshall. The task was assigned to Tom Redman even though he himself would not be part of the team.

Tom found their vehicular saviour in affable mood. 'I suppose I should have anticipated that it wouldn't be an early night. And I've got an early start the next day. Oh well, I've said I'll help you. I must keep my word. Would you settle for a midnight curfew? It should only take an hour to get back at that time of night.' Tom had his fingers firmly crossed in readily agreeing the deadline. If past form was anything to go by, an hour or two would be spent in the pub before moving on to the party. You never knew what might happen at a party. Watching the clock was unlikely to be uppermost in the minds of his friends when socialising in good company. He could only stress to Jon Palmer the need to keep a check on things if they ever wanted the help of Stephen Marshall on a future occasion. As he confided to brother Nigel he was on the whole relieved that he himself was not making the trip.

The Sink and Plumber had been fixed as the pick-up point. Departure time was later than the Outcasts' wont. Unsure whether the aversion to alcohol still pervaded thinking at Middle Daychurch Cricket Club despite the passing of Edwin Carter, they had ruled that there would be no pub stopover on the way to their destination. There was some expectation about the nature and style of the promised transport. The half-sized coach when it arrived looked to be in reasonable shape, but the inscription on the side raised eyebrows. In white on a lilac background were the words 'St. John's Free Church' and underneath 'Glory to God our Redeemer'. It was quickly found that this legend was repeated on the other side of the vehicle. On the rear panel the inscription was 'Going God's Way'. A sudden profanity escaped the lips of Kevin Newton, but had fortunately faded before Stephen Marshall bounded out of the driver's seat to beam a welcome to his passengers. 'What, ho!' he cried. The straw boater and gaudily striped blazer completed the Wodehousian image.

Getting over their surprise – and in some cases mirth – the Outcasts stowed their baggage and boarded the coach. It was well-appointed with a bible and prayer-book in every seat pocket. Affixed to each seat was a neat notice: '11th Commandment – Blessed are they who do not smoke'. 'Spitting seems to be OK then,' Kevin muttered to Colin Banks who was seated next to him. Colin was studying a leaflet about St. John's Free Church.

Pointing a finger towards the front, he suddenly exclaimed, 'He's only the bloody vicar.' As if on cue Stephen Marshall addressed his passengers, 'Shall we close our eyes and pray for a safe journey?' Not without exchanged glances the Outcasts complied. Throughout the journey the piped music was a series of hymns. The volume was not excessively loud, but just loud enough to make conversation difficult. The disturbance was occasionally made worse when the vicar of St. John's chose to join in the chorus of his favourite items. Only Harry Northwood, who was attached to his music player, was spared the Christian onslaught. The whole experience was a far cry from the Outcasts' usual pre-match preparation. Whether it would have an uplifting effect on their performance remained to be tested.

In all other respects the journey was uneventful. The prayer had been answered. Stephen Marshall proved to be a careful and competent driver. When asked what he would do until it was time to move on to Fenworth he answered brightly, 'Gosh, I'm going to settle down to watch the match and see how you chaps get on. In fact,' he said quietly to Stewart, who had posed the original question, 'I shall offer up a little prayer for your victory.' With straw hat clamped to his head he went in search of a vantage point. Stewart gazed after him in disbelief and then turned towards the pavilion and the serious matter at hand. He shot a glance at the balcony from which the wretched Douglas Carter must have launched himself into oblivion. The very thought made him shudder, but it was quickly banished when he entered the turmoil of the Outcasts' changing room. 'Those are my pads, you bastard.' 'Where's my bat?' 'I think I've left half my kit at home.' 'Do that again and you'll need surgery.' Comforting normality reigned.

First innings

Jon Palmer and Joseph Carter met to toss. The home team captain's welcome was formal. Jon felt glad he hadn't got drink on his breath. He felt unsure whether he should make any reference to the family's losses and was still thinking about it when his opposite number said, 'Call'. 'Tails. Look I was very sorry about your loss. We all were . . .' 'It's heads. We'll bat. Good luck. You'll probably need it.' Jon forbore to mention that luck was unnecessary when God was watching over them. Summoning his team, he addressed their fastest bowler. 'Colin, pavilion end or, or,' and realising that he had not known the ground long enough to be aware, 'or the other?' Colin pointed to the distance and began waving his arms around to direct fielders to their positions. His was a pretty standard approach. Middle Daychurch's opening batsmen were preceded from the pavilion by Simon Crossley looking a little chastened. Fatherhood was proving a tiring business. Greg Roberts, twelfth man for the day, had found him asleep in a corner of the changing room. Then came Joseph Carter and his son, Philip. They looked a solid pair. On this occasion, however, appearances proved deceptive.

Colin Banks had two great interests in life beyond the consumption of real ale. They were beautiful women and cricket. They need not be mutually exclusive, and Colin did his best to ensure that women played a full part in his life both in and out of the cricket season. Unfortunately he had hit a bad spell. Three successive rebuffs had dented his confidence and soured his mood. He could only give vent to his frustrations on the cricket field. From the first few steps it was evident to a keen observer that Colin was injecting extra effort into his bowling. For all that, the outcome was disappointing. Fast and furious maybe, but his first ball was also short and comfortably wide of off stump. It was dispatched square for four. The dispatcher was Philip Carter. When Joseph opened the batting he preferred to stand at the non-striker's end so that he could get a feel for the pace of the wicket.

After this unpromising beginning Colin's performance could easily have deteriorated. His captain was already thinking of dispensing with second slip so that he could reinforce the point boundary. He doubted whether Colin's scowl boded well. If the next delivery was any wilder, second slip might be needed after all. His doubts were soon removed as were three of the home team's batsmen. At the end of the over Middle Daychurch's score was 8–3. Philip Carter never saw the ball which sent his stumps flying. Nor did anyone else until it was retrieved from its resting place by the pavilion fence. David Carter came in first wicket down. In appearance he looked to be more of a cricketer than his cousin. This impression was confirmed when he put away another short-pitched ball from Colin. This possibly lured him into thinking that Colin had reverted to type. The look of anticipation on his face did not remain for long. An express yorker from Colin may only have grazed his boot, but it shattered his stumps. In the circumstances good old George, Joseph's cousin, was not the best man to be sending into bat in what was still the first over. A better batsman might have judged it wise to leave a ball that would have passed wide of off stump. Not George Carter. He loosely poked his bat towards the ball and connected. So too did Rashid Ali's gloves behind the stumps. George's successor at the crease refused to make the same mistake, but almost made a different one. The ball which he ostentatiously left missed the stumps by a hair's breadth. Charles Bell, sent in ahead of Michael Carter because he at least had strapped his pads on, uttered a deep sigh of relief.

Joseph Carter had watched these destructive proceedings with anger and disbelief. Ignoring his son, Michael, he rounded on his brother-in-law, Bert Love, who was doing umpiring duty at what was known as the river end. Bert had succeeded his father-in-law in this role on the basis that it was a job best kept in the family. Word on the circuit suggested that bias continued, but was not in the same class as that shown by the late Edwin. However, the home team had noticed that their new umpire was easily distracted. It was this feature of his performance which was currently provoking Joseph. Certain that Colin Banks had overstepped the crease when delivering the ball which had dismissed his opening partner, he grabbed Bert by the arm. 'It was a no-ball you missed. For God's sake pay attention.' Suitably chastened, Bert shuffled off to his square leg position for the second over, which was to be bowled by Stewart Thorogood.

The havoc caused by Colin Banks had been observed by Stewart with mixed feelings. How was he to follow that? At a stretch he was medium-fast, but he would need to find as much extra guile as Colin had found pace. He was helped to settle by Joseph Carter's obvious determination to steady the ship. So an over of no particular distinction was allowed to pass run-less. Maintaining pressure, thought Stewart. On seeing a quizzical look sent in his direction by Jon Palmer he mouthed the words to his captain, who did not seem convinced. However, Stewart felt emboldened in his belief when with the second ball of his second over Colin hit the stumps again. It was an unintentional slower ball which deceived Charles Bell although Colin was not making that widely known. 'I thought I might just throw one in,' he told his celebrating team-mates. Any craft which he was claiming seemed slightly less convincing when the remainder of his over had ten runs taken from it with relative ease by Martin Norwell, the interloper in the Middle Daychurch team.

'What are you doing here? It should be Richard.' Hardly the warmest greeting for a batsman who was needed to stave off a disaster and who looked as if he might have the capacity to do so. Martin Norwell bit his lip before saying, 'Richard wasn't around.' 'What do you mean, he wasn't around?' 'He said he had to slip out to do something.' 'Slip out, what the hell is going on? Anyway Andrew's a better bat than you. He should have come in.' It took a discreet cough from Syd Breakwell to persuade the batsmen to stem the exchange and allow the fourth over to start. Stewart Thorogood bowled very tight and straight. He gave Joseph Carter no scoring opportunities, but was not sure if the batsman was looking for them. When there was a clumsy mis-field at short third man by David Pelham permitting a single, Martin Norwell called his partner and was set to run, but a roar came from his captain, 'Stay where you are, you bloody fool.' It was not clear whether Joseph Carter stuck limpet-like to the principle that you never ran on a mis-field or preferred to avoid facing Colin Banks at full tilt.

On the latter consideration Joseph Carter need not have worried. After his dramatic and devastating opening burst Colin appeared to have shot his bolt. The run-up was more laboured, the pace had dropped a notch or two and the direction was now less concentrated. Martin Norwell was largely untroubled and enjoyed a productive over. In marked contrast at the other end Stewart Thorogood achieved a third frugal over. This was explained more by the passivity of the batsman than by the wiles of the bowler. Eschewing any conversation with his partner, Martin feasted on a distinctly lacklustre over from Colin Banks. The flourish with which he was able to hook Colin's last ball over the deep fine leg boundary probably signalled that it would be the last ball of his spell. If he had finished with a whimper more than a bang, Colin could (and did) regard his figures of 4–42 with some satisfaction. By now Jon Palmer was becoming restive about the level of runs conceded.

Stewart Thorogood's bowling, niggardly though it had been, did not put him in the same class as Derek Shackleton and Tom Cartwright. Even Joseph Carter could not go on resisting the scoring opportunities increasingly being presented. Cautiously he proceeded only in even numbers so that he could continue to occupy what he appraised as the safer end. He did at least open his account. With limited bowling resources at his disposal Jon Palmer adopted the standard approach of resting both his opening bowlers at that stage. He chose Winston Jenkins' medium pace at the river end in succession to Colin Banks. During the over, between retrieving balls from the boundary, he pondered whether it should be Charlie Colson (medium pace) or David Pelham (off spin) at the pavilion end. The dismissive way in which Martin Norwell treated Winston Jenkins made it an unenviable choice. Winston Jenkins' first over – on his own admission not the best he had ever bowled – had cost twelve runs. The batsmen had not yet changed ends. Martin Norwell was on the verge of reaching a half-century. Jon Palmer almost decided to ask Stewart Thorogood to carry on, but in the end stuck to his guns and summoned David Pelham into action. He gambled on a further change of pace.

In the circumstances only a harsh critic would question the tactic. Like Winston Jenkins, David Pelham seemed a bit rusty. It was quickly evident that the wicket was not taking spin. It took until the third delivery to make that clear as the first two had passed sufficiently wide of the stumps to make judgement unrealistic. Joseph Carter took his first single and then watched the greater appetite of his partner bring two boundaries and another single. Joseph Carter seemed almost to begrudge Martin Norwell's fifty, but there was a sprinkling of applause around the ground. Despite the aggression coming from only one of the two batsmen at the crease the home team could boast a total after ten overs of seventy. This was a healthy rate of advance.

And so it continued. Apart from striving for a breakthrough whilst chasing leather what the Outcasts noticed with some amusement was the deteriorating relationship between Joseph Carter and Martin Norwell as their partnership progressed. The older man appeared to share his late father's aversion to anyone who was not actually from Middle Daychurch. Having no relationship with the Carter family was a supplementary offence. The animosity was fuelled in the current match by the sharply different performances of the two players. For all his disdain over facing Colin Banks in his extraordinary opening spell Joseph Carter had revealed himself to be a competent if dour player, an accumulator not a cavalier. The worth of his approach to the game was downgraded by the powerplay being exhibited by the outsider. As Martin Norwell surged ahead, even aggressively pinching the strike, the expression on Joseph Carter's face blackened. When he should have been rejoicing in his club's surging counter-attack, the captain seemed to retreat into himself in curmudgeonly fashion.

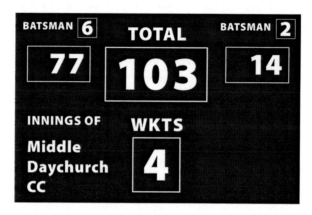

The Outcasts did not gain their fifth wicket until the twenty-seventh over. By this time their good humour had drained. Joseph Carter had been palpably run out when the score was 144. Unfortunately Bert Love standing at square leg was of the contrary view. Their understandable frustration was eased by a discreet word of sympathy from Martin Norwell, who by this time had 107 to his name. It was his second century this season, he confided to Rashid Ali, adding, 'I'll probably be dropped now.' In the meantime he kept on scoring whilst his partner made no more than a modest contribution. Still of a mind to keep his opening bowlers as his death bowlers, Jon Palmer had shuffled the other three around not with any particular design in mind. Charlie Colson had proved the most economical which Jon had some difficulty in believing. With Charlie it was always the next over that his captains feared. His four-over spell from the river end had cost only twelve which made his removal from the attack almost perverse. In fact it proved inspirational, because in what had to be his final over David Pelham bowled probably the finest off spinner of his career. It might have been good enough to have defeated Martin Norwell, but the victim was Joseph Carter, who played forward, but was deceived by extravagant turn. The score was 168–5.

It appeared that Richard Love was still not available. This added to Joseph Carter's annoyance. For the second time the perfect order (of batting) had been disturbed. There was no sign of him in the pavilion and no-one was able to advance on the vague excuse which had previously been offered. So it was Michael Carter, who had taken the initiative and was even now taking guard. 'It's far too high up the order for him,' snapped Joseph Carter before discarding his pads. His opinion was not borne out by the way his youngest son shaped up to the first ball he received from David Pelham. The excitement he had felt from taking Joseph Carter's wicket must have unsettled him for he greeted the new batsman with a short ball veering to leg. It veered a lot more to leg when Michael Carter went down on one knee and planted it over mid wicket. He hit it with such force that it dented the roof of the ice cream van, which had recently rolled into its appointed place. Its owner, Leslie Armstrong, let out a roar of disapproval, but was outdone for decibels by Connie Maxwell. 'Oi, watch what you're doing. That could have brained my Clarissa.'

The disturbance died perhaps never to be heard again had David Pelham not sufficiently forgot himself to send down a ball with no more merits than its predecessor. Michael Carter did not forget himself and applied the same treatment. The trajectory was remarkably similar. Its only imperfection lay in not hitting the same spot on the vehicle's roof. There were now two indentations almost classically spaced. Mrs Maxwell screeched, 'We 'aven't had bombin' like this since 'itler.' Showing the true grit which was the characteristic of that period, she marched towards the source of the bombardment. The boundary rope was no barrier to the intrepid lady. Waving her arms, she let rip at full volume, 'You bloody Carters think you can do what you like while us lot' (she looked around her for support from spectators) 'can go to 'ell. Well, it won't always be like that, I can tell you. You'll 'ave it coming to you, mark my words.' At this point the tirade faded. She saw coming towards her with calming expression the perpetrator of the offensive. This was one member of the Carter family she quite liked. Apart from anything else she did the cleaning at his home three times a week and she did not want that put at risk. With a 'Sorry, Mr Michael, I didn't know it was you. I didn't mean it,' she rapidly withdrew. But as she turned away her expression gave away her hostility.

The interruption had had a disturbing effect. Michael Carter, who had always felt undervalued by his father, was keen to impress whilst he could. The quality of the Outcasts' bowling seemed to provide a heaven-sent opportunity. Yet the venom of Connie Maxwell's outburst was startling. He thought of his two young daughters who were sometimes left in her care. It was an unwelcome distraction when he saw it as his job to build a total which would put the game out of reach of the visitors. For his part David Pelham with two balls left to complete his allocation of eight overs was unsure where and how to bowl if he was to avoid the consequence of serious injury to Mrs Maxwell's child. The image which floated into his mind was of a golden-curled little beauty with the face of an angel. He could not know that many of Clarissa's classmates at school would have been immensely cheered by the prospect of her suffering painful injury.

David strived for line and length, but did not noticeably succeed. A slightly hesitant Michael Carter limited himself to a one-bounce four. Faced with a batting combination which looked a serious threat Jon Palmer decided to depart from his original plan by bringing Stewart Thorogood back into the attack. Stewart's first four overs had cost only four runs, but this had been by virtue of them being bowled exclusively to Joseph Carter. A by now very well-set Martin Norwell might be an altogether more testing proposition. Stewart was as thoughtful a cricketer as the Outcasts possessed. Whilst fielding he had observed Martin Norwell's technique. He wondered whether there might be a weakness to a ball slanted across his body towards the slip area. He thought he might try bowling round the wicket.

The first four deliveries did not provide substance for the theory as Stewart's direction was awry. Having got the captain's permission to post two slips, Stewart's first ball was woefully wide and was crashed through a now less populated cover area for four. The second was a full toss driven straight and the third erred towards leg and was tapped away for two. The fourth ball at least had the virtue of being wicket-to-wicket. The surprise factor may have been the reason for the batsman doing no more than defend his stumps. Jon Palmer pointedly looked in the bowler's direction with an expression which said, 'Are you sure about this?' His answer came embarrassingly quickly. At the fifth attempt Stewart pitched right and the ball left Martin Norwell's advancing bat too late for him to withdraw. It flew at catchable height to first slip, but Jon Palmer was unable to pouch it. To give a batsman a life when he already had 137 to his name was a hard blow for the fielding side. This folly was counterbalanced by a second chance for the erring fielder. Having found the right delivery, Stewart managed to repeat it. Such a surprise might well have confounded Jon Palmer, but he caught the ball as neatly as his previous attempt had been clumsy. Martin Norwell silently cursed his folly. A masterly innings came to an end.

In the pavilion Joseph Carter was fuming over the whereabouts of Richard Love. His mood was not improved by virtue of most of his team's runs having been contributed by a non-family member and, worse, someone who came from outside the village. In that sense he had inherited all his father's narrow partisanship. Complain as he might someone had to be despatched to take the place of Martin Norwell. The choice was narrowed to Andrew Carter, George's younger son, as he was the only one padded up. Young Tom, Joseph's grandson, had just scuttled into the changing room guiltily to get himself ready.

Michael, aware that his cousin had played only occasionally for the club during the current season and shown no great form, greeted Andrew with a clear plan in his mind. 'Can you keep an end up while I try to get after this lot?' And before his new partner could answer he added, 'I'll take most of the strike, OK?' There did not seem room for much of a response. Andrew merely nodded and strolled to the non-striker's end. In view of Stewart Thorogood's success Jon Palmer had briefly considered giving Colin Banks a burst at the river end, but then felt that Colin probably needed a longer break if he was to be at his best in the closing overs. So Michael Carter found himself facing Charlie Colson.

Even though Jon doubted Charlie's ability to maintain the economy of his first spell he had not factored in the readiness of Michael Carter to throw the bat. Charlie managed two dot balls before the batsman let rip. There would probably have been four successive boundaries if Michael had not been determined to pinch the strike. The 200 mark was passed.

There was no doubt in Jon's mind that Stewart should be given one more over before returning at the death. They agreed that he would continue the round the wicket tactic. It was partially successful although the credit did not lie entirely with the bowler. Stewart could not maintain the line which had brought him Martin Norwell's wicket. He started well, but his third ball was loose and hit for four. The next was worked away for two. Then came a full toss which Michael drove straight back past the bowler. So sure was he of its destination that he sauntered a single. He had reckoned without Harry Northwood putting in a spectacular dive to save the boundary. Even more surprisingly by Outcasts' standards, Winston Jenkins arrived on the scene as back-up fielder and the ball was returned one bounce to the bowler. The batsmen had crossed and so Michael had got no more than one run and had lost the strike. 'Whatever you do,' he told his partner, 'stay at that end.' This was an instruction too far. Andrew felt he was being undervalued. He did not have to be strokeless to support his partner. He took his guard and checked the field placings, noting that there was now only one slip, who was standing fairly wide. Stewart reverted to over the wicket and produced a gentle outswinger. Andrew's intention was to nudge it down between wicketkeeper and slip with a good chance of a boundary. He so badly misjudged his shot that he contrived an inside edge gleefully caught by Rashid Ali. Middle Daychurch's seventh wicket fell with the score at 214.

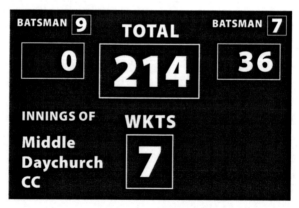

To general surprise and to Joseph Carter's fury the rest quickly followed. Michael Carter greeted his nephew, Tom, with rather more grace than he had shown towards Andrew, but the instruction was the same. 'Leave it to me.' Tom knew his place in the family hierarchy and was not disposed to argue. However, he did update his uncle with the news that Uncle Richard was nowhere to be seen. This left only his brother-in-law, Adrian Seymour, to bat if another wicket fell. This paucity of resources may have reinforced Michael's resolve, for there was no sign of any change of tactic. Charlie Colson's first ball was lifted straight back over his head for six. The next delivery was short and what Michael wanted to do with it was obvious. However, he must have allowed the image of a vulnerable Clarissa Maxwell to flit into his mind. He made a last-minute decision to steer the ball away from the ice cream van. It took a leading edge and went vertical. At first the fielding side was slow to react. As the batsman initially shaped to hit the ball the eyes of some of them had already turned towards the square leg boundary and what lay beyond. When the bowler screamed, 'Catch,' there was a startled reaction. If David Pelham had run in the right direction he might well have collided with Alan Birch who was backing himself into position. Fortunately for the Outcasts Alan's concentration was not broken. The catch was taken. Michael Carter's cameo was at an end. After one more delivery full and straight from Charlie Colson so too was the home side's innings.

Tea interval

An early tea might have been taken. It was clearly ready despite the somewhat precipitate close of the Daychurch innings. However, the door of the home changing room was shut. A team meeting had been convened. There were raised voices. One voice predominated. It was not possible to hear everything being said, but Kevin Newton picked out the sentence, 'Where the hell is he?' There was no doubt to whom this related. Why indeed had Middle Daychurch been reduced to ten men? The Outcasts were still pondering this question when the missing player cantered up the steps of the pavilion. 'Hello,' he said, 'what's happening? It can't have been rained off.' Stewart Thorogood was on hand to tell him. 'Oh, Christ!' said Richard Love, 'that's really not good.' But Stewart noticed that he made no move to go up to the changing room. Had Richard felt disposed to explain himself, he would have had a sympathetic audience in the Outcasts. There was a clue in the name.

The row of houses which fringed the ground was known as Cricketers Close which, without the apostrophe, was both a name and a warning. Despite the distance between pitch and housing balls did from time to time have to be retrieved from gardens. That this had not developed into a bitter dispute owed something to the fact that several of the properties were occupied either by members of the Carter family or their friends or employees.

Friendship was probably the most approximate word to explain why Richard Love had been drawn to number 10 Cricketers Close that afternoon in dereliction of his duty to the village cricket team. Shirley and her mother were new to Middle Daychurch. Mrs Simpson had become friendly with Richard's mother over a shared interest in astrology. A few months ago the Loves had given a drinks party to which Mrs Simpson had been invited. It was known that there was no Mr Simpson regularly in residence. Word was that business, the nature of which was not disclosed, meant long absences from home. On the day in question she had rung to ask whether she could bring her daughter, who had suddenly descended for the weekend. Maisie Love, who always brightened at the prospect of her son meeting 'some nice young girl,' said 'of course'. Unwittingly she had lit a fuse.

Shirley was a student nurse based at a hospital in Suffolk. Getting away from home had been a great liberation for her. Up to that point she had led a very sheltered life due to the excessive supervision of her mother and even more so of her father whenever he had been at home. Playing doctors and nurses for real had brought out a side to her character which hitherto had been suppressed. It had blossomed to her own great pleasure and, it had to be said, the delight of many others. Her visits home had become less frequent, especially since her mother had moved to Middle Daychurch, which she regarded as a backwater when contrasted with the bright lights and bright life to be enjoyed in her current place of work. However, when trouble looms, home is to where you instinctively turn. And trouble had loomed. It was trouble in the shape of a huge South African doctor who was trying to monopolise her attention. At first it had been fun, big fun. He was gorgeous and so very polite. But with familiarity she had seen him in a different light. Still gorgeous, but demanding, possessive and slightly menacing. She had needed a break. Hence the surprise phone call. 'There's always a bed for you here, dear,' her mother had said, although it took her daughter a little while before she could put it to ideal use.

Richard Love was not enamoured of his parents' occasional drinks parties. A few of his friends and relatives might be there, but all of them would probably prefer to be in The Cow's Corner with pints of beer in their hands and not glasses of sweet white or sour red wine. His sister, Barbara, was more dutiful and put pressure on her brother to be the same. Richard had reluctantly submitted, but was determined to escape as soon as he decently could. Entering the room, he thought the assembled throng looked much the same as ever. He nodded in the direction of cousin David and was edging in his direction when his eye caught a face which was not familiar. But it was strikingly attractive and almost by invisible force Richard was drawn to it.

This was the start of Shirley coming home more often. 'I'm finding it easier to study here away from the hustle and bustle of the hospital,' she lied to her mother. 'It's so much quieter here.' Mrs Simpson was surprised by this change of heart on her daughter's part, but was not disposed to argue. She did not notice that Shirley's appearances coincided with the cricket club's home fixtures. The friendship between Richard and Shirley nevertheless had to be conducted with extreme discretion as Shirley did not want her mother getting on her case. With Richard one of the more regular members of the team, their opportunities for unobserved whilst meaningful time together were extremely limited.

Finally the stars had assembled in the right constellation. It was a home match. Mrs Simpson had gone to visit a sick sister. Her husband was away as usual. Maisie was scoring. Even though his absence from the ground was risky, Richard's frustration had grown too much for him. It was time for him to score as well.

Tea on that day was an uneasy interlude. The Middle Daychurch team had eventually emerged from the changing room. They found Richard Love slumped in a chair. What followed was thought by the Outcasts to be a supreme piece of acting. They, of course, were as unaware of the truth as Richard's team mates, but they had seen him bound up the pavilion steps as fit as a fiddle. Joseph Carter's angry admonition on seeing his missing player was cut short by a hollow groan as Richard clutched his stomach. There was a grimace of pain. A stifled exclamation. Another groan. Richard then half rose from his seat before collapsing again. When Joseph tried to resume his interrogation Richard dramatically rose to his feet and made a bolt for the stairs this time with a hand on another part of his anatomy. The changing room door was slammed shut, but an extended wail began before fading away as Richard receded into its depths. Charlie Colson was so impressed that he could not help remarking, 'It must have been something he ate.' Richard could not have wished for better corroboration for the false impression he had attempted to convey.

Second innings

The tea itself was admirable in terms of refreshment and sustenance, but consumed largely in silence. Resumption of play could not come fast enough. There was no sign of the supposedly ailing Richard Love and so Brian

Stagden, the other man from Near Daychurch, was obliged to fulfil his twelfth man duties. Jon Palmer and Stewart Thorogood were the Outcasts' opening batsmen. They strode out in confident mood. 221 runs to win was not a daunting target even though they were largely unfamiliar with the strength of the home team's bowling attack. The pitch did not seem to possess any demons. Safety first was the approach on which Jon and Stewart had agreed. They recognised the bowler who pulled off his sweater to commence proceedings from the pavilion end. It was Philip Carter, portly and medium pace. With Richard Love presumably incarcerated in a lavatory cubicle, Stewart Thorogood realised that Middle Daychurch were missing their first-choice opening bowler. This seemed to augur well.

It was still auguring well after the first two overs. Philip Carter's bowling had held no terrors. As though they were having a net Jon and Stewart played a few gentle strokes and ambled four singles. To the evident disappointment of Tom Carter, who had been swinging his arms and engaging in loosening exercises, his grandfather chose one of his sons-in-law, Adrian Seymour, as the other opening bowler. This may have been because he was a left-arm bowler. It had certainly nothing to do with pace or, on the evidence of the first three deliveries, accuracy. Adrian opened with a wide and pitched his next two sufficiently clear of off stump that Stewart had no need to play a stroke. The third legitimate ball was straight but short and was square cut for a couple. The next was straight and overpitched. Stewart drove it for four. Then the bowler found his composure and the remainder of the over was runless.

Philip Carter's second over was much in the same vein as his first: not threatening, easily milked. The two batsmen repeated the treatment. Adrian Seymour's over was a vast improvement containing only one loose ball which yielded three runs. Then as Philip Carter's bowling began to improve so Adrian Seymour's performance declined. At first the change was barely noticeable, but it gradually became more pronounced. Five overs into his spell Philip actually achieved a maiden whilst at the other end runs were in free flow. The openers exchanged thoughts at the end of the tenth over. Their opening stand was worth 55. 'Leaving these two on,' said Stewart, 'suggests he must have fewer options than we reckoned. We know he's down one with Richard Love festering somewhere indoors.' 'Well, he can keep that left-armer going as long as he likes,' replied Jon, 'but that youngster over there looks as though he doesn't agree.' He pointed to Tom Carter, who was going through ever more frantic motions to gain attention.

In the pavilion the Outcasts were bored. Their opening batsmen were looking settled. The next two in the order were padded up. For the rest it looked to be a long waiting game without any entertaining distractions. The most usual distraction in this phase of a match would be a quick pint or two in the neighbouring boozer. Those batting at nine, ten and eleven would probably have set their sights higher than that. However, not being aware of any relaxation of the sobriety test following the passing of Edwin Carter, the Outcasts had resolved to play it safe. David Pelham sighed. 'Let's hope it's a good bash that Tim has lined up for us tonight.' Tim Jackson shifted uneasily in his seat. 'OK, guys, I've been meaning to mention, but I shan't be joining you tonight.' Seeing looks of surprise, horror even, on the faces turned towards him, he hastily added, 'No, don't worry, it's still on. You'll have a great time. But Alan's persuaded me to have dinner with him at the local restaurant. It's a bit of a special place.' Eyes turned to Alan Birch. His penchant for good food was well known, but to put it before a Tim Jackson-inspired party was a surprise even for a safely married man like Alan. Being next man in, Alan kept half an eye on the cricket whilst explaining that going off for dinner at Le Rêve Royal had not been the original idea. 'I'd tried to book, but they hadn't a table. Then I tried them on spec a bit earlier and they'd had a cancellation. It was just too good an opportunity to miss. I knew that Tim would appreciate it too. I'm sure you lot can get by without us.' And they would, but not in the way expected.

Stewart Thorogood had not entirely read the mind of Joseph Carter. The Middle Daychurch captain allowed his son to bowl another over in light of his increasingly economical performance. This was a mistake. He had bowled well, but had taken something out of himself in the process. His exertions now had their effect. Philip was visibly more laboured in his run-up and at delivery his arm drooped. The result was a mixed bag which Jon Palmer was able to pick off at will. Altogether sixteen runs came from the over, more than Philip had conceded in his previous five overs. He was not a happy man. Joseph Carter did not intend to make the same mistake twice. He had already made up his mind to relieve Adrian Seymour. The over just bowled reinforced the decision. He summoned David Carter whose accurate off spin was remembered by Jon and Stewart. This year it would be remembered with feeling.

David asked for and got an attacking field. Stewart, who was due to face him, did not believe that there was anything in the wicket to justify his being surrounded by four close fielders. David Pelham's performance earlier had not suggested that this was a spinner's wicket. The ball which had despatched Joseph Carter had been a surprise package to everyone. Stewart told himself to be watchful at first, but he had scanned the thinly manned outfield and thought there could be a harvest to be reaped. Six balls later he was less sure of himself. In one sense his assessment had seemed right. The wicket had not shown much sign of taking spin. It was in variations of flight that David Carter had posed problems. The faster ball which he had saved for the last delivery had completely deceived Stewart. He was saved not by his bat, but by virtue of Syd Breakwell being the umpire to whom the bowler had directed his appeal. 'Not out, I fancy,' replied Syd with the certainty he used to cloak his dodgy decisions. As David Carter took his cap Syd obligingly added that he'd heard a nick. David suppressed the response that formulated in his mind.

It was David's brother, Andrew, who was called into service at the pavilion end. Tom Carter was crestfallen. After Andrew's first over he had been given justification for his dismay. Andrew aspired to bowl leg spin. It was clear from the start that he had been chosen more for variation than for any belief that he was in the tradition of Shane Warne. The fielders were scattered. Joseph Carter seemed to be working on the theory of a catch in the deep. The first ball to Jon Palmer was short of a length and might well have been sent soaring into the deep. However, the batsman thought he would take a look at the bowling before turning to aggression. Seemingly one more ball decided him. This was a full toss suspiciously wide of off stump, but not called as such by Umpire Love. The next ball was straight, but asked to be hit. Jon swept it uppishly over deep fine leg. Ridiculously he got into a tangle with the fuller delivery which followed and they scrambled two leg byes. Jon's connection with the fifth ball was imperfect and he had to be content with three. A modest single from Stewart rounded off the over.

The spin combination remained in place for another couple of overs with an almost identical outcome. David bowled another maiden to Stewart Thorogood, who gave a half-chance to short leg. Andrew contributed another mixed bag from which Jon and Stewart plundered eight runs between them. The pattern then changed. Stewart at last stole a run off David Carter and gave Jon on 47 his first chance against the off spinner. The attacking field remained in place. David tossed the ball up invitingly. Jon looked set to launch it massively towards long on to reach his half century. Unfortunately he had not read the flight. The ball dipped on him and took a leading edge. It ballooned up for the bowler to take an easy catch. David could not resist turning to Umpire Breakwell. 'Another nick, eh?'

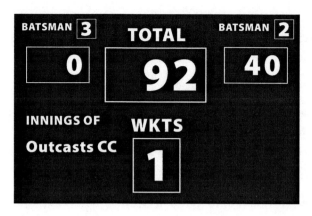

BATSMAN **3** **TOTAL** BATSMAN **2**

0 **92** **40**

INNINGS OF **WKTS**

Outcasts CC **1**

This brought two people to the wicket. Alan Birch, next in for the Outcasts, found himself accompanied by a sprightly Richard Love, who seemed astonishingly free of the malady which had convulsed him an hour or so earlier. Joseph Carter was unwelcoming to the supposedly restored member of his team. 'What the hell are you doing here? You can bugger off. You're not needed.' But in fact he was, because Richard had taken the precaution of advising twelfth man Brian Stagden that he should make himself scarce whilst the substitution was arranged. Brian was pleased to be relieved and slipped away for a quiet smoke. Joseph Carter realised that he had been outsmarted, but thought he would have the last word by saying, 'You needn't think you'll be doing any bowling today. I'd rather be struck down dead than use you after the way you've behaved.' Stewart Thorogood, who had heard this exchange, stirred the pot by saying that the Outcasts would have no objection to Richard bowling as his absence from the field had obviously (he emphasised the word) been caused by illness. Joseph glowered and the game resumed.

There was early evidence that denial of Richard Love's bowling would not have a crucial effect on the course of the match. Alan Birch played out the remainder of David Carter's over in an unconvincing manner. Whereas concentration was needed to blunt the bowler's accuracy, Alan was allowing himself to be distracted by anticipation of the dining experience which awaited him. Rather than giving one hundred per cent attention to flight and length his mind was wandering to choice of main course: beef or venison. He had memorised the menu, but, if he was to choose the venison, he would need to know a little more about the sauce. 'Are you OK?' asked Stewart having watched his partner deal somewhat unsurely with the bowling of David Carter. 'Fine, fine,' he was assured and after the next over might have been convinced.

Having wilfully denied himself use of his leading strike bowler and wanting to keep his impatient grandson in his place, Joseph Carter decided that he would have to risk another over of Andrew's leg spin. His only remaining option might have been Charles Bell. However, Charles had suffered a loss of form recently. His medium-paced cutters had lost their zip. Charles was nursing a niggle in his shoulder which would soon deny the team of a stock bowler capable of sealing up runs at one end. Andrew, who had resigned himself to spending the rest of the day patrolling the boundary, was delighted to have his spell extended. His delight was short-lived.

Despite the loss of a wicket the Outcasts in the pavilion remained upbeat about their team's prospects. They were ahead of the required scoring rate, almost halfway towards their target and had nine wickets in hand. Colin Banks, who did not expect to bat, said that he felt like a walk. His flatmate, Greg Roberts, whose twelfth man duties looked to be light or non-existent now that his team was batting, volunteered to accompany him. They turned in the direction of the main part of the village, passing Cricketers Close, and reached Le Rêve Royal where they paused to examine the menu which seemed to be of such attraction to Alan Birch. They were debating whether to walk on or turn back when they suddenly became aware of raised voices. They edged closer in the direction of the sound.

Wishing to stay concealed, Greg took no more than a quick glance round the corner of the building. In an area which he assumed to lie between the kitchen and an outhouse he made out the figures of two young men. One was in chef's attire, the other in blue jeans and a grey hooded top. As he withdrew his head Greg was sure that the next voice he heard came from the chef. 'But I'm the one who's taking all the risk.' 'Yeah, well, you're getting well paid for it,' – the other voice. 'It's not enough.' 'You've had long enough to think about it. You can't back out now.' 'I bloody could if you don't make it really worthwhile. I could go to the police and . . .' He was cut off in mid-sentence by his companion. 'I really wouldn't do that. It wouldn't then be just a matter of your mummy finding out what you really get up to here. You might end up at the bottom of the village well and you wouldn't be in a state to do any wishing. Funny things do happen here, you know.' His tone then changed. 'Now, look here Craig, I thought we'd got a deal. But tell you what, I like you and I want us to stay mates. How about I bung in another fifty? Will that do you?' There must have been a sign of assent, because the voice of the hoodie went on, 'OK brilliant. So it's half now and the rest when it's over'. There was a rustle of paper. Greg

risked another look and saw an envelope change hands. Then again it was the hoodie's voice, 'You goin' to give us a kiss then?' This was followed by a peal of laughter which Greg suddenly realised was coming nearer. With great presence of mind he propelled Colin quickly back in the direction from which they had come and then turned as though approaching the restaurant for the first time. When the hoodie emerged into the road he was wheeling a bike. Without a glance in their direction he pedalled off towards the end of the village and a prearranged rendezvous.

The match situation which Greg and Colin would find on their return to the cricket ground was radically different from that which obtained when they left. Off the second ball of his third over Andrew Carter conceded a single which brought Alan Birch on strike. However much Alan might have been preoccupied by gastronomic anticipation he could recognise bad balls which needed to be hit. Wherever Andrew pitched his deliveries they were all begging for severe treatment. Alan was not sparing and his account was opened with three fours and a six. But then the pendulum swung. Stewart Thorogood thought he was being watchful in dealing with David Carter. He blocked the first ball and intended to do the same to what looked like a similar delivery. He had not spotted a subtle variation and he edged the ball to slip. Catching it made Andrew Carter feel a little better. Next man in Rashid Ali had blossomed as a batsman once he had cast aside his defensive shackles and chosen to play his natural game. He had studiously observed David Carter's bowling and thought he was equal to the challenge. Without wasting time he used his feet to the first ball he received and thrashed it through mid on for four. Believing in rotation of strike particularly when he, a left-hander, was partnered by a right-hander, Rash took an effortless single from David's next delivery. With five runs already taken from the over he leant on his bat to watch Alan Birch cope with the remaining two balls. His composure was disturbed when Alan without using his feet groped at the next ball and it arched up to Charles Bell at silly point. Charlie Colson was pleased to be batting as high as five in the order, but his pleasure was not long-lasting. David Carter tried a top spinner first up and this proved too much for Charlie. The ball went between bat and pad and made a mess of his stumps.

Charlie's replacement was Winston Jenkins. There was time for a consultation between him and Rashid Ali as Joseph Carter was contemplating a change in bowling and taking his time about it. 'This guy's good,' said Rash ruefully, 'but there seem to be plenty of runs at the other end. I think our best bet is ultra caution against the offie and get our runs from the rest. Mind you, if we can keep rotating the strike we might disturb his line.' Winston had nothing to add by way of alternative and so agreed to take his cue from Rash.

Meanwhile Joseph Carter was in danger of being trapped by his own rigidity. Even the flurry of wickets did not persuade him that he could afford another over from Andrew Carter. He felt it was too soon to bring back one of his opening bowlers. He was denying himself Richard Love to make a point. He was missing Charles Bell. By process of elimination he was left with his precocious grandson, Tom. Maybe it would do no harm to give him an over, but he did not want him to get big-headed. There were a number of young ones in the family he needed to accommodate, but not all at once he reminded himself.

Tom had to bow to his grandfather's dictates in the matter of field setting. Having got his chance at last he was not disposed to argue. He had left school after a productive season. Physically he had filled out and was less willowy. He had drawn in knowledge from his school's new coach, who had played for Hertfordshire. In short at school level he had shown great promise, but apart from a short overseas tour with the school team he had been given scant opportunity to play any meaningful cricket since his return home. He urged himself not to let fly. Control was the watchword drilled into him by his coach. The outcome was a tidy over which Rashid

Ali had treated with respect. Had Tom been allowed a second slip the single which the batsman edged wide of first slip off the last ball might even have been a catch. Joseph Carter granted some encouraging words to Tom which seemed to be tacit admission that he would be allowed another over.

After facing the first two balls of David Carter's fifth over Rashid Ali formed the impression that he was less comfortable bowling to left-handers, which was surprising. The third ball went wide and Rash chopped down on it and got an easy single. The theory about rotation got some backing when David Carter's first ball to Winston Jenkins followed the same trajectory as his previous delivery. Without risk Winston was able to tickle it fine for a boundary. He exchanged an understanding nod with his partner. After that he was forced into eagle-eyed defence as David adjusted his sights.

Tom's second over matched his first. It was tight, steady stuff with nothing loose on which the batsman could feast. With another edge this time all along the ground Rashid Ali stole the strike. It took David Carter a couple of deliveries to get his line correct for the left-hander. Rash was able to get two runs off each and then called Winston for a very brisk single. Winston then got a couple as David erred down the leg side, but was made to look far less assured in the remainder of the over. Tom strode more confidently to his bowling mark, there being no sign that his spell was to be terminated. Without seeking a change in the field placings he pushed his mark back with the intention of upping his pace. He felt good and he looked good. As the ball whacked into his gloves Joseph Carter showed surprise, but did no more than take two paces back and gesture to Andrew Carter at slip to do the same. Rashid Ali survived, but his composure had been disturbed by a peach of a bouncer with which Tom had finished the over. Suddenly this looked like becoming a very different game.

The expectation quickly became fact. David Carter slipped back into the groove against the right-hander. Winston played and missed at two and then tried desperately to get off strike when the ball went off his pads down the leg-side. He yelled 'one' and set off. It was Rash's call and seeing the danger he instantly sent his partner back. It took a dive, but Winston made his ground. He mouthed 'sorry' in Rash's direction. Telling himself to use his feet, he advanced aggressively to an inviting flighted ball from David Carter. He missed it and was comfortably stumped by Joseph Carter. The off spinner had bagged five wickets. Winston's replacement was David Pelham coming in one place higher than shown on the team list. At the critical moment Harry Northwood had been scrabbling around in the visitors' changing room in search of his box.

Without giving any impression of permanence David Pelham survived the two remaining balls in the over. It was then time for a consultation with Rash. 'This lad Tom is good,' Rash acknowledged. 'He's not just a tearaway. God knows why he didn't bowl from the start. No offence to you, Dave, but here's what we'll do.' It was a sound plan, but successful execution could not be counted on in Outcasts' cricket. There was no question about Tom continuing his spell. The pendulum of authority had tilted in his direction. Three disciplined overs and he had visibly grown in stature. Rash sensed it too. He checked his guard. The first two deliveries he rightly judged could be left alone. Then Tom Carter decided to try his slower ball. Unfortunately for him it did not come out right. It presented itself to Rash as a very hittable ball and he went for it. 'Two' was his call, but when he turned after David and he had scampered the two runs comfortably Rash could see that the fielder had not yet gathered the ball. Instinct rather than cool thought overtook him. 'Come on,' he shouted to his partner, who did. Rash was witness to his own fate. Having scooped the ball on the run the fielder let fly an arrow-like throw which hit the stumps leaving Rash six inches short. Richard Love bellowed in triumph. With their best batsman gone the Outcasts were on the skids. 89 short of their target with, if they were honest, not a lot of batting to come.

It was at this moment that two members of the inadequate reserve returned to the pavilion with the situation transformed. Harry Northwood, box now safely in place, was on his way to the crease. Kevin Newton had just got himself ready. There was no time for Colin to be told what had been happening or to relate their little adventure. For Colin it was a race to the changing-room as he knew only too well that with six wickets already down his services might very suddenly be required. Out in the middle David Pelham found himself where it had not been planned that he should be. What had possessed Rash to try for the extra run? Now he was left to face half an over of quite sharp bowling. He took a deep breath to steady himself. Batsman/bowler? Bowler/batsman? After his performance with the ball (1–73 off his eight overs) his credibility now depended on some stickability with the bat. He took guard, swallowed hard and looked up to indicate he was ready to try to withstand Tom Carter.

Early optimism had faded. The Outcasts now expected defeat. The only question was how long it would take and then how long before they could discreetly transfer to The Cow's Corner for a few early evening bevies and maybe a steak sandwich before the main event, the promised party at Fenworth. They settled to watch in grisly fascination how David Pelham and

Harry Northwood would cope with the two very useful bowlers Middle Daychurch now had in combination. At this point Brian Stagden, the twelfth man from Near Daychurch, reappeared and sat down with them. With none of the rest of his team or their supporters in earshot Brian was prepared to get a few things off his chest. 'Bloody family,' he announced, 'Things haven't improved even with the old man gone. Some of the younger ones are a bit better, but they're still family. They have to kow-tow to their elders. If you ask me, the rest of the old 'uns should clear off if the atmosphere in this club's to get any better. Old Joseph's just as prejudiced as his father and he's not got an ounce of cricket nous. Just look how he's farted around with his bowlers. Probably not the blatant cheat his dad was, but you'll see he's kept the umpiring in the family. Bloody disgrace the way Bill Pledger was treated after all his service. He was furious not to be asked back after the old man died.' This litany of bile showed little sign of ending, unlike the innings of Harry Northwood. However, Rashid Ali interrupted the flow by asking why Brian continued to play at the club if he hated them all so much. Brian looked surprised. 'I wouldn't say hate exactly, but there's nowhere else round here to get a game. And anyway they need my batting. Well, not today obviously. Joseph seems to enjoy making Martin or me do penance from time to time. And . . .' But what more he had to say was interrupted this time by a spectator reaction outside and laughter from the Outcasts inside.

Whether it had been a reaction to being the indirect cause of Rashid Ali's dismissal or lack of concentration, Tom Carter's first deliveries to David Pelham had not been penetrative. The batsman had not been severely tested and had even managed to scramble a leg bye off the final ball. This postponed Harry Northwood having to take strike. Although it was fortuitous David Pelham told himself that as the senior batsman it was probably better for him to try to see off David Carter's final over. He succeeded in his objective, but it was not a model performance. He was totally deceived by the first ball, dropped off the second and given not out when the third cannoned into his pads having pitched, in the judgement of Syd Breakwell, outside, microscopically outside, leg stump. He got his bat to the next one, swished at the fifth without making contact and finally, as though a nerveless master of the batting art, drove the ball through a gap in the covers. They ran two.

Harry Northwood received two searing deliveries from Tom Carter which he knew little about. He thereupon adopted a different approach. He flung the bat at the next ball. Had he connected fully it would probably have carried to the next village. Instead it went off an inside edge in an unintended direction and Harry heard the shout of 'run' from David Pelham at the other end. And run he did, but it was only a single. Whether his partner was by now any better equipped to deal with bowling which seemed to be getting faster was not subjected to prolonged examination. David involuntarily edged an express delivery wide of slip and was relieved to race a single and observe what Harry would do next. He chose not to offer advice. Harry appeared to have settled on short but sweet. He slashed at a rising ball and it went over the wicketkeeper's head for four. He was rewarded with a short-pitched ball which whistled past the grill of his helmet and his flailing bat. With the over finished he trotted down the pitch and said to his partner, 'Well what d'ya reckon?' David was beyond words.

Having bowled his allotted overs and bagged five wickets for twenty runs, David Carter had to be replaced at the river end. Still angry with Richard Love, Joseph Carter chose Adrian Seymour. Once this became clear David muttered to Harry that orthodox should do. He was the first to demonstrate what this meant in practice. It was hard to tell. Two balls he was able to leave alone, two he steered towards fielders and two he despatched to the boundary, one with a handsome square cut, the other with a rather less handsome hoick over mid wicket. This left his partner to deal with the next over from Tom Carter. 'Cheers,' said Harry.

Tom had clearly benefited from being well coached at school. He had become a very promising quick bowler. What he lacked as yet was experience. It was not in Joseph Carter's nature, nor probably capability, to supply the missing ingredient. Middle Daychurch as a team did not operate in a collegiate kind of way. All eyes tended to be on the top man. It was up to him – even if he was not up to it. Left to himself the impatient bowler prescribed still greater speed as the means of overcoming Harry Northwood. It did not work. Harry was set on do or die. He was prepared to flash the blade. Tom's attempt to increase his pace led to a loss of accuracy. So Harry with his eye in was able to carve the ball away in all (not always intended) directions. When Tom petulantly flung in a couple of bouncers one was ducked, but the other top-edged for six. By the end of the over Tom was angry, but he was mature enough to direct the anger to himself. He had got it wrong and he knew it. He saw his grandfather move menacingly towards him.

The Outcasts needed 58 more to win the match. Eleven overs remained. After another Adrian Seymour over the target had been reduced to 53. Joseph Carter might not have been an acute cricketer or a sensitive man, but he was now torn. He wanted to win the match. That was a given. But he liked to do it his way. He had put trust in his grandson and he did not want to be proved wrong, particularly when his late uncle's grandson, David, had performed so well. So despite Tom's fears he was told to keep bowling and 'put your mark back where you started'. This had a sobering effect on the young man and he delighted his grandfather (although Joseph displayed no such emotion) by bowling a superb maiden over to David Pelham, who was scarcely able to put bat on ball. His discomfiture was completed when he fell over in trying to avoid a steepling bouncer and frantically rolled away to prevent disturbing his stumps. Now it was 53 off nine overs. The asking rate had risen.

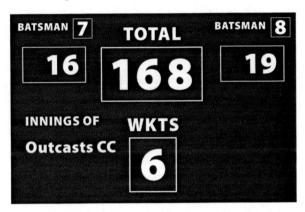

BATSMAN **7** **TOTAL** BATSMAN **8**

16 **168** **19**

INNINGS OF **WKTS**

Outcasts CC **6**

Joseph Carter had the wit to realise it could easily go in the opposite direction. Tom had only one over left. Adrian Seymour on current form looked well capable of conceding six an over. If he wanted to win, the inevitable threatened. Stubbornly Joseph put it off and gave the ball to his son, Philip, who he hoped had recovered by now from his previous exertions. He had not had too much chasing to do in the field. If he could contribute a couple of tight overs or better still get rid of that scything school kid, Joseph reckoned that the match could be put out of the Outcasts' reach. The way in which Philip Carter walked back to the end of his run did not underpin his captain's expectation. Nor did his first ball, perhaps understandably a loosener. It was crashed backwards of square by Harry Northwood. The bowler did not hurry himself in returning to his mark. His second delivery was as uncontrolled as his first and Harry feasted off it. Philip was breathing heavily when he passed David Pelham to prepare for the next ball. But it never came. Just before leaping into his delivery stride Philip crashed into Umpire Breakwell. Both fell to the ground. Syd quickly recovered himself, but the bowler lay motionless.

Joseph's stentorian cry roared across the ground. 'Is there a doctor here?'

A figure detached itself from the ring of spectators in the vicinity of the pavilion. 'Quick, man, quick,' barked Joseph, although the elderly, white-haired man was doing his best. Alan Birch was a pharmacist, not a doctor, but he had sufficient medical knowledge to recognise a serious situation when he saw one. 'This is an ambulance job,' he said, getting up. He took it upon himself to make the call. In the middle a small confused circle surrounded the prostrate figure. The doctor, excusing himself for being long retired, said there was a pulse, but he recommended that an ambulance be summoned in a case of this kind. 'Of what kind?' demanded Joseph bulging with impatience. 'He may have had a heart attack.' 'Nonsense,' said the patient's father. 'He's just not as fit as he should be. He'll be all right in a few minutes. He probably had too much lunch.' He had to be held back from toeing his son in the ribs. In the pavilion Colin Banks stretched and said, 'That's obviously put the kybosh on it. No more play today, lads. Well, not that sort anyway.' He laughed and went up the stairs.

When finally they were able to assemble in The Cow's Corner the Outcasts had much to talk about on what had been an extraordinary day. After their dismissals one or two of them had taken the opportunity to shower and change whilst others had lounged around in their whites or tracksuit bottoms. After the interruption had happened Stewart Thorogood thought to take his bag out to the coach and commiserate with Stephen Marshall about the game being spoilt. The vehicle was unlocked, but there was no immediate sign of the vicar. Stewart clambered aboard for all to be revealed. The smell of the distillery hit him first. The source of it was a quick second. Stretched out in the gangway was the recumbent and motionless figure of Stephen Marshall. Unlike in the case of Philip Carter, no doctor was required to diagnose the cause. There was very little left in the whisky bottle which lay by his side. Clearly not all of it had found its way to his stomach as there was a small pool of the liquid about level with his neck. Multiple thoughts rushed through Stewart's mind as he turned still clutching his bag to break the news to the rest of the team. As he descended the steps of the coach he was almost mown down by an ambulance which arrived at high speed.

The paramedics had taken a more serious view of Philip Carter's condition than was evinced by his father. They made it clear that Philip needed treatment and observation in hospital. By this time Philip's mother had been called to the scene. She was deputed to go in the ambulance with her son whilst Joseph declared that there was a match to finish. 'He's going to be all right. He wouldn't want us to stop playing on account of his little upset.'

This verdict was greeted passively by his team, but with incredulity by the Outcasts. Most of the spectators had gone, apart from those with a morbid outlook. Signs that the game would shortly recommence was too much even for them and they drifted off for an early tea or in some cases an early pint.

'Are you sure?' Jon Palmer had asked of his opposite number. 'Oh yes,' replied Joseph Carter, 'we don't let a little setback like that ruin a match! We got rained off last year, didn't we? The light's OK and we've got time to finish this one. Boiling up nicely, I'd say.' Seeing the doubting look on Jon's face, he went on, 'You're not in a hurry to go, are you?' Jon shook his head. In light of what Stewart had told him that was the least of their problems. Nevertheless Jon made one more try. 'But don't you need to get off to be with your son? It looked bad to me.' 'No, no,' Joseph said, 'I don't think it's more than a funny turn. Anyway his mother's with him. Now should we get on?' Jon gave up. He turned away so that Joseph could not see the expression on his face. What surprised him was that the rest of the Middle Daychurch team seemed to acquiesce in their captain's decision. There was no sign of protest, except from Brian Stagden who had thought his job done for the day and had surreptitiously downed a can of ale in the changing room. He returned to the field keeping well clear of Joseph Carter.

The outstanding four balls of the thirty-second over were delivered by Adrian Seymour. More out of respect than anything Harry Northwood played them quietly, making no real effort to score. Whatever he may have thought about the situation it was clear that Tom Carter intended business as usual. It was his last permitted over and he was determined to go out on a high. David Pelham was left in no doubt about that. First up Tom managed a ferocious bouncer which without a lightning reaction on David's part might have taken his head off. This had the effect of dictating terms for the rest of the over. Awareness of another short-pitched ball governed the batsman's approach. There was no eagerness to get in line. David scratched around, was lucky to survive a dropped catch, but ended the over runless. Equally Tom was left wicketless, but it had been a fine spell of medium-fast bowling. His grandfather unbent to the extent of giving him a pat on the back. Tom went to his assumed fielding position with now nothing to think about but the welfare of his father. A sense of unease prevented buying wholeheartedly into his grandfather's breezy assurance.

His son's wellbeing had not appeared to trouble Joseph Carter. His furrowed brow had more to do with how he marshalled his depleted bowling resources. Adrian Seymour had to be discounted as he had only two deliveries left to him. The unthinkable loomed. Despite what he had said and what he felt Richard Love would have to be used if he wanted to keep alive the possibility of winning the match. He postponed his U-turn for another over by calling up Andrew Carter to bowl at the river end. It was a risk. Three balls and ten runs into the over Joseph began to think callously that even an out-of-form and apparently injured Charles Bell might have been the better choice. Harry Northwood gave the impression of liking leg spinners, particularly if they failed to bowl line and length. Andrew's fourth ball was a little better, but Harry was still able to caress it towards deep mid wicket for a gentle single. David Pelham was relieved to be facing bowling which contrasted sharply with his experience in the previous over. Batting made easy, he thought, after watching how Harry had gone about his business. The ball was straight, looked too full and was too full. David decided it was going places. He took a mighty heave without using his feet. All he succeeded in doing was edging it into his pads with a sound like a rifle crack which reverberated around the ground except it seemed to the ear of Syd Breakwell. In his excitement Andrew Carter had appealed and Syd's finger had been raised. David Pelham was stupefied, but had to go. His partnership with Harry had been worth 55.

Kevin Newton had skipped out to the middle, quickly taken guard and slammed the remaining ball of Andrew Carter's over for four. Then he had sauntered down the wicket and slapped Harry Northwood on the shoulder. 'Another 30, no problem. Three overs should do it.' This was said in such an exuberant voice that Joseph Carter could not help but hear. That settled it. Richard Love it had to be. Richard saw this as a little victory. He was disinclined to defer to his captain. He set the field himself as he might have done had he opened the bowling. Harry Northwood sensed that it might suddenly be a different game. Richard tested Harry with three balls which shaped away towards the slips. And then he threw in his slower ball. He was sure Harry would go for it. Harry obliged and was caught at mid off.

Colin Banks had played in the manner to which he was most accustomed. To his first ball he achieved no more than an air shot, but his bat had connected with the last delivery of the over and it went one bounce into the seats at the front of the pavilion. This cavalier approach had only served to encourage Kevin Newton. In recognition of his wicket in the previous over Andrew Carter had been retained in the attack. He had not morphed into a better bowler, but with batsmen bent on a kamikaze approach to batting it became a more even contest between bat and ball. At first it had gone the batsman's way with Kevin stealing seven runs off the first four deliveries.

Persevering, Andrew found two better balls which left Colin Banks floundering and runless. It proved to be his most economical over. The Outcasts' score passed the 200 mark. Four overs remained. 21 runs were needed. On paper it should not have been a difficult proposition. As ever there was a gap between hope and reality.

Richard Love had shown that he knew his business against tail enders who seemed set on swinging the bat. Kevin Newton would have bridled at being so classified. On most appearances for the Outcasts he expected to bat higher than nine. The record showed that his expectation was not always fulfilled. What happened next provided a reason why. Richard tested him with a short, rising ball which forced him back on his stumps and followed it with a perfect yorker. The ball went straight through his defences and hit the base of middle stump. Tim Jackson was no man for this situation. His journey to the wicket had occupied far more time than his presence at it. At least his bat had connected with the ball, but only to steer it into the hands of Joseph Carter behind the stumps.

Close of play

Unsure whether on this occasion they would be joined in The Cow's Corner by any members of the home team, the Outcasts' principal talking point after ordering the first round, was not so much a review of the match but their unexpected transport problem. 'Is it right to curse a man of God?' David Pelham asked, 'because that's what I feel like doing.' There were murmurs of sympathy before Jon Palmer said, 'We can blast the bugger all we like, but it doesn't get us any nearer home, let alone to that party. None of us is qualified to drive that coach.' 'In the last resort,' Charlie Colson intervened, 'we could always order cabs to get us to the nearest train station. I've done it myself. But I don't know how late the trains run.' The landlord, who had no real interest in denying himself the drinking capacity of the Outcasts, said that he would look for a timetable. He had already obliged them by finding some space for them to dump their kit. 'It's a bloody expensive option,' was Harry Northwood's response, underlining his indeterminate student status. 'And unless we leave our bags behind,' said Winston Jenkins, 'we'll need an extra cab or two to squeeze everything in.' Heads nodded at that, because those set on partying had brought an extra change of clothes for the evening. The gloom deepened, mitigated only by a second round, when the landlord returned with the news that the last train was 9.35 p.m. 'I hadn't got a timetable,' he said, 'but I've checked on the internet. If you are prepared to go to Long Southworth though, the last one from there is 10.20 p.m. Mind you, it's another 15 miles.'

Ian Birch was feeling desperate. He could see his gourmet evening slipping from his grasp. Addressing the landlord and explaining his situation, he said, 'Do you have rooms?' 'We're not an inn in the old-fashioned sense, you know. We don't do overnights. I'm sorry. Can't help you there.' Perhaps it was the agonised look on Alan's face that stirred him. 'Course, we do have a spare room. I suppose I might persuade the wife to make up the bed. You'd have to share it though.' He laughed, but then he could see that Alan and Tim were prepared to go to such lengths. 'Let's see,' he added – and disappeared again. This desperate ploy amused rather than annoyed his team mates. They felt it was no skin off their nose if Alan and Tim wanted to splash extra cash in this way. Greg and Colin exchanged glances. They had seen the prices on the menu at Le Rêve Royal. Another round was purchased as the Outcasts continued to bemoan their situation. However, it did cheer up for Alan and Tim when the landlord told them they could have the room. 'For 100 quid, I can't guarantee you breakfast, but I will throw in a ride to the nearest station unless, of course, you'd prefer to ride with the reverend gentleman, always supposing he's sobered up by then.'

The afternoon's events were brought back to them with the arrival of Club Secretary, Michael Carter. He was followed by his cousins, David and Andrew, together with Charles Bell and Richard Love. Polite enquiries were made about Philip Carter, but Michael expressed confidence that his brother would be fine. Tom had gone to the hospital to check up on him and be with his mother. The Outcasts did not press the point despite the misgivings which some of them felt on seeing Philip collapse as he did. Their first instinct had been to abandon the match, but Joseph had been insistent that it be played to a conclusion. Compliments were paid to Tom, David and Richard's bowling. Andrew looked suitably abashed. There was no talk about Richard's mysterious absence and the Outcasts did not like to raise the subject.

It was not long, however, before their plight entered the conversation. There was general laughter about the drunken priest, but then Michael Carter cleared his throat and said that he had an idea. 'There might be one way of getting you all to the station, but I think you'll have to forget about your party. 'Why don't you buy a round and I'll make a phone call?' To the Outcasts that seemed a worthwhile investment. Michael was away 15 minutes, but when he returned he was smiling. 'Sorted,' he said. 'Your carriage will be here at eight o'clock and you'll be at the station in ample time for the last train. In the meantime you might want to get some bar food to keep the ale company.' There was such a degree of relief that no questions were asked and the advice readily taken.

Over a few more rounds snippets of information about Middle Daychurch Cricket Club's affairs were revealed. The Outcasts sensed that there were starting to be cracks in the formidable family facade. There were internal jealousies and the younger members were impatient for a greater share of the action. 'But, sure,' said Michael, who seemed to have a level-headed approach, 'we still want to field the best eleven, even if it does mean putting up with the odd outsider.' The exchanges remained good-humoured. Excellent ale was copiously drunk. Alan and Tim slipped away for their gourmet treat. Prompt at eight the Outcasts' transport arrived. It was probably as well by then that they were in no state to discriminate. Mine host at The Cow's Corner wished them a hearty farewell and an early return. His takings had received a significant boost.

The morning after had been selected as one of the dates for an informal get-together at The Sink and Plumber. Charlie Colson had been charged with issuing reminders. This must have been to good effect, because the turnout within five minutes of opening time was impressive. Charlie himself, however, was not one of the assembled throng. Syd Breakwell had given apologies. He had promised his wife a trip to Hastings ('God knows why' would have been a sentiment he might currently be sharing with the rest of the Outcasts). Despite Brian Sachin Crossley being not much more than two months old he had settled into a very predictable pattern of waking and sleeping. Sophie had therefore released Simon from domestic duties ('but don't make too much of a habit of it'). Two absentees without leave were Alan Birch and Tim Jackson. Too much after-dinner Cognac, it was reckoned, would have led to a lazy start. Or it could have been Sunday trains up the spout. Little more was thought of it.

Those who had not been involved in the outing to Middle Daychurch were given an account of the day. It was the latter part which commanded most interest and amusement. God's representative had indeed conducted himself in mysterious ways. There were suggestions that Bill Blimp might not have been so bad after all. As to the manner of the team's final exit from Middle Daychurch there was a fair amount of hilarity. 'Farmer Giles' (actually Tom Goodwin) had turned up trumps. He had fired up his tractor and the trailer which served to convey his shooting parties and local carol singers. Sitting on bales of straw with their kit piled between them, the

Outcasts had travelled at sedate, but ultimately reliable pace to the nearest station. At the time of night when they reached the station there was no possibility of buying tickets. With the entrance to the booking office firmly locked, they had access only to the platform. However, it proved to be not too late at night for them to encounter a Revenue Protection Officer, who lived up to his company's expectations. His determination to impose penalty fines was robustly proof against the Outcasts' pleadings. The fact that they had been having a boozy evening whilst he was on late duty had in no way helped their cause.

Due sympathy was expressed by yesterday's absent friends. Cheeriness took over as more ale was consumed. Particular pleasure was gained from the week's guest bitter which came from a niche brewery in Windsor. The name 'Royal Taste' was most probably a coincidence. The mood, which had lightened, darkened again with the arrival of Charlie Colson whose expression was strained. Without preamble he accounted, 'He's dead'. There was silence. John Furness was the first to react. 'Who's dead?' A fair question. After all it might have been anyone. 'Philip Carter,' Charlie blurted out. 'I've just taken a call from his brother. It was heart failure. Poor guy. They got him to hospital OK, but then he had another massive heart attack and he was a goner. I hope his father's regretting his callous attitude. And to think we were all sloshing it back in the pub without so much as a thought.' This was a long lament from Charlie which the rest heard in silence. Then the questions and comments resounded.

Gradually the hubbub reduced in volume. Contemplation took over. Another death. Out of respect a further round was purchased and solemnly consumed. Slowly the conversation resumed a more normal course and the session might have drifted to an unremarkable end if the door had not burst open in dramatic fashion. An unkempt and white-faced Tim Jackson lurched into the bar. The usually suave and well-turned out Tim looked such a mess that the reaction he provoked from his friends was laughter until it rapidly became clear that he was expecting sympathy. 'Not such a good night then?' David Pelham queried without being able to banish the smirk on his face. 'Terrible,' gasped Tim. 'And it's not a laughing matter,' he added seeing the looks around him. 'Alan's had to go straight to bed. Margaret says she's never seen him so bad. She's called the doctor.' The reaction of the Outcasts began to adjust and Tim was pressed for an explanation.

It seemed that the restaurant had taken delivery of a consignment of oysters. These were being heavily promoted by the staff and heavily discounted into the bargain. 'Well, you know what Alan's like,' said Tim. 'He was up for it and I was persuaded. So was half the clientele. It was after I'd finished my main course that I began to feel a bit off-colour. I looked at Alan. He'd gone quiet and seemed to be sweating. I was just about to ask him if he was all right when he suddenly got to his feet and made a rush for the gents. He was unlucky to collide with another guest who seemed in a hurry as well. This allowed someone else to squeeze past both of them, with unfortunate results for Alan.' Seeing the expression on the faces around him, he said, 'You know what it's like in these chi-chi restaurants. There's only one WC in the bog. A urinal did not fit the need'. He paused as if disapproving of the humour that had provoked, before he continued. 'A bloke at the next table to us suddenly slumped forward into the remains of his boeuf bourguignon. There was an awful sound behind me. I turned to see that a woman had vomited into her risotto. That was the last straw for me. I made for the front door. A couple from the table by the window were close behind. I'm afraid we were a very undignified trio, but there was no fighting it.' 'So it was an attack of duff oysters,' said Jon Palmer. 'I hope you got your money back. So anyway have a pint. That should clear out your system.' The suggestion was too much for Tim, who put his hand to his mouth and moved with surprising speed to the loo. He was gone a while.

On the whole the Outcasts found the tale quite funny. Pretentious fine diners brought down to earth. Should have stuck with pie and chips. But Greg Roberts spared a thought for Alan Birch and made a call to his wife. The doctor had been and whilst he only had broken English he had assured Margaret that sleep and a diet of water would probably put things right. Tim came gingerly back into the bar and surprised his friends by saying that he might try a pint after all. That raised a small cheer. After two hearty gulps there was more he had to tell them. There had been a chaotic scene inside Le Rêve Royal. No-one who had eaten the oysters had been spared. The proprietors were distraught, fearing ruin. The evening had been wrecked for everyone. In the case of one patron an ambulance had had to be called. Wishing to be spared further details, Dean Faulds asked, 'So what happened to you then? How did you make out?

'I just wanted to get away,' said Tim, 'but I was equally worried for Alan. I had to go back inside. He was in a terrible mess.' Dean Faulds rolled his eyes, bracing himself for some truly awful revelations, but Tim showed restraint. 'Well, we both were and we just wanted the hell out of there. To say we walked back to the pub would be an exaggeration. It was a punctu-ated journey. Without me I reckon Alan wouldn't have been able to do much more than crawl. I didn't feel we could go in the pub in the state we were in and so we made for the coach. We found 'his holiness' sitting on the step, waving an empty bottle and attempting to sing 'Onward Christian Soldiers'. Here was one person in no position to criticise us. So that was our refuge. Neither of us got much sleep. I won't say more than that.' The Outcasts exchanged glances, some suppressing mirth. When Stewart Thorogood asked how they had got back home there was all-round amazement when Tim said, 'On the coach'. Stephen Marshall had sworn that he was fit to drive and Tim and Alan had been desperate enough to let him. He explained that he had a service to conduct and that quite often he took whisky the night before to steady his nerves. He had shown no disposition to apologise for his lapse the previous evening. In fact he made no reference to it. 'It was as though,' said Tim, 'it had wiped from his mind. And we were in no position to complain. The landlord settled for £50 when we collected our kit.' At which point Tim downed the rest of his pint and pronounced himself much better. Then he added, 'Can't help wondering what the sermon was like.'

After dispersal Charlie Colson felt that it fell to him to pass on condolences over the death of Philip Carter. So after he had eaten a round of sandwiches prepared for him by Liz and discovered that the limited overs match to be shown on TV that afternoon had been rained off, he reached for the telephone. Michael Carter was not at home. Charlie left a short message on his answering machine. After that he must have succumbed to a post-prandial snooze. He woke to see Liz looking at her most attractive. He was instantly attracted. It was not ideal to be interrupted by the telephone. In the heat of the moment he had forgotten to turn it off. The caller was Michael Carter. As if by some sixth sense he asked, 'This is not a bad time, is it?' 'No, no,' spluttered Charlie. 'Fine, good of you to return my call. We were all so sorry to hear about your brother. That must've been a helluva shock.' Michael agreed. 'You can say that again. And then to lose Uncle Paul as well. It's knocked us all back.' 'Your Uncle Paul. Why, whatever happened to him?' Michael sounded surprised. 'Haven't you heard? There was a bad case of food poisoning at our local restaurant. My uncle was badly affected. It must have triggered some reaction and (Michael's voice broke) he died early this afternoon.' Charlie found this hard to take in and was stumped for words, or at least for adequate words. Gabbling apologies, he promised to ring back the next day.

Two deaths in a day to add to the two others were too much to restrain the headline writers in the tabloid press. 'Blighted village' was the mildest

of the front page storylines. One paper had a picture of the main street in Middle Daychurch with the Grim Reaper superimposed on it. In worst taste was a manufactured picture of a team of cricketers in which four players had been replaced by skeletons. Michael Carter was understandably in a poor mood when Charlie managed to get hold of him. Anger had begun to chase out grief. There were no more details to glean. A funeral ('I guess it'll be a joint affair,' Michael had said) had not yet been arranged. Word of these latest disasters spread quickly round the circle of Outcasts. Alan Birch was much better and counting himself lucky that there had been no complications in his case. Tim had congratulated himself on the remedial qualities of real ale. Circumstances had cast Charlie in the role of liaison man with the Carter family. He had mourned twice with them and felt obliged to do the same again. For some reason that he could not quite fathom he was drawn to the event as well.

Death certificates had been duly issued. The doctors attending both Philip and Paul readily identified both deaths as caused by sad misadventure. Philip's death was straightforward heart failure. Seemingly Paul had never eaten an oyster in his life before and so even a sound oyster might have been too much for him. However, it had been clear from what had happened to so many guests at Le Rêve Royal that the consignment had contained a bad batch. The supplier had been contacted by the restaurant proprietors. He had admitted nothing, but promised a rigorous investigation. There had been only half a dozen oysters left over to be subject to examination, but the cause of the trouble, and in one case the tragedy, was generally recognised as all too obvious. So obvious that Greg Roberts did not even consider reminding Colin Banks of the transaction they had witnessed on the day of the match.

The double funeral which Charlie attended was a sombre affair. This time there was no wake. Even the young members of the family looked in no mood to get wasted. Charlie moved among those of the Carters whose names and faces he could by now recognise. He spread the Outcasts' sympathy as wide as he could. Before leaving, a strange sense of curiosity impelled him to look at the floral tributes which were arranged separately for the two deceased. It was in the row related to Paul Carter that he found a wreath with the mysterious 'K' and the snake-like mark. On a more appropriate occasion Charlie thought he should ask Michael Carter if he could throw any light on it. However, before the opportunity arose there would be a shock development – and the Outcasts' remaining fixtures of the season.

The re-emergence of Bill Blimp was also something of a shock. The Outcasts were introduced to his remarkable double-decker bus with integrated bar on the visit to Doredell CC. The experience had proved too much even for the Outcasts (*Incidentally Cricket* 2003). Yet they still had the fixture at Weasden to fulfil. For this match they absolutely had to have transport. Both the niche brewery in the village and the beer fanatics who made up the Weasden team made it the ideal place for an end-of-season celebration. It was the more compelling for the previous year's visit having fallen victim to the weather. Rashid Ali, who was to captain the team against Weasden, struck a deal with Bill Blimp. There was to be no alcohol on board the bus and Bill's son, George, was on no account to be the driver. Having no alternative client on that day, Bill had agreed. Some of the Outcasts were not entirely in favour of this arrangement, but a stern reminder by Winston Jenkins that the excellence of Weasden ales did not deserve palates possibly compromised by beer of lesser nobility. At this heads had nodded. And after all it was not far to Weasden.

It was only at the tea interval that the Outcasts received the sensational news. By then they had batted. Rash had won the toss. It had not taken more than one visit to Weasden for the Outcasts to realise that batting first gave you the best chance. There was less time for the beer to take hold.

Experience had taught the Outcasts that at Weasden the first pint came early. On the day of the last match of the season it was apparent that the social side of the visit asserted itself at a very early stage. Availability was helped by what the Outcasts considered to be a unique system. A conveyor led directly from the brewery building into the bar area of the cricket club. Plastic crates each capable of holding twelve pint glasses shuttled to and fro as necessary. It was a slick operation. The consortium that had founded and maintained ownership of the brewery included the chairman and captain of the cricket club.

There had been no difficulty in assembling a team to play Weasden. Fifteen Outcasts had signed up and were determined to make the trip whether or not they were in the final eleven. So the regular pairing had been chosen to open the innings. Rash, who always paced himself in the beer stakes, opted to bat at three. Thereafter sobriety had declined. This was demonstrated by the scorebook, but for one exception. In a whirlwind innings of comedic character David Pelham, going in after the fall of the sixth wicket, had contributed 41. This had made him second highest scorer. David had metaphorically puffed out his chest on being passed this information. His mood quickly changed when Charlie loudly proclaimed that he had better not be put on to bowl as he would probably give that many away in two overs. The Outcasts' innings expired in the fortieth over. They had made 173.

The tea interval was respected as such. The beer supply was temporarily suspended whilst a mountain of sandwiches and assorted pies was reduced. In a momentary silence when most mouths happened to be full the Weasden secretary, sitting opposite Charlie and Winston, suddenly said, 'Rum business at Daychurch. You don't expect anything like that.' Seeing blank expressions across the table, he went on, 'You mean you guys haven't heard?' Blank expressions remained in place. 'They're only going to exhume the body.' That produced a reaction, Jon Palmer saying, 'But it was only food poisoning. Alan over there had a day in bed and then he was all right. It took only two or three pints of best bitter to settle Tim.' His voice tailed away as he saw the look of impatience on the Weasden man's face. 'Not him, the other one, the one who collapsed whilst playing.' Incredulity reigned in the Outcasts' camp. Yet apparently it was true. The police had received an anonymous tip-off asserting foul play. There was no more information, but it seemed definite that an autopsy would be performed on Philip Carter.

The inevitable lively discussion which followed this sensational news delayed the restart of the match, but not the restart of the conveyor. The

Weasden opening batsmen went out to the middle having had scarcely a pint between them. That gave them a significant advantage over Colin Banks and Stewart Thorogood who in differing proportions had spent much quality time in the pavilion. Stewart, who had consumed less than Colin and bowled less fast than his partner, was way below his best. By contrast Colin, seemingly untroubled by his consumption, bowled with the pace and vigour he had displayed at least for a short period at Middle Daychurch. The period on this occasion was shorter still, but two devastating yorkers got their reward. A third wicket had been much harder to find. The man who batted at four for Weasden carried a lot of weight. This had enabled him to add power to the strokes he played against the off spin of David Pelham and Basil Smith. However, it began to tell on his speed between the wickets. A run-out was duly obtained, but by then the home side needed less than fifty to win. The beneficial effect of the long and productive partnership had been counteracted by the dwell time of the rest of the batsmen in the pavilion.

Weasden's fifth man in had just looked unsteady. He did not seem to adopt the guard he had asked for and been given. Basil Smith, still capable of summoning some concentration, took no more than a pace and bowled probably the slowest ball of his life. But it was straight and so Weasden were four down. Basil had two deliveries left in his over. The new man gave him a broad smile which seemed to say that he would not be fooled so easily. Basil fed the vanity with a ball that invited to be smote far and beyond. In normal circumstances it might well have had that treatment. But late in the afternoon and late in the season normality had suffered some decline. The batsman's lunge sent the ball some distance towards deep midwicket where Harry Northwood was patrolling without a care in the world beyond the wait for his next pint. There was no certainty that he would take the catch. First, he had had to be alerted to the ball's approach. He did not so much as catch it, but obstruct it. The ball struck his chest. He clapped his right hand to it. The ball slipped. Harry fell to his knees and got his left hand under the ball before it hit the ground. Not wishing to lose the strike in the next over, Weasden's opening batsman, with his sights set on a half century, had refused to run. This was a show of confidence in Harry's fielding skills which had not been shared by Basil.

The last ball in Basil's over had to be faced by a batsman who had obviously been hurried in his preparation. A pad was flapping and there was something about the way he was fiddling with his gloves which suggested that they were not his pair. Having taken guard, he faced Basil with a glassy-eyed stare. Altogether it was a minor miracle that he hit the ball. It was not perhaps in the direction he had intended, but it went into a gap in the field. That was sufficient for the newcomer. Yelling 'one' he charged down the wicket. Reluctantly his partner was forced to run. It was a fateful single. Similar drink-fuelled enthusiasm in the next over led to the senior batsman being run out. Batsmen eight, nine and ten were in no state to match such straight balls as David and Basil were able to purvey. Although some runs were plundered Weasden were ten runs short at the fall of the ninth wicket. At that point the Weasden captain conceded the match. Their eleventh man was recorded as absent hurt – his pride, not his body, despite the latter being prone on the changing room floor. An empty beer glass lay testament to his club reputation.

There was a post-match celebration from which the Outcasts with more men standing also emerged victorious. Finally came the retreat to the double-decker. They had not been long down the road before a voice was heard shouting, 'When's the bloody bar opening?'

In the sober light of another day grim reality resurfaced. Charlie was unsure what to do or say in reaction to the news from Middle Daychurch. It had to be true, but he for one had seen nothing in the press about it. He thought it might be awkward, insensitive even, to ring Michael Carter. He discussed it with Liz, but she agreed that it was difficult to know what if anything was appropriate. In bed a couple of nights later the thought suddenly came to him. Roy Groves. He could call him. And so the next day he did. Although it was a year since he had last phoned his office the rigmarole in getting through to the man himself was this time foreshortened. 'Yes, it's a ghastly business,' agreed Roy Groves. 'It's shaken the whole family. The police must have taken leave of their senses, but I suppose they have to be so careful these days. Apparently the message they got was so bizarre they felt they couldn't ignore it. And Philip had kept it pretty quiet that he might have had something wrong with his heart. He'd been to the doctor once, but was told it was something else. I don't know. Indigestion or something. Philip was a great trencherman. The autopsy is tomorrow as a matter of fact. Do you want me to let you know?' Charlie slipped in a yes. 'Better remind me of your number. Right. Must go now. A client's waiting.'

Three days later Roy Groves kept his promise. Not a trace of anything untoward had been found in the body of Philip Carter. The pathologist had found clear evidence of natural causes even if a healthier lifestyle might have averted them. Philip's body would be recommitted. It was concluded that the tip-off had been either mischievous or malicious. In truth it had been neither.

Charlie left it another week and then rang Michael Carter to commiserate. His call was obviously appreciated. Charlie's attentions had forged a closer bond with the Outcasts than Middle Daychurch Cricket Club had enjoyed with any other club. Michael told Charlie that it would not surprise him if his father resigned the captaincy and hung up his boots. 'He's just not the same man.' The subject was then changed to Uncle Paul. 'Seemingly there was just something in his constitution that reacted very violently to the duff oysters,' said Michael. 'It makes you think, doesn't it? Who knows what any of us have got lurking inside of us? Fit and well one minute and for some completely unforeseeable reason gone the next. I know I'll never touch the bloody things. But then it could be anything. That's what is so frightening. I heard of someone who never thought he had any kind of nut allergy and then one day he bit into one of those cereal bars and keeled over. He was dead within an hour.' 'What's happened to the restaurant?' asked Charlie when Michael paused. 'It closed for a week, but it's open again now. I think it's accepted that what happened was nothing to do with them. I believe there's some talk of them suing their supplier. But some bargain offers seem to be bringing the punters back.' Discussion then turned to more general cricket topics. At the end Charlie said the Outcasts would look forward to their next visit. Michael Carter laughed. 'Let's hope there's enough of us left to get up a team.'

Third encounter

THE CLOSE SEASON HAD PASSED uneventfully for the Outcasts. As was their wont they would gather in varying numbers on a regular basis at The Sink and Plumber. Good notice would be given for certain formal meetings such as those needed to approve fixtures. The landlord liked to be aware of the occasions when a maximum turnout was expected. He would time deliveries from the brewery accordingly. The Outcasts' fixture list was subject to constant revision. Some clubs were less forgiving than others after the Outcasts had visited them. A core of clubs had remained faithful either because they played cricket in much the same style and spirit as the Outcasts or because they were desperate to maintain a full fixture list. The Outcasts themselves were desperate to retain the loyalty of the places where they had found the social ambience, if not always the cricket, to their taste. Despite its idiosyncrasies they were keen to build their relationship with Middle Daychurch. The village club had in its turn been increasingly accommodating. A deal had been struck between Winston Jenkins and Michael Carter to bring the next match forward to a date in July.

In Middle Daychurch there had been a number of developments. Within the cricket club there had been much heart-searching. There was never any of that kind of thing in Edwin Carter's day. He had reigned supreme, which had meant without challenge. Nominally there was a club committee, but in practice it did not meet. When Joseph had succeeded his father the rigidity was eased – a little. Joseph would air his thoughts with one or two of his intimates. Whatever might have been said it was usually his thoughts which prevailed. But the double loss of his son and his brother had had its effect. The stuffing seemed to have been knocked out of him. If Michael had need to approach him for a decision, he was all too often dismissed with a weary gesture and the words, 'You decide'. Just when Michael was beginning to despair and under pressure from Roy Groves, who had his duties to discharge, Joseph Carter called a meeting.

A small circle of his peer group in the family was told by Joseph that he was quitting the club chairmanship and captaincy. His cousin George would take over. George must have been primed, because he did not dissent. Some words of sorrow and thanks followed. Joseph then took his leave saying only that he would expect to continue playing. What he had probably not expected was the significant liberalisation of governance on which George chose to embark. He announced the formation of an executive consultative committee comprising his brother-in-law, Henry Bell (club groundsman), cousin Maisie (scorer), her husband Bert Love (umpire) and his nephew Michael (fixtures secretary). Michael was then admitted to the meeting thus reducing the average age of its membership by an appreciable amount. George announced that he would pursue a policy of encouraging youth. He was also ready as necessary to recruit players from beyond the parish boundary. There was surprise, but no protest. The others present had no track record of arguing with the chief.

Change was not confined to the cricket club. The owners of Le Rêve Royal had been considering their position. The oyster fiasco, let alone the death connected with it, was a serious blow to a country restaurant of widening repute. Whatever the explanation there was bound to be talk, no doubt encouraged maliciously by rivals. The owners themselves were troubled. As Marty said to Pete, 'The odd one, yes, that can happen, but a whole load of them?' The kitchen staff had been interrogated to try to trace how and by whom the offending shellfish had been handled since arriving on the premises. Had they been stored correctly? At the right temperature? Could they possibly have been contaminated? All these questions and others had been answered satisfactorily. So when Marty and Pete had been as sure as they could be as to what had happened at their end they had had to turn their attention to their supplier. He had been as adamant as they themselves were. No blame attached to him. Hadn't he always supplied top quality product? Had they ever previously had cause for complaint? Had there been any oysters left over to examine? To the last question Pete had been forced to admit that the half dozen remaining had been sent for analysis and been given the all-clear. 'Well, there you are,' said the supplier. 'I think this is just one of those freak circumstances. The chances of it happening must be millions to one. There's nothing you can pin on me, but I tell you what. We've done a lot of business together. I'll make some enquiries among my staff and handlers, but, as I say, I think it's just one of those things.'

'You sure you were tough enough with him?' Marty asked Pete. The matter continued as a niggle between them. However, within a few days the supplier rang them. 'I've spoken to all my people bar one who's off sick – and anyway he's been with me for years – and no-one can throw any light on this business. Everything checks as normal as far as we're concerned. Sorry, mate, if you were looking for some excuse.' It was Marty who had taken the call and the last remark had incensed him. A testy altercation took place. A neutral witness would have said it was a case of two proud men trying to defend their reputations. 'I don't like it,' Marty said to Pete afterwards. 'We should sue him.' His partner demurred. 'But we can't prove anything.' 'Yes, but what if someone sues us?' 'You'd expect the Carters to be the first,' replied Pete, 'but they 'aven't. They've as good as said it was incredible bad luck.' 'There's a reason for that though, isn't there? Others might take a different view, especially if they get some scheming lawyer involved.' The partners continued to worry even though a writ was neither delivered nor indeed threatened. They preoccupied themselves with rescuing the business. There were always issues to confront: promotional offers to be planned, a junior chef to be recruited following a sudden vacancy and, more ambitiously, a conservatory addition where they might develop a bar food menu.

Coincidentally an extension was on the mind of the landlord of The Cow's Corner. He did not doubt that Le Rêve Royal would get over its bit of bother. The place had begun to put Middle Daychurch on the map. If visitors came, they would not all be wanting to eat fancy food at London prices. He could see a gap in the market for sensible food at sensible prices without having to eat it in a crowded bar atmosphere.

The parish church was another village institution on the verge of a construction project. However, St. Michael's was far from needing an extension. The regular congregation had dwindled to single figures driven by a succession of uninspiring vicars coming to the end of their careers, a direction of travel accelerated by their experience at St. Michael's. What they had failed to achieve in arresting the decline in church attendance, inadequate heating made up the difference. But then at the end of the previous November the living had been entrusted to a young, precocious and distinctly evangelical priest. Had he been canvassing for votes as a politician he could not have been more active in knocking on the doors of his parishioners. His pleading had a beguiling charm to which elderly ladies were susceptible. Attractive, unmarried and in his mid-twenties he was an attraction to young women not all of whom were unmarried themselves. Something about him appealed to young men as well. The congregation at St. Michael's swelled and remained swollen as people were captured by his mesmerising preaching style.

His powers of persuasion did not stop there. He went after potential money-givers with the tenacity of a terrier. He sought out charitable trusts and grant-making bodies. He wanted a replacement heating system although in the short term the crowds he was attracting from well beyond the confines of Middle Daychurch helped by their presence to increase the temperature. More urgent was the church roof in which severe structural defects had been identified. He was successful in obtaining a grant from the Almost Redundant Churches Restoration Fund. The roof was in reach of being saved.

When the new chairman and captain of the cricket club applied to build new cricket nets on a piece of land adjoining the club it was a case of action on all fronts in Middle Daychurch.

News of the internal affairs of the cricket club had filtered through to the Outcasts, but neither Charlie Colson nor Winston Jenkins had had any direct contact. That was until June. Winston returned home to find a message from Michael Carter, who sounded agitated. Asking Winston to call him he said no more than that the fixture which they'd brought forward to July would now have to be put back to August. When Winston got through to him he learned that there'd been an accident. George Carter had been walking along the street as he regularly did to pick up his Saturday papers. It was an extremely windy day. As he was passing the church a large piece of masonry must have been loosened by a sudden gust. It fell off the building and poor George was in the line of its descent. He was struck on the head and was flattened. Although an ambulance had got to him within ten minutes and he had been alive when they got him to hospital he had never recovered consciousness. Despite the surgeon's best efforts he had died two days later.

'We're in some trouble at this end,' said Michael after Winston had expressed suitable condolences. 'Another death has sort of deflated us. We obviously cancelled the next two fixtures whilst we were dealing with the situation. But then my dad announced he would step in again. I think he'd begun to regret he'd given up the reins. I could tell he didn't particularly like Uncle George's approach. Frankly, and I'm telling you this very privately, his marching back in again hasn't gone down too well with the rest of us. So there's a bit of a confrontation taking place. How are you lot off for dates in August?' Winston tried to question Michael further about what was going to happen, but it was clear that he did not want to be drawn. It proved relatively easy to settle on a Saturday in August and Winston duly reported the news to the other Outcasts.

With Bill Blimp and Executive Sporting Coachways in baulk and the Reverend Stephen Marshall in purgatory for all the Outcasts cared, transport arrangements throughout the season had been mixed and makeshift. For this year's visit to Middle Daychurch some research had been done. This had largely been carried out by Adrienne Palmer, Jon's wife, who had begun to take life more quietly as her pregnancy advanced. She had compiled a list of coach companies and taxi firms within a given radius of Middle Daychurch and its nearest train station. The broad decision had been taken to use the train to get near so that the cost of vehicular transport to complete the journey could be kept to a containable level. Michael Carter had been asked if he could pinpoint a likely contractor. Having been by now exposed to the Outcasts' drinking capabilities on two occasions, Michael was able to make an informed recommendation. Two mini-buses were arranged to be at their disposal for the July date. Fortunately they were able to fit in with the altered date.

There was high anticipation on the part of the Outcasts ahead of their next trip to Middle Daychurch. Speculation too. The latest news was at the heart of discussion at a gathering in The Sink and Plumber. It was Alan Birch who observed that they had never played a club where the body count was so high. That remark was picked up by Kevin Newton. 'You're not suggesting there's something funny going on, are you?' 'Not really,' replied Alan now laughing, 'but you've got to admit it's a bit weird.' Ray Burrill chipped in, 'But there's been no . . .' to be interrupted by a 'Welcome back, Ray' taunt from Dean Faulds. The Outcasts had seen much less of Ray socially since the match at Doredell. 'Yes, how is she, Ray?' enquired David Pelham with a look of innocence on his face. The 'she' in question was Andrea Firbrook to whom Ray had taken a shine from their first encounter at Doredell. Being a trainee vet he had given attention to her dog and then very much to Andrea herself. His friends had noticed.

Some further questionable ribaldry followed before Ray was able to get back on track. 'What I was trying to say about the deaths at Middle Daychurch was that there's been no pattern to them: a car crash, suicide, heart attack, food poisoning and an accident. I agree it's quite a sequence, but there's been a perfectly rational explanation in every case even when that poor bloke (Ray had not yet been to the village to be able to tell one Carter from another) had to be cut open.' 'Yes, but,' said Tom Redman, another who had not played at Middle Daychurch, 'you could argue that someone deliberately dropped that stone from the roof of the church and suicides have been known to be staged. When his brother retorted that Tom had read every detective novel their shop had ever stocked the discussion dissolved into general mirth. 'Let's get back to Ray and Andrea,' said Colin Banks, 'that's much more interesting.' More laughter. More pints. But Charlie Colson looked pensive.

The day arrived. The weather was set fair. The transport arrangements worked without hitch. John Furness was at the helm for this match. The team he led was not perhaps the Outcasts' strongest line-up. Their main strike bowler, Colin Banks, was missing. He had met 'this gorgeous girl' and they were spending the weekend somewhere. The season's most prolific batsman, Jon Palmer, had also declared his non-availability, being conscious of the need to spend more time with Adrienne. Selection had been affected by curiosity on the part of those players who had not previously been to Middle Daychurch. On the whole though, as he had checked the list of names, it was not a badly balanced team. How it would perform against the village side was another matter, but they had at least maintained the no drink rule. John was first out of the first vehicle as they came to a halt in the club car park. First to greet him was a familiar face. What was unfamiliar was the smile which it wore.

'Greetings,' said Joseph Carter. 'It's been good of you to fit in with the altered date. We've had a few changes here, as you may have heard.' John emitted a kind of grunt which did not commit him either way. He smiled in an enquiring manner and Joseph continued. 'I am still the club captain and my sister Maisie is our new chairman following the untimely loss of my dear cousin George. You may have heard about that tragedy.' This time John gurgled. It seemed to suffice, for Joseph went on. 'We're still a family-centred club, but we decided we had to bring on the youngsters.' By this time the rest of the Outcasts had debussed and some were standing close enough to pick up what was being said. Charlie Colson whispered to Winston Jenkins, 'He had precious little choice with their rate of attrition.' 'So,' Joseph was saying, 'I think you'll find that we'll give you a tough game. May the best side and all that.' John Furness managed a word. 'Great,' he said. And with that the Outcasts headed for the changing room.

As soon as they had privacy Charlie, whilst trying to divest himself of his jeans, announced as loudly as he dare, 'We must have a plan.' 'Cow's Corner soon as,' said Alan Birch, 'I'm not risking that restaurant again.' In fact he gladly would have but for time and, more potently, wife constraints.

'I mean before that,' Charlie retorted. 'Michael Carter's probably our best source, but we could pick up what we can from the others. If we get some of the young members of the family into the pub, I don't think it'll be too difficult to loosen their tongues. But we don't know yet who's in their team. Has anyone seen Michael?' 'Yes, I spotted him,' said David Pelham, 'and he was in whites.' 'OK, David, if we're fielding, you're our twelfth man today so you had better man-mark him. If we're batting, let's look out for whoever their twelfth man is.' And to Simon Crossley, who had put his head round the door, 'There's a job for you, Si. Your opposite number is now their club chairman, so find out what you can.' When Charlie had finally shut up John Furness sidled across and said, 'I thought we'd come to play a game of cricket. That sounded a bit like we're conducting a police operation'. 'Ah,' said Charlie, 'good intelligence is never wasted.'

First innings

Out in the middle John took a cursory glance at the state of the pitch. It looked firm enough to him although he would readily have admitted to being no expert. He thought, given the chance, he would bat. However, he lost the toss, but was then surprised to be told by Joseph Carter that Middle Daychurch would field first. John made the appropriate gesture towards his players so that the openers could be ready. It had already been agreed that Stewart Thorogood and Alan Birch would go in first. Joseph Carter had scribbled down a team sheet and John retreated to confer with his team to assess who and what they were up against.

'Yes,' commented Charlie Colson, 'I can see we're getting to the bottom of the Carter barrel. It's probably as well it's August with their young lads not at college. Otherwise they'd be in quite a fix. We've got to find out what's going on here.' 'But why is it so important?' asked Harry Northwood. 'I don't know,' confessed Charlie, 'but you've got to admit it's an odd set-up. Anyway you're right, we've got to get on with the game. Let's see if they're any easier to beat this time round.' As Stewart and Alan set off to open the innings some of the Outcasts sat on the balcony whilst the others sprawled outside on the grass. Amongst them was Charlie who positioned himself close to James Carter. 'Hi there, Uncle James, remember me?' The reply was 'All right, mate, are you on for a few vodkas later?' A promising start, thought Charlie. After a while he ventured, 'Have you had much cricket this year?' What he heard in reply only fuelled the doubts that continued to nag him. Something – he did not know what – was not right.

In the score box Maisie stole a sidelong glance at Simon Crossley. It was not entirely approving. Young men should not wear earrings was her view. She was not over-enamoured with ripped jeans and felt that Simon's t-shirt might have covered a higher proportion of his upper body. She softened a little when he showed her a photograph of his infant son, Brian Sachin. On the strength of that they were able to settle down in cooperative spirit to record the events of the match. To his approval Maisie was a neat and meticulous scorer. That set Simon at ease. As they went about their preliminary business Simon threw out a friendly remark to test the atmosphere. He complimented her on becoming club chairman. 'Someone had to do it,' was Maisie's reply. After a short pause, 'Someone sensible, that is.' Simon let that sink in before venturing, 'Joseph didn't want it back then?' 'He may have done,' she said and left it at that. Simon was contemplating how to follow that when he heard Bert Love call 'play'.

An immediate sign that youngsters were being brought on came when Lee Lingrove was directed to open the bowling. In terms of cricket capability little was known about him. Charlie was aware of his capability in another direction, but news from the circuit was sparse. Lee looked to be of student age and so his cricket, if there had been any, would have been played mostly in different circles. He was tall (taller than Charlie remembered), loose-limbed and glowering. After one over the Outcasts knew a great deal more about him. For Alan Birch, who had received it, the yield was two painful bruises, a dented helmet and no runs. An early conference with his partner took place. Stewart Thorogood's observation that Alan had been lucky not to get his bat on any was possibly not the most tactful in the circumstances as Alan rubbed his arm and another even more sensitive part of his anatomy. Seeing who was about to operate from the pavilion end, Alan muttered, 'Watch it, mate, it could be your turn next'. Tom Carter was marking out a run which seemed to have added a metre or so since last year. Alan's parting word of advice was, 'I thought they'd left a bit of grass on.' Thus encouraged Stewart took a middle stump guard. Whether it was the pitch or the speed of the bowler or a combination of the two Stewart did not have long enough to judge before the next mid-pitch meeting.

Stewart missed three, blocked two and edged (undeliberately) the final ball for a single to third man which his partner had seemed the more anxious of the two to run. 'Thanks, mate,' Stewart said with heavy emphasis. 'Not at all,' replied Alan. 'It looks as though we'll need to scrape every run. Those were two bloody good outswingers he let you have. It's as well you spotted the one that went the other way.' Stewart said nothing. They touched gloves. It might have meant good-bye, Stewart thought as he walked back to take guard in readiness for Lee Lingrove's second over. The young man had obviously been fired up by the relative success of his opening over, because enthusiasm overtook him. He began with a well-directed bouncer which Stewart evaded, but not with grace. In attempting to repeat the dose Lee went wide. Stewart top-edged it over the slips for a boundary which third man was stationed too square to intercept. If Stewart felt mildly satisfied by that he was soon put in his place by a sharp rising ball which he had to perform contortions to avoid. The next ball struck his pad, but out of line with the stumps. That did not prevent a loud and long appeal being emitted by an excited bowler. Not even family feeling could allow Bert Love to accept it. Goaded into striving for extra pace, Lee's next two balls might have been express, but they passed harmlessly wide of off stump and in the case of the second between the wicketkeeper and first slip for four byes.

This examination by pace in the middle was testing. In the pavilion it was greeted by the Outcasts with undue hilarity. Although at any time they might be expecting to face the music the waiting batsmen, perhaps to avoid nerves, derived amusement from the sight of Stewart and Alan hopping around in attempts to quell the opening salvos. As the two openers again paused for a mid-pitch exchange Kevin Newton could not restrain himself from shouting out, 'Come on then, give it some wellie'. This was greeted by another raucous laugh amongst his team mates. If Alan and Stewart heard the call, they chose to ignore it. 'I don't think he's moving it,' was all that Stewart could impart to Alan, who was about to face Tom Carter for the first time. He too came out of the experience not a lot wiser. Tom was provably into his stride and decidedly quick. Fortunately for Alan he was able to watch most of them pass the off stump. When Tom overpitched Alan was able to push for two, but then took a glancing blow on the shoulder when a short ball at the end of the over took him by surprise.

The aggressive barrage continued through the next four overs. With their eye in, the opening batsmen became better able to judge the pace, but it remained a battle for survival. Run-scoring was a secondary consideration. For Middle Daychurch it was Tom Carter who claimed the first success. Having played with great care and some luck, Stewart Thorogood received a short, wide delivery which asked to be put away. It was too good to be true and put it away he did straight down the throat of Michael Carter fielding in a deep gully position. An objective observer would have said that the bowler deserved the wicket. Stewart was nevertheless very cross with himself. He felt that he had weathered the storm with rich pickings ahead. He said as much to Dean Faulds as they crossed. They were very soon in a position to reassess as Dean shouldered arms to a ball pitched just outside leg stump and saw it clip the bail. Back in the pavilion he was quick to challenge the notion that there was no movement out there.

A new batsman came to the middle. A new bowler entered the attack. Fourth was higher in the order than Harry Northwood usually found himself batting, but John Furness was inclined to give him the chance. In his relatively few appearances for the Outcasts to date Harry had shown himself to be a gutsy if at times impetuous player. He had not taken long to pass the beer test, but John thought this might be the time to see if he could prove himself at the crease. The captain himself felt no urge to lead the way. He would confine himself to a tactical role. His opposite number was thinking tactics too. His call-up of Richard Love to take the next over at the pavilion end seemed to suggest that last year's spat had been forgotten. Lee Lingrove had bowled very well in tandem with Tom, but Joseph Carter wanted to keep his remaining overs until nearer the end of the innings. He knew that he owed Tom at least one more over as he was on a hat-trick. His other options took him into doubtful territory.

Events last year had been such that the Outcasts had not seen much of Richard Love in any capacity. However, the nine balls he bowled had accounted for three batsmen. If memory served Alan Birch, Richard's bowling was pacey with a good measure of control. He was therefore pleased to receive for starters a lacklustre loosener which he was able to punch for four between mid on and mid wicket. He was surprised when the second delivery was not a lot better. With a hit in the same direction they were able to run three. To Harry Northwood, Richard tightened up a little. Harry, mindful of his promotion, was content to be watchful and settled for a single off the last ball of the over. 'Mind not on the job,' was the verdict Alan passed to Harry as they took stock.

Alan Birch's judgement was spot-on. Richard Love's mind was elsewhere, much as his body had been for a good part of the previous match. A message he had received on his mobile shortly before play began had jolted his equilibrium. It had come from Shirley Simpson with whom he had formed a relationship a year ago. Distance and her hospital duties had limited the number of occasions when they could get together and derive the maximum pleasure from their friendship. The intervals between meetings increased the anticipation of them. For a while. Once Shirley had found excuses to travel home more frequently Richard's ardour had begun to wane. Greater exposure to her company led him to doubt whether they had much in common. What he had initially found attractive in her now seemed less alluring. He wanted to end the affair, but was unsettled as to how to do so bearing in mind that his mother and Shirley's were on good terms. He had gone to great lengths to conceal from his mother quite how close his relationship with Shirley had been. So he wanted the break to be polite and discreet. That prospect had been shattered by Shirley's message. She was pregnant. And she a nurse, Richard had ruefully reflected. Matters were made worse because he had recently acquired a new partner. What he did not as yet know was that so too had Shirley.

Tom Carter put a lot of thought into his hat-trick ball. He had bowled at Harry Northwood in the previous match. Since then he felt he had improved. He did not know how far this was true of Harry. He reckoned that Harry would expect something fast and so finally he thought he would opt for his slower ball. He did not want to make a change in the field which might signal his intention. That proved to be a mistake. It was a good slower ball. Harry was outfoxed, played at it too soon and sent it looping to where a closer-in mid off might have been standing. Tom himself could not react quickly enough to make a leap for the catch. Harry resolved to capitalise on the life he had been given. The rest of Tom's over was not up to the standard of his first four. The batting began to acquire a little momentum.

So too had the conversation in the pavilion between Charlie Colson and James Carter. It was clear that Charlie did not have to rely on vodka to loosen the young man's tongue. He had obviously made a good impression on James in their previous encounter. Am I becoming a father figure? was the thought crossing Charlie's mind. There were two factions in the Carter family, James had told Charlie. When Grandpa Edwin was alive he ruled and there was no scope for division. Once he was dead sides had begun to form. Not everyone was ready to accept that Uncle Joseph should simply take over the reins. That was what had led after a struggle to the splitting of the club chairmanship from the captaincy. At first there had been a move to keep Joseph out of both. 'My dad and Uncle Douglas should have been in charge, but,' and here James stopped, trying to control his emotions. Charlie put his arm round the young man's shoulder. Father figure, he thought, and half withdrew it.

There was an awkward pause. But the moment passed. James resumed: 'Aunt Maisie was the surprise. She stepped in. I hadn't realised she took much interest apart from doing the scoring, but she acted as something of a peacemaker. Mind you, I don't know whether it would have worked without the vicar.' The expression on Charlie's face posed a question. 'Oh, you don't know,' said James. 'Garry has had something of an impact in the village. In fact he seems to have had an impact on Uncle Joseph. Cousin Philip's death affected him very badly. It sort of gave him a God-rush. The vicar came on him in the church one day and they must have got talking. Uncle Joseph's been acting differently since. He's been a bit more accepting of us younger ones although,' he hesitated, 'I can't say I've had too much benefit from it. Twelfth man again.' 'But things are better?' Charlie ventured at that point. James shrugged. 'It's still a bit of a tyranny. I wouldn't want him to catch me round the pub tonight. Know what I mean?' The question was accompanied by a wink. The worldly wise Charlie knew exactly what he meant. He had got to know a circle of young men carved in the image of the Outcasts Cricket Club. Apart, it seemed, from the drink of first choice.

Charlie had reached a degree of intimacy with James which might have yielded further information when an enforced interruption occurred. Harry Northwood batting against an off-colour Richard Love had struck a full toss straight back in line with the stumps. The bowler stopped to put his hand in the ball's way. The hand failed in its purpose. The foot involuntarily did not. Richard was poleaxed. Cursing somewhat uncharitably James leapt into action clutching the club's first-aid bag. There was little that James's ministrations could do to ease Richard's condition. It was impossible to tell whether he was suffering from more bruising or a possible fracture. Such was his pain that Richard believed in the more severe prognosis. What was not in doubt was Richard's inability to stay on the field. An emergency call had to be made. Richard was helped off the field by two of his team mates and James was told to look sharp about returning in Richard's place. 'Bum deal,' he whispered to Charlie after making the necessary phone call. Charlie knew what he meant. All the hard work, but none of the satisfaction of being able to bat or bowl.

Adrian Seymour was called on to complete the interrupted over. Alan Birch and Harry Northwood both saw this as a lessening of pressure. On the evidence of the past they reckoned that Adrian was no more than a trundler. However, he surprised them. Teased by his wife about his weight, Adrian had gone in for a mild degree of fitness training. He had not drawn attention to this, but at least in the privacy of his home he had won some plaudits. In the course of the season his bowling had gained some zest. He was deceptively sharper than he had been when last seen by the Outcasts. Any improvement was not immediately noticeable. Adrian used his initial five deliveries to get into rhythm, concentrating on accuracy rather than guile. A couple of singles were scored off him and his captain was then left to decide in the absence of any other pace bowler whether he should let Tom have another over or turn to spin.

Past recollection of Joseph Carter's captaincy was that he was not a man to consult. A further mark of his change of approach was when he called up Tom for consultation. Tom was smarting from the treatment his last over had received. He was more than eager to keep going and pointed out to his grandfather that he had been able to take a breather while they had been dealing with Richard. This swung the argument and in the deed Tom certainly showed no lack of pace. Neither did he take a wicket although he twice caused Harry Northwood to play and miss. Four runs came from the over, but three of those were leg byes. Tom was reasonably satisfied with the outcome. The satisfaction was shared by his captain, but that had to be it. Tom's final two overs would be reserved for the end of the innings.

Joseph had momentary cause to reconsider that decision in the course of the next over. He had become aware during the season that his son-in-law Adrian was turning in some useful performances as a change bowler. It was nevertheless a surprise when in the space of four balls he removed both Alan Birch and Harry Northwood. His first ball deceived Harry through the air, took the edge of his bat and flew into the slips. Only one slip had in fact been posted, but that sufficed. The ball travelled straight to Brian Stagden, who took a regulation catch. Winston Jenkins was next in. Any consistency on Adrian Seymour's part was not immediately apparent when his next ball was driven past him for four. The next would have suffered the same fate but for an inspired piece of fielding by Tom Carter. The batsman was limited to one. This put Alan Birch back on strike. Perhaps lulled into believing that the ball which dismissed Harry Northwood had been pure luck and that normal mediocre service had been resumed, Alan aimed an expansive drive at a well-pitched up ball. He knew he could have left it, but he had been lured into presenting a thin edge which not even as senior a wicketkeeper as Joseph Carter could fail to snaffle. This left the Outcasts' innings in a mess.

This was Ray Burrill's first visit to Middle Daychurch. Since joining the Outcasts Ray had established himself as a potent all-rounder. He rarely failed to contribute with either bat or ball. On some occasions he had contributed tellingly with both. With four wickets down cheaply and a poor scoring rate consolidation competed with aggression in Ray's priorities. Perhaps over-elated by his double success Adrian Seymour helped to resolve Ray's dilemma by serving up two short wide balls. 'I'll have those,' said Ray to himself and the score advanced by eight taking the total past fifty. But by now Kevin Newton and Charlie Colson were padded up.

An obligatory mid-pitch exchange took place between Winston and Ray. Winston also laid claim to being an all-rounder. His West Indian roots and commanding physique could inspire dread in opponents. Yet Winston would be the first to concede that he did not consistently punish with the bat or threaten with the ball – and only rarely did he succeed in both disciplines in the same match. Nevertheless he was an imposing presence. 'Consolidation,' said Winston; 'Aggression,' countered Ray with the two boundaries fresh in his mind. After discussing how they rated Adrian Seymour their attention turned towards who was to bowl at the river end.

If he was to conserve the two overs left to be bowled by Tom Carter, Joseph was left with little alternative but spin. His determination had wobbled during Adrian's over. He wondered whether a quick kill might be possible. On seeing the ease with which Ray had struck Adrian's last two balls for four he stuck with his original idea. Actually a variant of it. He suddenly remembered the presence in the team of his nephew Brian, elder brother to James. Joseph's apparent conversion to the potential of youth was given further emphasis by his calling up Brian to bowl the fourteenth over ahead of either David or his brother Andrew. Like Andrew, Brian aimed to bowl leg spin, a considerable ambition for one of tender years. David looked at Joseph as if he had gone mad. The game could be at a turning point and the captain was prepared to take this risk. Brian himself seemed unfazed. He discussed field settings with his uncle, marked out quite a long run and tossed the ball from hand to hand. First time in the village team. This was his moment.

Sadly for the young man it was not. Nevertheless the over was not without incident. Maybe it was nerves, but Brian began with two wides. As he finally corrected himself in finding direction he produced a full toss which Winston Jenkins showed no mercy in launching straight back over his head for six. It was all credit to the young man that he did not go to pieces, for his next delivery was perfectly pitched. It was a classic leg break from which Winston withdrew his bat. Brian tried again. It was a bit less than perfect, being too full. Winston, who had counselled consolidation, struck it powerfully through the covers with two fielders converging in vain. Brian tried to look unconcerned, but there was a frown of concentration as he ran in again. It was a pretty good leg break, but Winston had time to dab it down wide of the only slip and set off for a single. There had been no call from the other end. Ray Burrill's eye had been caught by the flashing blue light which announced the arrival of the paramedic. Winston was almost halfway down the track before he realised that his partner was otherwise engaged. For a big man he performed a remarkably sharp about-turn. A clean piece of fielding would have caused a run out, but Winston dived successfully for the crease. The commotion at the other end re-engaged Ray's attention. 'Hell, mate, sorry,' stuttered from his lips.

The bowler was on something of a high. He had not been scheming a run out, but he derived some satisfaction from the near fatal error. Reckoning on Winston being shaken up by his desperate effort to save himself, Brian thought he would try his quicker ball. The idea was good, the execution bad. It was short and it was inviting. Winston took a step to the off, swivelled and sent the ball soaring in the direction of the mid wicket boundary. It was an area in which Adrian Seymour was patrolling and gathering as he did so some words of praise from a line of spectators in portable seats or deckchairs. The ball that rose and then began to seek him out was hard to judge. It was going for six. It was not going for six. It might just clear the rope. It would land just short of the boundary. No, it would be a six. There was nothing he could do. In the last seconds he realised it was making straight for him at shoulder height. Or was it just a bit higher than that? He made a final decision to fling himself arms outstretched in its direction. He lost not just the ball, but his balance and crashed into an adjacent deckchair, flattening it and its occupant to the ground.

There was a groan (his) followed by a scream (high-pitched) although there were some in recounting events later who asserted that the scream had preceded the groan. However, every witness agreed as to the placement in the sequence of the raucous bellow which was the next disturbance of the peace. 'If 'e's bloody killed 'er, 'e'll never live to tell the tale. Oh, my poor darling,' added Connie Maxwell as she rushed to rescue Clarissa from the writhing heap of canvas and flesh. The girl's instinctive effort to rescue herself led to the deckchair being turned over. This time the scream came from Adrian Seymour as his hand became trapped hard between two moving pieces of wood. The pain was momentarily quelled when something cold was applied to the imprisoned hand. It later transpired that this was the ice cream which Clarissa had been consuming. Later still Adrian discovered that the chocolate flake which was part of the confection had applied itself embarrassingly to another part of his anatomy. With the deft assistance of neighbouring spectators, and none from Connie Maxwell who confined herself to wailing and cursing, the two bodies were freed. The more damaged was Adrian whose hand, his bowling hand inevitably, was bruised, swollen and lacerated. The well-cushioned Clarissa seemed to be suffering from no more than shock. At least that was the judgement of the paramedic who had been summoned from the pavilion after his examination of Richard Love. Connie was eventually quietened down and made to see that the inadvertent perpetrator of the accident was suffering more than her daughter. As the paramedic led Adrian away to the pavilion for treatment her last word was, 'You'd better buy my poor little girl another ice cream.'

Middle Daychurch were now a man down. In a generous act of sportsmanship John Furness told his opposite number that David Pelham would be pleased to make up numbers for the fielding side. This was not an accurate reading of the situation. With his side batting David had planned to spend the first half of the afternoon in more leisurely fashion. There was a respectable turnout of spectators, not all of whom to distant inspection were in the twilight of their years. Quite the opposite. So David had slipped off for a circuit of the ground to see what talent could be found. Borrowing a pair of binoculars John located David at a point on the boundary behind where third man had been fielding before the interruption. He appeared to be in close conversation with an attractive-looking young woman with long auburn hair. She seemed disappointed when John raced across the ground and detached David from her. He thought he heard her say, 'See you later,' as they moved off. David was quite sure and muttered to John when they were out of earshot, 'You bastard, can't you see that I was . . .?' John cut him short. 'Hour of need, old son, hour of need.' Those sentiments David shared, but in an entirely different sense.

Richard Love meanwhile was experiencing mixed emotions. Whilst his foot was being examined by the paramedic his mother's friend, Mrs Simpson, had strolled into the pavilion en route to finding her. The resultant fussing was what he did not need. 'You'll be relieved to know,' said the paramedic, 'I don't think there's a fracture. As far as I can tell it's just a bruise. It'll be painful for a few days. Try to avoid walking as much as you can. I'll apply some of this cream and then put a crepe bandage round it.' He was about to carry out the aforementioned tasks when the commotion at square leg occurred. 'Stay there,' commanded the paramedic although Richard had no early plans to move. 'It looks like double trouble for me today. This village has a bit of history, hasn't it? I'd better take a look.' He shot off leaving the cream and the roll of bandage behind him.

'Well, isn't that lucky?' said Mrs Simpson. 'I'll give Shirley a call. She'll love the hands-on practice, especially as it's Richard.' Feeling an explanation was necessary, she added, 'She's just turned up. Quite a surprise, really.

But I expect you knew about it, dear.' Dear Richard did not. Instead he was filled with alarm. What did this mean? Had she come home to confront him? Or, worse, to confess to mum? 'No, no,' he managed to say. 'Honestly there's no need. The paramedic will be back in a minute. I'm sure she must be tired. We'll catch up later.' 'Nonsense,' said Mrs Simpson, 'she's bound to want to come to the rescue.' And there was no stopping the call being made. Richard put his head in his hands, a move misinterpreted by his would-be benefactor. 'You must be in such pain, dear.' He was, but his foot was the minor part of it.

Before the match could be restarted there was another matter to settle. Had the ball despatched by Winston Jenkins scored four or six? The umpire whose call it was, Syd Breakwell, seemed not to be sure. He consulted Bert Love, but he had not been looking in that direction. More in hope than conviction the bowler volunteered that it was four. Winston held out for six. Syd insisted on moving at his usual measured gait to check if the man on the spot could settle the matter. For the man with the throbbing hand it was the final insult. 'Of course it was a bloody six. Why do you think I fell over the line trying to catch the bugger?' Feeling slightly chastened Syd marched back to give the appropriate sign to the score box where in fact Simon and Maisie had already accurately recorded it.

For Brian Carter the enforced interval had done no favours. He had one ball left to bowl and he was desperate to get it right. Too desperate. He released the ball early and it presented to the batsman as a high full toss. Without pity Winston thrashed it through the on side. Lee Lingrove made a heroic dive, but the ball evaded his fingers (which was probably fortunate) and crossed the boundary line at speed. Spectators were quick to make way for it. The extended over had cost twenty-two. Brian looked haplessly towards Joseph Carter, who preferred for the moment to avoid his gaze. The captain now had plenty on his mind. His two fastest bowlers had between them six overs left to bowl. There were two regular spinners in the shape of the brothers, Andrew and David, but their potency on this day had not yet been tested. If the visitors' innings ran its full course of forty overs, that left him four overs short. He looked at the retreating figure of Brian with speculation. Perhaps he had ruined things by pitching him prematurely into the fray. He cast a mean glance in the direction of Winston Jenkins.

Joseph knew that David with his off spin preferred to bowl at the river end and so it was Andrew with his leg spin who prepared to operate from the pavilion end. The passage of play which followed was testing. Between giving away runs when he lost his length and imposing wariness on the batsmen by sometimes achieving extravagant turn, Andrew's bowling gave the batsmen more chances. David complemented this with a very tight, economic spell. The Outcasts found it difficult to lift the scoring rate. The fact that both Winston and Ray were given chances increased their feelings of impatience that they were finding it difficult to capitalise on the fielding errors. The hundred came up in the twenty-third over and they had put on more than fifty when they decided that new tactics were required. 'You just keep going,' said Winston to his partner. 'I'm going to have a go at this leggie.'

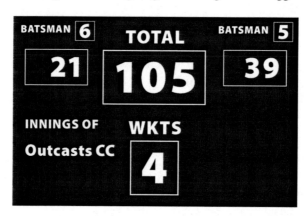

The change was dramatic and Andrew Carter was not prepared for it. After Ray had taken a quick single off his second ball Winston gave the next two deliveries the charge and sent them soaring to left and right of the pavilion. 'That's better,' he said to himself and got ready to repeat the treatment. But Andrew had steadied himself, foresaw Winston's intention and slipped a quicker ball past him. It was an easy stumping. 'That's better,' Andrew murmured with satisfaction. But Winston had reached a half-century with his final blow. He hoped the shackles had been broken allowing Kevin Newton to engage in some powerful strokeplay. It is surprising how in cricket a new batsman can sometimes change the tempo. Ray met Kevin with a few observations. Kevin nodded, took guard and waited for the leg break. He stepped back, gave himself room and punched it to the extra cover boundary. A disgruntled Andrew pitched short and was cut hard to the boundary backward of square. Twenty-one off the over. 'That's better,' agreed the batsmen.

In the case of Adrian Seymour the paramedic's conclusion matched his assessment of Richard's foot. 'Nothing broken you'll be glad to hear, but I think the hand is going to need some supporting because you won't be able to use it for a while. You were lucky not to lose a finger.' He then turned to his other patient, who was still clutching the crepe bandage. Of Shirley there had been no sign despite her mother's assurance that she would be round in a minute. Mrs Simpson had then taken herself off to the score box for a natter with Maisie Love. The paramedic said that he might as well bandage the foot, greatly to the relief of Richard. Before he left he told both the casualties that they ought to show their injuries to their GP on Monday morning. 'Help me upstairs, Adrian, there's a good chap. I think I could do to lie down.' What Richard really meant was that he wanted to put himself out of Shirley's reach.

Simon Crossley in the score box noted that Maisie Love appeared to have taken her son's injury in her stride. 'He'll be fine,' she assured Simon. 'He may make a drama out of it. I've seen that before, I can tell you. It's the team I'm thinking of. They'll miss his bowling.' When the accident involving Adrian occurred her first concern was again for the team. 'Oh, that's gone and done it,' she exclaimed. 'I can't see him bowling again today. Nor next week neither.' With the game paused Simon ventured, 'But it looked quite a nasty injury. It certainly hurt him.' 'He'll bounce back, I'm sure,' she replied, 'but the trouble is it won't be today. Joseph's got quite a problem on his plate now. Two bowlers down. That's bad.' Giving up on the welfare angle, Simon tried again to get Maisie to open up about her brother. 'Joseph seems to have brought on some of the younger players in the club.' Maisie remained silent for a moment and then in a soft voice said, 'Well he had to, hadn't he? We told him that the club needed to look to the future, open its doors a bit. If he wasn't prepared to go along with that, we wouldn't have let him stay captain. It was a bit of a gamble, because we didn't want him to walk out of the team, at least not until we'd found ourselves another wicketkeeper.' At that point Maisie's previously expressionless face broke into a broad grin.

Simon silently congratulated himself on achieving a breakthrough with his opposite number. He decided not to sacrifice this advantage by persisting with enquiries into the internal affairs of Middle Daychurch Cricket Club or for that matter the Carter family. He turned the conversation to the state of the match and cricket in general. There was no opportunity to revert to those other matters before the resumption of play and the arrival of Mrs Simpson. Simon could not help admiring Maisie's capacity to cope with the visitor whilst maintaining an accurate record of the match. True, she was not called upon to say very much, because most of what was said came from the mouth of Joyce Simpson. If her monologue was not distracting to Maisie, it certainly played on Simon's patience. He found that he could not stop himself picking up some of the flow of words.

Didn't expect her – seemed excited – wonder what's up – engagement – lovely boy your Richard – bruised foot – women's institute – Reverend Garry – that Frenchy restaurant – don't know what's happening – Joseph OK these days – haven't seen your Barbara – seems like months – dinner party soon – vacancy – might do for her – blame it on the Government – rely on no-one these days. And on she went until finally she said, 'Look at the time. It's been nice talking to you. Better dash. I need to know whether Shirley's in for a meal or going out with you know who'. With an ingratiating smile she slipped away. Her departure brought relief in equal measure to both the scorers. 'I'd better just check I got that last over right, Simon.' The Outcasts' scorer noticed pleasurably that Maisie had used his name for the first time.

Although Kevin Newton believed that Ray Burrill would set out to anchor the innings while he tried to up the pace, this was not the observable pattern as their partnership developed. After five very tight overs David Carter began to slip and Ray Burrill took six runs from his sixth, exceeding the number he had conceded to that point. So few were Joseph Carter's options that he allowed Andrew Carter to continue from the pavilion end despite the high cost of his previous over. However, Andrew seemed to have drawn strength from capturing a wicket and he managed to limit the batsmen to four singles between them. David Carter continued from the river end, regaining his length for the first five balls of the over, but finding himself half swept, half pulled for six at the end. Andrew's final over proved to be one too many. Feeling shackled for too long, Kevin Newton determined to dominate. Unfortunately for the home side Andrew gave him too much of an opportunity. An ugly heave at the first ball led to four leg byes. Kevin connected robustly with two out of the next three deliveries scoring a boundary in each case. A third looked likely from the next ball, but smart fielding by Tom Carter pegged him back to a couple of runs. Andrew's final ball earned him a moral victory. It was flighted well. Kevin read it as a leg break, but it went straight on, narrowly passing over the stumps. Standing behind, Joseph Carter had also read it as a leg break. Two byes resulted. The stand was now worth forty. The two batsmen reassessed. There was little reassessing to be done by Middle Daychurch's captain. His room for manoeuvre had been almost completely eliminated. He tossed the ball to David Carter for what would be his final over. 'Make it count,' his captain pleaded.

Joyce Simpson returned to 10 Cricketers Close to two surprises. The fact that the house was empty she might have expected, having herself called her daughter out for first aid purposes. What seemed odd was a note on the table in Shirley's hand which read, 'Don't wait up'. If Shirley had gone out in a hurry in response to the emergency call, her mother wondered why she would have got dressed up for the night out. Then again young people these days put on jeans and a top and regarded it as good for anywhere. Still it did not seem quite right. Not her Shirley. This speculation was cut short by a knock on the door. She looked out of the window and saw a police car in the road. She put thoughts together and rushed to the front door. However, the uniformed officer standing there had a broad smile on his face which did not presage bad news. 'Hello, Joyce,' said Constable Eric Hillgate, 'I wouldn't be calling at tea-time, would I?'

David Carter did his best to oblige his captain, but he was finding it hard work against Ray Burrill. He was pleased with his first three deliveries. Although they did not threaten to penetrate Ray's defences some sharp fielding ensured that he had no scoring shots. Then David's concentration lapsed. What amounted to a slow half-volley was eased through the covers for four. David recovered himself with the fifth ball, but this time the fielding was less than sharp and a single ensued. Final ball. Kevin Newton, bent on belligerence, abandoned first principles of batting, essayed a cross-batted heave across the line and missed. 'How's that, umpire?' In weariness David's enquiry was distinctly low-key and unsupported by any other member of the team. Nevertheless all eyes turned to Syd Breakwell. There was silence.

Syd's mind had been elsewhere. It had strayed elsewhere intermittently throughout the afternoon. A small legacy from a distant relative had been notified to him in the morning post. It afforded the opportunity to fulfil a long-held ambition: a cruise in the Caribbean during the coming winter coinciding with a tour by the England Test Team. He would be able to see England play in Barbados and Antigua. Everyone he had ever spoken to had said that a Caribbean holiday lived up to expectations. There was only one snag: what he had promised his wife. As recently as last week she had reminded him of his words: 'If we ever come into some money I'll see you get that new three-piece suite you've been wanting.' How, he kept wondering, could she be persuaded that there was more to life than a new set of springs encased in velour?

'Pardon,' said Syd, mentally setting down his glass of rum punch on the counter of the poolside bar. Not wanting to make a scene over it, David said, 'I simply asked how was it?' How indeed, thought Syd as he suddenly came to terms with his situation. And what was 'it' for that matter. Caught, lbw, stumped all flashed through Syd's mind as possibilities. He stared at Kevin Newton, who was down on one knee. He looked guilty. Syd had been impressed by David's bowling and anyway he was a polite young man. 'I'm afraid that's out, Kevin,' Syd announced in a booming voice which belied any suggestion of hesitancy. He was encouraged when Kevin departed without any hint of doubt or dissent. Syd made a note to check with the scorers during the tea interval how Kevin had been dismissed. Simon would be bound to know.

There was a brief period of confusion in the Outcasts' quarters. Charlie Colson had been listed to go in at the fall of the sixth wicket. At the critical moment there was no sign of him. John Furness as skipper was prepared, but doubted whether he was the man for the hour. With ten overs to go his side needed quick runs. This was not John's forte. Some might have said unkindly that slow runs could sometimes be too much for him as well, particularly if he was up against quick bowling. Without appreciating exactly how far the bowling resources of the home team had been stretched John had assumed that Joseph Carter would revert to his opening bowlers sooner rather than later. He ordered a search for Charlie and told Basil Smith and Tom Redman to pad up. Thereafter he set forth to do his captain's duty.

The slight delay had given Joseph Carter time to think. There were ten overs in the innings left to bowl. Lee Lingrove and Tom Carter could bowl six of them. He did not fancy Brian Carter bowling the other four. Equally he was unsure which of the non-bowling regulars in the side could do better than Brian. On the other hand he could gamble on bowling out the Outcasts inside the forty overs and save his side embarrassment. Or he could compromise. There was evidence of the new attitude being displayed by their captain when he called up Brian for a second over. Giving the boy a second chance was the thought that had prevailed. Brian was surprised and so too was John Furness, who wondered whether after all his luck was in. There would be surprises all round.

'That went down well, I don't mind saying,' PC Hillgate told Joyce Simpson as he placed his cup (emptied for the second time) on the tray. 'And that there lemon whatsit cake were to die for.' His host smiled at him. 'Lemon drizzle cake. It was my mother's recipe.' 'Well, she certainly taught you right, I must say.' They had had quite a chat. Few village stones had been left unturned. In answer to Joyce's question the policeman said he was unaware of any funny business at the French-style restaurant. 'Well, no more than usual,' he had added, 'if you know what I mean.' He hesitated. 'Come to think of it there was some talk of a tiff between the two of them about a member of staff who left. Or it may have been over the design of the extension they're doing. And while we're on the subject I hope The Cow's Corner doesn't lose its character with what's being done there.' The conversation moved on to the Carter family, but there did not seem to be anything new on that front beyond Joyce blurting out that her Shirley was seeing one of them. The vicar was next in line for a mention. 'He's a one that Reverend Garry. He's made a hell of an impact – oh, perhaps I shouldn't say that.' Before Joyce could register her opinion on that point, Eric Hillgate swept on. 'Do you know, I was at the school the other day to give my talk on road safety. The vicar had just done his RE bit. He must have left a right impression on those kids. Do you know what one of them asked me?' This time Joyce got as far as shaking her head before the narrative continued. 'The little blighter asked me if Jesus would have worn a helmet when he was riding his bike in Jerusalem.' For all the reaction he got the constable might have been a first-time comedian on the stage of the Glasgow Empire.

'Goodness me, is that the time? I'd best be on my way. But there was just one matter of business I'd meant to mention.' Joyce Simpson suddenly looked alert. 'I just wanted to remind your husband that his shotgun licence needs to be renewed pretty soon. It's my job to carry out a routine check that he's obeying the regulations and keeping it safely under lock and key. So if I can just take a look I'll be able to tick the box when his renewal application comes through.' Joyce Simpson was obliged to think fast. 'He's away at the moment on business. He's been on a long trip. I suppose that's why he's left the renewal to the last minute. I'll show you where he keeps the gun, but I can't open the cupboard. There's only one key and he's taken it with him.' She gave a nervous laugh. 'I don't think he trusts me. The ammunition's in the safe. I do know the combination, but it's a double one and so I better just check it on the computer.' She saw his expression. 'Oh, don't worry, it's under a special password protection.' PC Hillgate took a cursory glance at the sturdy cupboard and the padlock. 'No, you're all right, Joyce. I'm sure everything's in order. Just needed to see it, that's all. I think I know you both well enough.' And with thanks for the tea and the chat he was out of the door. He left Joyce Simpson a relieved woman counting the lies she had told.

Since his one calamitous over, Brian Carter had been brooding in the field. He kept going over in his mind where he had got it wrong. He tried to remember everything his coach at school had told him. Mostly it had been negative, don't do this and don't do that. An hour passed and it came to him: don't do such a bloody long run-up. Brian had dismissed the advice. He was comfortable with his run-up. And anyway he'd taken a few wickets. At school level it was true, but someone else had said he showed promise. Perhaps though he should do some experimenting in the nets. He was thinking about how to approach this: cut off a couple of paces or start with just a couple of paces. He was deep in self-analysis when he heard his name called. He could not believe it. He had to bowl again now. There was a moment of panic and then as if by a miracle his head cleared. He marked out a run of only three paces. A field was set for him with no-one except the keeper close to the batsman. Brian came into bowl and was hit for six. Feeling sorry for him Uncle Bert suppressed a call of 'no ball' which by a generous margin it was.

Without prompting Brian moved his mark back before delivering the second ball. It was swung for six more by Ray Burrill giving him a half century. Again Brian had overstepped and again the umpire took pity on him, giving him nevertheless a quiet warning. Brian adjusted his mark again trying to suppress panic. As much to his own surprise as that of anyone else the delivery was legitimate and accurate. Ray was not prevented from taking a quick run which allowed John Furness to have the strike for the first time. Having observed half the over from the non-striker's end, John fancied his chances against the nervous leg spinner. With no pressure applying he felt he had a chance. Although he had avoided a no-ball Brian was not altogether happy with the run-up he had now created. So again he retreated. He felt easier as he moved in. With a twirl of his wrist he released a high flighted ball which pitched on the batsman's foot and knocked back his off stump. John Furness had been yorked. Perhaps surprise had been the key element in the dismissal.

Charlie Colson bounded on to the field of play in a show of impatience that his appearance had been delayed. Probably as much out of sympathy as of joy, Brian had been surrounded by his team mates. It was his first wicket on debut even if it had cost thirty-five runs. Despite his success the bowler was still fretting over his run-up. Whilst Charlie was taking guard and having a look around the field Brian was undertaking another re-pacing. In he came and pitched one on a good length without upsetting the umpire. Charlie scuffed the ball away and because the fielders were so scattered he was able to take an easy single. He was disappointed when Bert Love signalled a leg bye. 'I'm sure I got some bat on that,' he said on arriving in conversational distance of the umpire. 'Didn't look that way to me,' replied the protective Bert Love.

By now Brian had worked his way back to where he had started the afternoon. Capturing the wicket seemed to have relaxed some inner tension. He came loping in. Now on the charge Ray Burrill advanced only to be deceived by a classic leg break. Stranded too far down the pitch for recovery he could only anticipate that Joseph Carter would have all the time in the world to gather the ball and remove the bails. Ray departed shaking his head. He felt he had let the side down. He had shown himself to be on song. He ought to have carried his side through the remaining overs. It was now left to Charlie Colson, Basil Smith and Tom Redman to get the Outcasts up to a competitive total. Ray was not the only Outcast to reckon the odds were long against their achieving it. Yet as ever cricket proved itself unpredictable.

Meanwhile a conversation was taking place at Le Rêve Royal between the owners, Marty and Pete. They were sharing a brief interval between lunch service and dinner. Lunchtime had been busy and dinner was fully booked. They felt that the oyster incident had been overcome although there had not been any contact from Michelin. They were impatient to get their new facility open and had got over their artistic divergence regarding it. 'Funny thing,' said Pete, 'I meant to mention it sooner, but I thought you might fly off the 'andle.' Marty looked puzzled, but his expression cleared when his partner resumed. 'That sous chef, Craig, who walked out on us, the one you thought fancied . . .' Marty cut him short with a gesture. 'Yeah OK I'm not going back over that. It's just that I got a call the other day from Ken Norman. You know, 'e 'as that restaurant Ipswich way. 'E was moaning about staff problems. 'E's had some trouble as well. 'E was telling me that 'e took on a young chef with no references, but because 'e was desperate just on the basis of a trial in the kitchen. Thought 'is prayers 'ad been answered. Then after just two weeks the lad vanished. Strange, I thought. So I asked Ken to describe 'im. 'E sounded very like Craig, except 'e wasn't called Craig. It was Ben. 'E left no word. Didn't even take 'is wages. Coincidence, I thought. Anyway, because I was so inquisitive Ken said 'e'd send me a photograph. It came this morning.' Pete fished an envelope out of his pocket and handed it to Marty. 'Bloody hell,' his partner said, 'that's Craig, no doubt about it. Strange or what?'

Charlie Colson found himself facing Lee Lingrove. There was no question in Joseph Carter's mind that he would let Lee bowl his four remaining overs from the river end, even though his opening spell had been from the opposite end. However, there was a question mark over Brian Carter. His two wickets had been a bonus, but there was no denying that the cost of

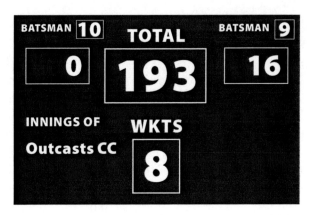

BATSMAN **10**   **TOTAL**   BATSMAN **9**

0   **193**   **16**

INNINGS OF   **WKTS**
Outcasts CC   **8**

his two overs had amounted to thirty-five runs. Yet it would be a slap in the face to take him off after he had captured two wickets in three balls. And, of course, he was two bowlers light. He had the space of an over to come to a decision. He had willingly given Lee the attacking field for which he had asked. It would be perfect for him to grab the last two wickets in double-quick time. The bowler had much the same idea. The Outcasts would not want to have to rely on Charlie's batting skills in a crisis, but he was not the rabbit his innings last year at Middle Daychurch might have suggested. And Charlie was at the crease with a sense of responsibility enveloping him. Middle Daychurch had won the last time with an innings of 220. The Outcasts' present score was well short of that. Charlie did not anticipate Basil Smith contributing many. This meant he must take the lead.

The innings which Charlie played could only be described as streaky and it got streakier as it progressed. Having previously bowled four overs for no more than five runs, Lee became increasingly disgruntled to see his figures ruined. Charlie had seen the first ball whistle past his off stump and immediately decided that a defensive innings would be short-lived. To lead meant to attack. He waved his bat at the next ball and managed to loft it over the three slip fielders who had been posted. With no third man in place there was no-one to stop the ball reaching the boundary. Lee's next delivery was of a better length and did not permit the same treatment. Charlie wound himself up as though intending to drive. He had completed the stroke before any part of his bat intercepted the ball. It went high in the air over Charlie's head, over the wicketkeeper's head and again reached the boundary. The next ball from Lee was an absolute beauty, but the adrenalin in the batsman was high. He played not quite an air shot. There was the thinnest of edges which might have led to a catch if keeper and first slip had decided between them whose it was. In the event neither moved, but the ball did. Another four resulted.

The situation in the Middle Daychurch camp came under some strain. Joseph Carter chose a bad moment to tell his grandson that he was taking Andrew out of the slips and putting him at third man. Had his last delivery gone to hand the original plan would have been vindicated at a cost of eight runs. Lee did not say this, but his glare conveyed ample meaning. The disturbance of his temper probably contributed to the next delivery being full and wide. It asked to be hit straight or through the covers. Charlie was unable to oblige. Instead he slashed the ball at catchable height through the recently formed gap in the slips. Despite a despairing dive by Andrew it gained him another four runs. The bowler was fuming. There was only one ball left, but matters could only get worse. It could be said that for a young man he managed to compose himself remarkably well to produce a very fast yorker which crashed into Charlie's pads plumb in front. Lee's spirited appeal rent the heavens. This time Umpire Breakwell did not have to snap out of a Caribbean reverie. He would claim he was all attention, but evidently not all ears. 'Not out,' he retorted, 'there was a bit of bat on it, I fancy.' Composure deserted Lee as quickly as it had been attained. His arms went up in the air again, but this time the cry from his mouth was very rude indeed.

Joyce Simpson had had time to collect her thoughts. She was seated at the kitchen table with a sheet of paper in front of her, beside which she had placed the application for the renewal of a shotgun licence which she had just downloaded. She had armed herself with a drink. Gin this time, not tea. She felt there was no immediate danger. The neighbourhood police officer had been easily fobbed off. She would not have wanted him to see inside the gun cupboard as it was in its way a veritable arsenal. In particular the presence of a sleek handgun would have attracted his interest. So far as she was aware it had never had a licence since the day her husband gave it to her for her protection when he was away from home. 'The business I'm in, ducks,' he had said, 'you never know who might come calling.' Chilled by that thought she had located an isolated spot where she could undertake some target shooting and satisfied herself she was proficient enough to hit someone where it would hurt. But, if the shotgun was not covered by a current licence, it would be the police who would be the first to come calling.

Lee Lingrove's explosion meant a hold-up before play could continue. Joseph Carter had advanced thunderously towards his exasperated grandson. The rest of his team appeared unshocked. The Outcasts were amused.

Surprisingly Syd Breakwell was totally unfazed. For Joseph Carter, however, this was as much a family matter as anything else. The spectators, most of them local, would have seen and heard the bad language and poor sportsmanship of a representative of the Carter family. 'You must apologise to the umpire immediately,' snapped the captain to his frustrated grandson. 'Or else . . .,' but then reality must have kicked in. He could not afford to lose another bowler and from his vantage point Charlie must have been out. And so 'I don't want to see that kind of behaviour ever again or there'll be no future for you at this club. Now go and speak to the umpire.' This involved a visit to square leg where Syd had already taken up station in readiness for the next over. In seconds after his outburst Lee knew that he had seriously transgressed and was in knots as his grandfather dressed him down. He cantered over to Syd to do the necessary. The umpire still seemed unfussed. Having listened to the young man, Syd nodded and said to him, 'Just not so loud next time.' And then he winked.

His captain's anger with Lee had the effect of making him feel the more sympathetic to Brian. Calling him across, which Brian had not really expected, he patted him on the shoulder and said, 'Try and get me another.' It was a well-intentioned gesture and a far cry from the Joseph Carter of old. It also turned out to be futile. Basil Smith was an off spin bowler, probably the Outcasts' best in that department albeit he now faced some rivalry from Ray Burrill with his sometimes penetrative mix of off spin and cutters. On the strength of his record Basil's batting was not something on which the Outcasts could rely. His string of modest scores (with downright failures thrown in) did not mean that Basil's ambitions as a batsman had been extinguished. Having watched Brian Carter's two overs, Basil reckoned that he might have a chance to strike a few blows. Brian by contrast was a mixture of optimism and confusion. He had got himself into a muddle with his run-up, been hit for two big sixes, but had taken two wickets. He looked at Basil, whom he had never previously encountered, and decided that this was no batsman.

After he had bowled a brisk leg break which completely fooled the batsman, he was sure he was right. Basil had been fortunate in keeping both bat and pad out of the way. Joseph Carter behind the stumps had the misfortune of failing to keep either glove or pad in the way. They ran three byes. Brian saw Charlie Colson eyeing him in a rather different way, raising and lowering his bat to suggest that he was intent on smiting the ball to the furthest extremity of the ground. Worst of all, as he reached the end of his run and turned he saw Charlie smiling at him. He sensed that his run-up was out of kilter and he must have delivered the ball at least a metre earlier than he should. Charlie, whose first thought had been to give him the charge, went on to the back foot and cracked a very short ball square on the off side for four. Feeling hot and bothered, Brian re-marked his run and tried again. This time Charlie did give him the charge and got a one bounce boundary. It was bad luck for the bowler, because the bounce had taken place after the ball had passed through the hands of Brian Stagden. Another boundary would have followed if the same fielder had not pulled off an amazing one-handed stop to a ball which had been travelling faster than a spectator's eye could see. The batsman had to be satisfied with a single. His partner was relieved to have the chance to get back on strike with two balls left in the over. Brian Carter's tail was drooping, but he was lucky to concede only four more runs. Two uncharacteristically powerful hits by Basil were met by two very good pieces of fielding. But by now the Outcasts' score had gone past 200.

Feeling that there had to be a further gesture of reprimand to Lee, Joseph Carter changed his plan and ordered Tom Carter to bowl from the river end. On a distant boundary Lee sulked. Charlie Colson continued to see himself as the man who had to carry the Outcasts to a decent total which might put pressure on the home side. In this mood he was averse to dealing in singles. Tom's first ball was a loosener which whetted Charlie's appetite and he chopped it backward of square for four. He wound himself up for a big hit to the ball following and lost his off stump. Tom Redman was last man in. He had a brief word with Basil mainly to indicate that he would be aiming to get off the strike as soon as possible and by any convenient means. Fortunately from the point of view of prolonging the innings the opportunity was immediately presented. Tom did not know much about it, but Basil shouted 'Run' and he did. A ball he did not see grazed his thigh and a leg bye was obtained. Basil survived Tom Carter's next two deliveries without scoring, but just managed to scramble a single off the last ball of the over when he saw Tom Redman already halfway down the pitch in his direction.

In the face of reality Lee Lingrove's exclusion could not be further extended. The young man was wise to wear an expression of penitence as he answered Joseph's summons. He accepted patiently the skipper's advice and agreed his field settings. He told himself that he had to bowl his way back to approval. These were not now the most propitious circumstances so to do. There was only one wicket left to take and the batsman facing him gave every impression of wanting to have a go. No, this was far from perfect. It was even further from perfect when Basil edged his first delivery through the gap in the slips which Joseph had perpetuated. Lee ground his teeth, but otherwise tried to stay calm. He had minor revenge when his next ball nearly took Basil's head off. Lee gave him the look which he had seen famous fast bowlers use. The intimidatory gesture had a temporary effect. Basil adopted a very cautious approach in fending off the two following deliveries. Then Lee dropped short. Basil knew it was hittable, but his timing was wrong. The result was half-hearted, in fact very nearly his dismissal, as the ball lobbed just over the mid on fielder. 'Can we make it two?' asked Tom as they crossed. 'No,' said Basil. As Tom prepared to face, it was hard to judge whether he or the bowler was the more anxious.

Shirley parked her car where he had said. Had to be discreet. It was a bit further to walk to the flat than she imagined from his description. Before she arrived she had begun to regret her choice of footwear. And then there it was. The yellow entrance door. She took from her bag the key ring which he had given her: two shiny metal keys which looked to have been recently cut, with a gold pound symbol as the makeweight or, she wondered, was it a talisman? She identified correctly the key which opened the outer door, made her way up a flight of stairs and she saw it on the right: his place. She had been told to make herself at home as he would not be back till later. She should help herself to anything she fancied, but be ready for him on his return. A quiver of excitement ran through her which became all the more intense after completing her exploration. Admonishing herself to be patient, she made a cup of coffee and settled down in front of a large-screen television. The first picture which appeared was a cricket match somewhere on earth. With a grunt of disapproval she channel-hopped until she found a rom-com featuring one of her favourite hunks. She reckoned it would help to pass the time until her hunk arrived.

Tom Redman's account of his innings could be said to have magnified his performance. To his brother later it had acquired further lustre. Tom's first boundary had been an unconscious deed. He would not have been inclined to argue if the umpire had signalled leg byes. Lee Lingrove had managed on this occasion to contain his immense frustration. He had bowled the unplayable ball and a number eleven batsman had somehow got something on it and picked up four extremely lucky runs. So it was back to Tom Carter to try to end the innings. He was not proud of his first ball, only thankful that Basil Smith scored no more than one run off it. He was more proud of the next which flew through Tom Redman's defences narrowly failing to clip the bails. This in no way contributed to the batsman's comfiture. He decided on death or glory. It was glory (or at least a pale version of it) which visited him. He swung the bat. There was a connection of sorts. Had any member of the fielding side anticipated in which direction the ball would go it might have been interrupted in its passage to the boundary. Tom Redman had doubled his score. Tom Carter swallowed hard.

Someone describing the over from Tom Carter's perspective might have said of his fourth ball that it was a perfect inswinger, but it also turned out to be a four ball. Tom Redman somehow got his bat down on it. The ball found a way through without disturbing the stumps and was moving at such pace that the fine leg fieldsman had no chance of stopping it. What particularly hurt Tom Carter was that Tom Redman smiled. He began to feel the emotion which had overcome his cousin Lee. Basil Smith felt the need to steady his partner. 'Steady,' he said to Tom and without saying more trotted back to the non-striker's end. Tom was unsure how to react, but as the bowler's remaining deliveries, although fast and on a length, were wide of off stump he held back from offering a stroke. He then wandered up to Basil and said, 'What do you mean?'

This improbable last wicket stand – it was now worth 20 runs – had begun to attract closer attention from the rest of the Outcasts in the pavilion. Informal bets were being made about how long it might last. Cruel jokes were exchanged regarding the comparative abilities of their comrades at the crease. There were four overs left to be bowled. The Outcasts seemed not to appreciate the paucity of the home team's surviving bowling talent. There could be no doubting that Lee Lingrove would be used for two of them. He was already at the end of his run impatient to get at Basil Smith. For his part Basil was realistic. He could hardly lay a claim to senior batsman status just by virtue of coming in ahead of his partner. There were no other grounds. Yet Basil felt himself in charge, despite the fact that Tom's score already exceeded his own.

Was 'steady' the right answer Basil wondered as Lee Lingrove raced towards him? He had time for further thought as the ball whistled harmlessly past his off stump. The second delivery was straight and just short of a length. Basil got his bat on it, but only to block. Third ball. Basil wanted a single, but Tom registered no enthusiasm for being on strike with three balls of the over to go. Slightly peeved, Basil showed more aggression to the next delivery. The fielders were sufficiently surprised that the shot eluded them and Basil collected a boundary. A loud cheer came from the pavilion and those sitting nearer heard the clinking of coins. A single followed and this time Basil insisted on the run. Tom found himself again facing Lee Lingrove with one ball of the over left.

Tom was still puzzling over the command 'steady'. In the match situation he reckoned his side was short of runs. A streaky four was surely better than a dot ball. In truth he never saw the ball. Lee had let himself go. It was a superb delivery and deserved the wicket. Tom had swung the bat defiantly, but the ball had taken the edge and flown through to the massive gloves of the wicketkeeper. Unfortunately the hands inside the massive gloves were unequal to the task. The fumble did little to impede the ball's passage. Tom collected his fourth boundary. Lee bottled his curse as another cheer emanated from the pavilion.

The stand between Basil and Tom was stretching credulity, first, amongst the Outcasts who knew them and their capabilities too well and, secondly, amongst their opponents who knew them too little. Joseph Carter saw little alternative but to turn again to Brian, his young nephew, to plug the bowling gap. Even at this level of cricket forty-eight runs off three overs could be reckoned to be expensive, but he had got two wickets to his name. He was to bowl the thirty-eighth over and even though the Outcasts' two lowest order batsmen were at the crease the field placements favoured boundary protection as against quick singles. It made no difference. Brian's first delivery was a high full toss. Whether Basil Smith recognised it as such was beside the point. From what he had seen previously of Brian's bowling he was intent on swinging the bat. Steady was not in it. His connection may not have been altogether perfect, but he got enough bat on ball to send it soaring over the boundary well beyond the capacity of any earthly fielder to intercept.

'Are you sure about this?' questioned Tom whilst complimenting his partner on the achievement. 'It was there to be hit,' replied Basil with a show of defiance. Tom was sure that the stroke had been made by Basil with his eyes shut, but he did not demur. His doubts were confirmed when Basil also seemed to swing blindly at the next ball. This time there was no semblance of majesty about the shot. Bat unquestionably met ball, but it was an inelegant consummation. The ball somehow squeezed between the stumps and the keeper without disturbing either. On Tom's insistence the batsmen collected two runs and the Outcasts' score reached the 250 mark. Having collected eight runs off the first two balls, Basil then seemingly chose consolidation. He played a good-looking forward defensive stroke when at last Brian produced a length ball. Whether his bat actually grazed it would remain a talking point in the Outcasts' changing room, if only at Basil's insistence, but the bowler's enthusiastic appeal was rewarded by

Syd Breakwell's upheld finger. Thirty-seven perhaps crucial runs had been added for the last wicket. Maybe this time the Outcasts had a sufficient total to have a chance of inflicting their first defeat on Middle Daychurch.

Tea interval

Once again it was shown that the quality of the tea provided in the pavilion would have placed Middle Daychurch high in the order of the *Annual Guide to the Best Cricket Teas*, if such a publication had existed. What was also noticeable, and pleasing to the visitors, was the greater integration between the two teams as they enjoyed the break. The segregation first encountered, and for which Middle Daychurch had been notorious, seemed to be a thing of the past. The Outcasts were unsure whether this was now the norm or something which had developed from their own deliberate charm offensive which had been spearheaded by Charlie Colson. At any rate cordiality reigned amongst those who were gathered. Indeed such was the cordiality that it masked the fact that a full complement of players and umpires was not actually present. Remembering a previous visit, Winston Jenkins said to David Carter who was sitting next to him, 'Don't the lads from Near Daychurch stay for tea?' 'Yes, of course, they do,' replied David, 'look, there's Martin over there, although, now you come to mention it I can't see Brian at the moment. He may be in the loo.' But that was a false assumption.

Richard Love had also made his escape. Had anyone seen him hobbling away and remarked about it his answer would have been that he had needed to pop back home for some painkillers. However, home was not his destination. Nor was he in search of Shirley. The very reverse. She was the last person he wanted to see. How bloody ironic he thought to himself that the girl who had supplanted Shirley in his thoughts and desires should be living only two doors away. Debbie Mason had moved into 8 Cricketers Close a couple of months ago. It was a house share with her elder sister. Debbie was a solicitor and her sister a barrister. Both had done sufficiently well for themselves that with assistance from their father, a judge, they could afford to have a place in the country. Richard had spotted the new arrivals from the perspective of the cricket ground. An upstairs window had been thrown open and a vision had appeared. An introduction had occurred when a ball bowled by Adrian Seymour had been deposited by a visiting batsman into the garden of number 8. Fortunately this had happened without injury to the occupants who had been sunbathing at the time. By chance Richard had been the nearest fielder to retrieve the ball. It was handed back by Debbie without any trace of reproach and with every appearance of pleasure. The exchange lasted just long enough for introductions to be made. And it had all begun from there.

An assignation had been fixed for the afternoon of the match against the Outcasts. Debbie's sister was away on a troublesome case in the north-west. The coast theoretically was clear, but Richard still needed to skirt number 10 and the possible eye of Shirley's mother. The unexpected appearance of Shirley herself and the worry of the message preceding it were complicating factors. However, as Richard limped furtively along Cricketers Close he could not know that Shirley was otherwise engaged whilst her mother was far too preoccupied to be gazing inquisitively out of her front window.

If she was entirely honest with herself, Joyce had known from day one that Frank Simpson was not entirely honest. Yet the realisation somehow added to his attraction. He was a very handsome man and he made Joyce feel good, excited even about their relationship. There seemed no difficulty in providing her with creature comforts, but his best gift had been Shirley. Devotion to her daughter diverted Joyce's thoughts from how exactly their rising standard of living was being financed. Frank showered her with gifts. She wanted for nothing. There were fabulous holidays, the house in Northern Cyprus and the yacht in Florida. Just one thing Frank demanded. No ostentation at home. 'We don't want attention drawn to ourselves and I want Shirley to grow up with her feet on the ground.' So they had lived in relatively modest style in a suburb of Birmingham until Frank had announced that it would be better to be buried away somewhere deep in the English countryside. Hence the move to Middle Daychurch. Although modesty had been maintained in the purchase of 10 Cricketers Close it was nevertheless a pleasant, well-appointed property. The Simpsons' real luxury was enjoyed elsewhere. And Joyce, who had taken to Middle Daychurch, had given up asking questions.

Frank Simpson's absences from home had become more frequent and longer. He would rarely phone, but Joyce had been used to receiving occasional letters and postcards which were always affectionate and full of endearments. Now she had no real news, but at least she noticed that their joint bank account maintained a healthy balance. So in the wake of PC Hillgate's visit she went methodically about her business, forging her husband's shotgun licence renewal. With that job done her mind reverted to more disturbing thoughts. Where the hell was Frank? Was it pure chance or had there been some meaning behind the strange phone call a week ago? It had made no sense. She had been unable to discern any message. She thought the language might have been Spanish. There was music in the background. She had tried to respond to the flow of words from the other end, but without more ado the caller had hung up. The call had not been repeated. Then Joyce's mind turned to Shirley. Something was not quite right. Where was she if she was not with Richard?

Unknown to Joyce, Richard himself was in close proximity, but not in the company of her daughter. The discomfort of covering the distance from the pavilion to 8 Cricketers Close had quickly proved worthwhile once he was across the threshold. The inhibitions which might have attached to a prim and precise professional were cast aside once Richard was in her presence and in her arms. Debbie was in no way attired for a court appearance or an afternoon tea party. Richard knew before he was sure that she was intimately close to him. His whites made him overdressed by comparison. There was only one snag. With the damage to his foot the stairs would be an obstacle. Before much time passed an alternative arrangement had presented itself. When Debbie said, 'Oh darling I've so been looking forward to this moment,' Richard's reply surprised her. 'What's that vibration? Is it your phone or mine?' It turned out to be his and what he heard was a serious blow to his plans.

No such disturbance affected an encounter elsewhere. Shirley did not hear the sound of an approaching car, but she heard footsteps on the stairs. She held her breath and waited. Then a key was inserted in the lock. The door opened and he was with her. They embraced passionately. When they eased themselves from each other's arms a flow of endearments poured forth from his lips, but ended anti-climactically. 'We must make the most of these moments, precious, because I cannot stay long. I have to be elsewhere or I shall be in big trouble. But I will return to you later.' She hid her disappointment as well as she could. Having had the time to acquire a clear knowledge of the layout of the apartment, she took a determined lead out of the living room in order to enjoy their rendezvous to the full. He apologised profusely on leaving, but he need not have worried. His partner lay back in contentment. This was definitely the better life that she badly wanted.

'What the hell is all this about?' demanded Richard as he dragged himself towards the pavilion, play not having yet resumed after tea. Joseph Carter confronted him. 'Your dad's had a funny turn whilst we were having tea. I can't send him out there to umpire the second innings.' This was the new caring Joseph Carter. 'So you'd better do it. You're bugger all use for anything else today.' This was a flashback to the unreformed Joseph Carter. 'There's a fold-up chair you can use.' Caring captain. 'Make sure you don't get in the way.' Less caring captain. 'Hurry up, we're late starting.' But Richard wanted to check on his dad first before he donned the white coat. 'I'm sorry about this, lad,' said Bert, 'it may just be a touch of sunstroke. I left my cap at home.' Richard hoped he was right, but he could not altogether rid his mind of the cavalier attitude which his uncle Joseph had shown towards his son a year ago. However, realising he had been given no option, but resenting the interruption of his intended pleasure, he paired up with Syd Breakwell in slow progress to the middle, lightweight chair in hand.

Second innings

There was early indication that the 251 runs needed to overhaul the Outcasts' total might not be beyond the reach of the home side. Neither Stewart Thorogood nor Winston Jenkins made any impression in their opening spell. After eight overs Joseph Carter and Lee Lingrove (an unusual choice to open in the circumstances) had posted a handy partnership of forty-five runs. Winston had been noticeably off-line. He grumbled that Richard

124

Love's chair forced him to bowl from wider of the stumps than was his custom. He offered that as the reason for so many balls going down the leg side and being called as wides. This had affected Kevin Newton's keeping. In trying to guard against the deliveries going wide of the leg stump he was putting himself out of reach of anything wide of off stump which the batsman failed to hit. The extras mounted as did Winston's impatience.

This steady unbroken partnership owing most to Lee Lingrove (desperate to prove himself) and extras had acted as cover for the late return to the ground of Brian Stagden. He was fortunate that his absence had not been noticed by Joseph Carter preoccupied as he had been by the collapse of Bert Love. Brian was able to get kitted and ready to fulfil his role as fourth in the batting order. To an enquiring glance from Martin Norwell he merely said, 'There was something I had to fix'. Martin shrugged. 'You're lucky we lost no wickets.' It was Brian's turn to shrug. He was saying no more. Meanwhile John Furness had been in lively discussion with the bowlers at his disposal as to what to do next. After taking 2 for 31 last year at Middle Daychurch Charlie Colson was keen to press his claim, but his captain was all too well aware that Charlie had done little comparable since then. He opted for Ray Burrill, suggesting that his cutters might be more appropriate than his off spin.

It proved to be a shrewd decision, because within the space of five balls both opening batsmen were back in the pavilion. They were even denied a half century opening partnership which had looked distinctly attainable when Ray's first ball pitched short and was cut savagely to the boundary just backward of square. However, Ray was quick to recover. His next delivery looked similar, but was a little fuller in length and came on to the batsman a little quicker than he had expected when he shaped to cut. Lee Lingrove succeeded only in dragging the ball into his stumps. Ray leapt in delight. Lee swung his bat with annoyance, worried that he had wasted his chance. He had felt in such good form. Martin Norwell shared his feeling and was further buoyed by the memory of the century he had taken off the Outcasts in the last match. He was determined to show intent from the start. His first ball from Ray was too full and he played a fluent on drive. This was followed by not such a convincing stroke, but he scrambled a single. Ray's deceptive pace – he bowled his faster ball – accounted for Joseph Carter. Syd Breakwell took an agonisingly long time to answer the appeal. Joseph glared at him and shook his bat as if to plant the thought in the umpire's mind that the ball had hit bat before pad. Finally Syd worked it out in his own way and managed to reach the right decision. It had been plumb. The fifty mark had been passed, but the loss of two quick wickets took the edge off it. Joseph Carter departed examining his bat, but no-one was fooled. He had contributed eight singles.

His replacement was Brian Stagden who was greeted by Martin Norwell with a smile. 'Just in time after all.' His reward was an unwarranted scowl. 'Button it.' An altogether inauspicious start to a partnership. Brian still wore a scowl having hit his first ball to the boundary. He might even have been preoccupied. With two new batsmen at the crease John Furness was tempted to give Winston another over or even bring Stewart on at the river end. Yet when he saw Richard Love sprawl into his chair he could see the risk and concluded that one of his slower bowlers might find it easier to work round the obstacle of the sedentary umpire. He thought he would try Basil Smith's off breaks before Tom Redman's leg spin.

This was the first time that the Outcasts had seen Brian Stagden bat. Whilst it was equally true that this was Ray Burrill's first visit to Middle Daychurch, it became quickly clear that the balance of advantage lay with the batsmen. Martin Norwell was as elegant as the Outcasts recalled from their previous encounter whereas Brian was in bludgeoning mood. Another eight overs passed without a wicket falling, but in this passage of play eighty runs were scored. They might not have been had catches been held. Brian was far more ready than his partner to play elevated shots relying as much on brute force as on placement. Twice he should have been taken, but instead of catches Alan Birch and Dean Faulds were left with stinging hands. Both Ray and Basil had suffered and their captain was forced into another double change. Charlie Colson's medium pace did not in any way stem the flow of runs from Martin Norwell's bat. After twenty-three runs had been taken off Basil's fourth over the introduction of Tom Redman could only be seen as a desperate last throw of the dice.

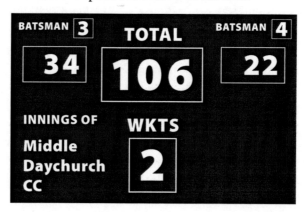

BATSMAN 3   TOTAL   BATSMAN 4

34   106   22

INNINGS OF   WKTS

Middle Daychurch CC   2

In all honesty the fact that Tom Redman's bowling had not previously been seen by Middle Daychurch batsmen was not thought by John Furness to have any special significance. He just needed to change the bowling. Continuing rotation of his attack was the strategy looming in his mind in the hope that changes of pace and bowlers at different ends might do something to hold these two dominant batsmen in check. Middle Daychurch required another 113 runs from twenty-three overs. This meant approximately five runs per over. The most economical of the last nine overs had cost that number of runs and most of them rather more. 'It may just be one over, Tom. I think I've got to mix it up a bit.' With that ringing endorsement Tom prepared to bowl the eighteenth over of the Middle Daychurch innings. It brought instant success. At least Tom had the grace to refrain from saying that he had been bowling for it.

A leg spinner, unless the very best, often takes a while to settle into his stride. So Tom did not avoid early punishment. His first two balls went for four and two respectively enabling Martin Norwell to record his half century. Now he felt thoroughly well set. The third ball appeared to be on its way to the boundary as well. The batsmen had run two whilst Harry Northwood was chasing round to intercept the ball. At this point Brian Stagden was guilty of ball-watching, which was also Harry's thought as he gathered the ball, and shouted 'no'. He then turned to see Martin bearing down on him intent on a third run. 'Get back,' yelled Brian in despair without moving an inch himself. Martin tried desperately to recover his ground, but Harry's return was good enough to find Kevin Newton, who calmly removed the bails. Whatever Martin thought about his partner he kept to himself, but he was not a happy man after picking himself up from a fruitless dive and making his way back to the pavilion.

Michael Carter was next man in for Middle Daychurch. He played himself in by treating his first two deliveries with circumspection and taking a gentle single off the third. When he asked his partner what he thought he found Brian Stagden taciturn as though his mind was elsewhere. 'Well,' said Michael brightly, 'I reckon we should make these runs pretty easily.' 'I've already got a few myself,' replied Brian. 'I might get a few more.' Michael broke off the exchange and went to take guard in readiness to face Charlie Colson, who had been allowed another over. It did not go well for the Outcasts. There was no consistency about Charlie's bowling other than in his production of boundary balls. Michael languidly stroked the ball through the covers twice, added a single and then watched Brian power his way to a half century. The over cost Charlie seventeen and his spell.

Tom was given another over in view of the 'success' of his first. Although he bowled tidily there were two lapses which received severe punishment. This meant that by the halfway mark the home side had harvested 174 runs and needed no more than 77 from the remaining twenty overs. It was not a situation which the Outcasts found easy to recover. John Furness tried Basil Smith at the pavilion end and, after a third Redman over, Ray Burrill at the river end, but it was all to no avail. The total passed 200 in the twenty-fourth over. In desperation John turned to his opening bowler, Stewart the reliable, and he was not let down. No more than two runs were taken off him, but that had to be seen in the context of Middle Daychurch not needing more than three runs an over to win. Whether this easy formula relaxed the batsmen or made them careless was hard to gauge, but at the end of Ray's next over in which he had taken some punishment his arm ball induced a mistake on Michael Carter's part and at the second attempt Kevin Newton caught the edge.

David Carter marched to the wicket with purposeful strides. He had not been best pleased at being dropped down the order. 'It will give you time to rest up after your stint with the ball,' Joseph had said. David could not help wondering whether there was some other motive. He thought that he had enjoyed a good season with the bat. With his side needing only thirty-one runs to win he knew he would not be able to get many on this occasion. As the player he was joining was batting like a man possessed David reckoned he would be lucky to get to double figures.

Concentration is the key to success in any sport. In David's case it had become diluted which may have accounted for the fact that his innings lasted two balls. Stewart Thorogood had bowled a beauty to Brian Stagden which had the batsman in a tangle from which a leg bye was retrieved. Given this early chance David was keen to make progress. He slashed at his first ball, got an outside edge which went through the vacant slip area and was fast enough to elude Tom Redman at third man. Recalling how David had perished last year at the hands of Colin Banks, Stewart strove to up his speed. He was rewarded by an airy drive and the clatter of ball into stumps. David was aghast at his folly. His mood was not improved when Joseph greeted him on his return by saying, 'I obviously sent you in too soon.' David snapped a regrettably rude response before stomping up to the changing room.

He was succeeded by his brother Andrew, who had also bowled eight consecutive overs and, as David silently noted, at rather greater expense than his own performance. Andrew was in no mood to rush. Unlike his brother he saw no need. So he played defensively through the remainder of

Stewart's over. Ray Burrill at the other end had been reprieved after capturing Michael Carter's wicket. He decided to switch to off spin despite Basil Smith's lack of success in that mode. This gave Brian Stagden something different to think about, but he thought about it for no more than half an over before taking two steps down the wicket and hitting Ray's fourth ball high, straight and long. However, he had miscalculated. Ray had spotted his initial movement and had held the ball back. The consequence was that in the stroke height triumphed over length. Had the deep fielder not also been guilty of a miscalculation Brian would surely have been out. Unfortunately for the bowler John Furness first back-peddled, then came forward and finally two steps back. In the end he did not get even a finger on it – which was probably just as well – and the ball went one bounce for four.

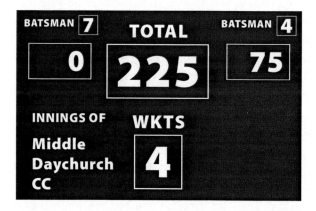

It seemed to be all over bar the shouting and so Ray thought what the hell. He would try the two card trick. His fifth ball was a cutter bowled at a brisk pace. It almost yorked Brian Stagden who scowled in Ray's direction. And then Ray tried a slower ball. It was a technique which he had not yet mastered, but the gods must have wanted justice done. Brian played too soon and obligingly spooned up the ball into Ray's joyful hands. Despite having top-scored with a hard-hitting no-nonsense type of innings Brian gave Ray an almost murderous stare before turning on his heel and marching to the pavilion whilst muttering repeatedly to himself. Tom Redman recalled later that it sounded like 'Job not done, job not done'. Sadly there was a sound not unlike a bat being thrown to the floor as he disappeared from view.

John Furness gathered Stewart, Ray and Winston around him and said, 'What do you think? They haven't got much left, have they? I guess he won't be contributing.' John had gestured in the direction of Richard Love. 'If it's a choice between winning and losing, I wouldn't bet on it,' said Stewart. 'I don't believe that Joseph Carter's new-found benevolence runs that deep.' 'Hmm, well we'll see. Just try and slip in a few quick ones, mate.' This last remark was addressed to Stewart and with that John gave him a couple of slip fielders. 'Let's sharpen up, lads,' he said loudly as Andrew Carter had readied himself to take strike. Thinking of John's hapless dropped catch, Ray admired his captain's chutzpah.

There was no doubt that Stewart strove hard in his next over, but his maximum achievement was to staunch the flow of runs. Only a single was conceded. Ray in his final over fared only slightly worse, giving away a couple of singles. Stewart ended on a high with a wicket maiden. It was clear that the bruised Adrian Seymour was bent on defence, but Stewart's fifth ball would have tested anyone. From somewhere he found a fraction of swing which neither the batsman nor the bowler in truth had anticipated. He looked ruefully at his shattered stumps. Brian Carter leapt at the chance of an innings. Richard Love swivelled uneasily in his seat at square leg. He was not going to have to do a Cowdrey (Lord's 1963), was he?

So rarely did his opportunities arise that Brian was inclined to see himself as the man of the hour. He made no effort to confer with cousin Andrew. After all, what could he say? He had been there only five minutes himself. Brian looked round the attacking field settings, stared in particular at the two slips and sliced his first ball through them for four. Game on, he thought. 15 runs needed. Nine overs left. No problem.

Nor was there. The Outcasts had reached the summit of their achievement in this match. It was all downhill from that point. Winston Jenkins was brought back at the end from which he had previously bowled. Whether deliberately or by chance Richard's chair seemed fractionally more obtrusive than earlier. To compensate Winston bowled from wider of the crease and again the ball went wide of leg stump. Four wides were thereby gifted to the opposition. And that was not the end of it. Despite John Furness posting a fine leg fieldsman two more extras were added to the score. Winston took deep breaths, steadied himself and finally got his line right. To his chagrin once the batsman could lay his bat on the ball, he did. Andrew first getting two runs and then a single. Six runs then lay between Middle Daychurch and victory. Andrew could see the glint in Brian's eye. The young man took an almighty heave at Winston's next delivery and was fortunate to miss. His second attempt was no more successful. Winston ran in again going closer to the stumps. Too close. His brush with the umpire's chair disconcerted him and he lost control of the ball. It flew out of his hand as a high full toss. It may have been a cross-batted heave, but it flew majestically out of the ground. Brian dropped his bat. His fists pumped the air. He had won the match. Magic.

Close of play

The handshakes were cordial. Words of praise were exchanged. For the Outcasts Ray Burrill had had a good all-round match, but the two best innings had been played for the home team. The top scorer, Brian Stagden, seemed curiously muted in his response to the compliments which came his way. For one, Brian Carter could not understand this. He knew that, if he had scored 79 with 16 boundaries, he would have been manic. But then he had taken three wickets and won the match with a six and so probably in an hour he would be manic anyway.

Once back in the Outcasts' changing room the atmosphere was a bit depressed. In the kind of cricket they played winning was not a necessity, but from the beginning Middle Daychurch had presented a particular challenge. Although these opponents were not now as tricky and ruthless as they had first found them, the Outcasts realised that there was still deep down a determination to win. They told each other that they would have to give a lot of thought to tactics before the following season. In the meantime there were the excellent ales of The Cow's Corner to smooth away their disappointment.

Once the competitive tension had eased camaraderie was re-established. It struck the Outcasts as interesting that members of the home team now had no problems about walking directly to the pub with their opponents. The prohibition of former years had gone. There were one or two exceptions. Joseph and the older generation were still inclined to slide away to their domestic situations. Those below the age of eighteen still found it necessary to undertake a detour to The Cow's Corner although once inside there seemed little restriction from either side of the bar about what they drank. Richard Love used the excuse of his foot to miss the post-match wind-down. He explained that he found standing very painful and that he would find lying down more comfortable. He then made his way to 8 Cricketers Close to effect that very cure. Brian Stagden, hero of the Middle Daychurch innings, seemed to have shaken off the surliness which he had exhibited earlier and made himself a prominent life and soul of the party.

For no special reason Alan Birch had been ahead of the pack in reaching the pub. He had changed quickly and left the pavilion so that he could put in a call to Margaret at home as he had left her feeling under the weather.

However, the number was engaged and Alan was left to wonder with which of her friends his wife was having one of her usual gossips. The Snug bar when he reached it had only one customer whom he immediately recognised. It was Pierre from Le Rêve Royal, but very much Pete when off duty. Alan felt a twinge in his stomach as the memory was revived. The chef was in animated conversation with the pub landlord and the language employed was conspicuously not French. 'Conspiring with the enemy, I see,' said Alan in a light-hearted tone, also in English. 'You could put it like that,' said the landlord, 'but we were just comparing notes on the progress of our little ventures. We don't see them as too much in competition, do we Pete?' 'Nah, not really,' said Pete slipping back naturally into Estuary English. He went on, 'Do I know you, mate?' Alan mentioned that he had been to the restaurant, but did not specify the occasion.

The landlord chipped in with the explanation that Pete was enjoying a half-night off. He and his partner had taken on an additional chef in anticipation of the opening of their brasserie. After a period of familiarisation he was this evening being put on his mettle by being placed in sole charge of the kitchen. Pete had got out of the way for a while, but would return as back-up should it be necessary. He seemed relaxed with time to make conversation with Alan. What was Alan doing in the village? 'Oh, cricket, right,' Pete acknowledged, 'I used to play a bit myself. Mind you that was a while ago before I went to France. There wasn't much chance of cricket in Paris. And anyway I met Marcel, Marty actually, and we got down to some 'ard graft. It was a career changing moment.' He paused. 'And no way I've regretted it, but I sometimes think back. Essex were quite interested in me when I was sixteen.' Alan asked him if he had not considered turning out for Middle Daychurch. 'Nah,' said Pete, 'I 'aven't 'ad time. Running a restaurant is knackering and anyway word is the local side's a bit of a closed shop.' Alan could hear noise indicating the arrival of the rest of the crowd. He just had time to say, 'Well, if you're taking on more staff, you never know. They might be pleased to hear from you especially if ever they're a man short.' These last words were to prove eerily prophetic. Pete looked doubting and after a further word with the landlord excused himself. 'Better check, to be on the safe side.'

The 'ifs' and 'maybes' of the match were discussed in lively fashion. The youngest Middle Daychurch players seemed to be having their own post-mortem on the match with some of those who had not been picked trying to take the rise out of those who had. Occasionally one of the group would detach himself, sidle up to Charlie or one of the other Outcasts to indicate that another round would be much appreciated. Sometimes a banknote would accompany the request. Charlie told Harry to attach himself to the group later on to see if he could pick up any intelligence that might serve the Outcasts' interests in next year's match. This plan was frustrated when the landlord called out John Furness' name and said he was wanted on the telephone. It was the owner of the minibus firm. 'Tried to get you on your mobile, but seemingly it was switched off. So in the end I guessed you'd be where you are. There's a bit of a problem. I've just heard that the last train tonight will be 8.30. Network Rail are having to bring forward some maintenance work otherwise it will be havoc on Monday morning. If you lot have to get back, I'll need to pick you up no later than eight o'clock.' This news led to another three rounds being disposed of on an accelerated schedule. The landlord offered pie and chips to anyone interested. There were a few takers, but the other Outcasts began to think of a late night curry at the Balti Temple or the arms of their beloved where applicable or even a combination of both.

There were hurried farewells as the Outcasts piled on to the two mini-buses, interspersed with some banter about next year's fixture. As the lead vehicle moved away Tom Redman turned to Dean Faulds in the seat behind him. 'There was a lot of noise, but just before we went out of the door back there I'm sure I heard some sort of distant roar. It might even have been an explosion. Did you notice anything?' Dean's reply was non-confirmatory. 'More likely your guts. You cleared that pie and chips faster than Usain Bolt does the 100 metres.'

The journey was not many minutes old when a fire appliance with lights flashing swept past them in the other direction. It was followed by another and then an ambulance. In the rear minibus Winston Jenkins nudged Ray Burrill. 'Look back,' he said, 'Can you see something?' Ray turned his head. 'There seems to be a glow in the sky. I guess it must be' – and here his words were drowned by the noise of another fire appliance racing past – 'a fire. Hope it's not the pub.' After this profundity he lapsed into silence for the remainder of the journey to the railway station. Once they were all on the train speculation about the emergency vehicles gave way to talk about how they might occupy the remainder of the evening.

On Sunday morning Charlie Colson was late to rise. In fact it was already afternoon when he did. The previous evening he had persuaded himself that it was too late to inflict himself on Liz. He was therefore easily per-suaded, principally by David Pelham, that there was still time to get a few in at The Sink and Plumber. Six of the others readily agreed. The session had ended late. The encounter with the fire appliances had exited his mind. There was nothing in either of the papers he'd got from the shop on the corner to revive the memory. After two black coffees and an effort to make himself faintly respectable he had got in touch with Liz and spent the rest of the day with her. He saw nothing in his national newspaper on Monday morning of particular interest and so it was a shock when two days later he got a call from a very excited Jon Palmer. Under the headline 'Village of the Damned' one of the tabloids was reporting another death in Middle Daychurch. Charlie was on the road at the time and sought out a service station where he could get a copy of the paper. He bought a coffee at the same time and settled down to absorb the news.

The story, written in lurid and sensational terms, was splashed over two inside pages with a provocative trailer entitled 'Welcome to Middle Diechurch'. Six deaths all in the same family deepened the suspicion of a curse or even some malign hand. There were photographs, mostly blurred, but the names were clear enough. It was the name of Joseph which leapt out at Charlie. Several paragraphs into the report he found the hard news. Joseph Carter had died in an explosion on Saturday night. After playing and winning a cricket match against some nondescript side from London ('thanks a lot,' breathed Charlie) the Middle Daychurch captain had retired as was his habit to the workshop he maintained at his allotment. It was larger than the normal shed and had the benefit of electricity. Joseph kept more than garden tools there. There were also gas cylinders together with some creature comforts. He would sometimes spend hours working away on what he called his little projects.

The fire and safety people had said that the most probable cause of the accident was a gas leak. Just switching on the light would have been the spark to cause the explosion. It had been massive. The late Mr Carter had kept more cylinders in the workshop than would be considered prudent. Virtually nothing was left, least of all the unfortunate Joseph Carter. There had also been collateral damage to the allotments which the newspaper described as devastated. The boots and equipment of the fire and rescue service had laid waste to many lovingly-tended root crops. These facts such as they were took second place to a torrent of journalistic hype.

Charlie put aside the paper, deep in thought. He felt an urgent need to talk to Michael Carter, whilst recognising the sensitivity of the moment. This was his father who had died and Michael was now the oldest surviving son. Charlie knew that he must respond to Jon Palmer. A special meeting of the Outcasts beckoned. He had the unsettling feeling that they were in strange territory.

It was not until later in the day that he was able to reach Michael. It was obvious from the sound of his voice that he was a deeply troubled man. Charlie thought it wise to keep questions for a later occasion. He expressed sorrow on behalf of himself and the other Outcasts, asked how everyone in the Carter family was bearing up and enquired when the funeral might be expected. The last point was particularly awkward in view of the nature of the tragedy. Charlie wondered whether forensic investigations might hold up funeral arrangements, but then, if reports were correct, there was a paucity of evidence to try to analyse. It would seem cruel to extend the family's agony by delaying the formal act of burial. These were hardly details Charlie wanted to trawl over with Michael, but equally he felt it was an occasion which the Outcasts would want to mark in an appropriate way. In the end he got little more from the conversation than a promise to be kept informed.

Charlie reported back to Jon. They agreed that an email should be circulated to the others, but Charlie felt more was needed. 'I agree,' said Jon, 'yet another death stretches the bad luck theory, but I assume you're not flirting with witchcraft nonsense or anything of that kind.' 'All I'm saying,' Charlie insisted, 'is that we sit down and talk about it.' 'But what do we know beyond the bare facts? We can do no more than gossip . . . or fantasise. Look, I tell you what. If it'll keep you happy, a few of us will go out on a Sunday morning to try out a decent pub we haven't previously tested. Then we can pool what little we know and you can try out your theories. At least we may have found some good ale. But we shouldn't do this until there's been a funeral. Then there might be a few more crumbs of information.' That was how it was left between them and Charlie had to be content. Nevertheless he could not shake off his unease.

Joyce Simpson was another enveloped by unease. She had sent out the secret coded message to her husband. It was their agreed way of letting him know that she needed him to get in touch. His absence was longer than usual and she had not received so much as a postcard from him. What had been very unsettling was that she had received a postcard from Northern Cyprus. It was a picture of their home on the island and in a hand which was not her husband's was the word 'going'. By now she was desperate to speak to him. Better still for him to be home with her. Why wasn't he getting in touch? She had the feeling that something had gone terribly wrong. Not for the first time a woman's intuition would prove to be perceptive.

Her worries extended to her daughter. On the night of the match Shirley had come home extremely late. Her nights out with Richard had never extended beyond midnight. At breakfast when finally she had surfaced she was unusually tight-lipped. Asked if she was all right, she had said very firmly that she was. Asked about Richard, she had been noncommittal. Asked about how long she could stay, she answered 'not long'. Asked about how things were going at work, she told her mother that they were going fine. Joyce made one further effort. She tried to make her question as natural as possible. 'Have you heard from your dad recently?' Shirley looked at her with astonishment. 'No, why, there's nothing wrong, is there?' 'No, no, I was just wondering.' And with that her mother gathered up the used dishes and disappeared into the kitchen. Within ten minutes Shirley had left.

At the funeral of Joseph Carter the Outcasts had more than a sole representative. On this occasion Charlie Colson was accompanied by Jon Palmer, Stewart Thorogood and Greg Roberts. Other clubs were represented as well, a sign that generally there had been a thawing of relations over the last couple of years. Charlie, who had become a practised mourner, could see at once that more than just grief was affecting the surviving members of the Carter family. Etched into even the youngest faces were signs of stress. In one or two cases it might even have been fear. So many funerals in so short a time made it more difficult than usual to find the right words to offer. Eventually Charlie cornered Michael, who had had the melancholy duty of delivering the eulogy. The emotion, which he had held at bay, now broke over him. Embracing Charlie, he wept. For perhaps two minutes not a word was exchanged as they remained locked together in a quiet corner of the churchyard.

Finally Michael stepped back, but gripping Charlie's arm he blurted out his appreciation for his being there. 'I just don't know what to say,' Charlie admitted. 'Nor do I, nor do I,' responded Michael, 'it seems like one long nightmare. You can't help wondering' and his voice tailed away. 'Wondering what?' asked Charlie. 'Well, dad was always so careful. He used to bang on to us kids about safety, respect for tools, you know, that sort of thing. It's almost unbelievable that he wouldn't have made sure that a gas cylinder was sealed.' 'Did you mention this to the police?' Michael looked at him. 'You're not suggesting foul play? Who'd ever do something like that? I just felt he must have been distracted. My brother's death weighed heavily on him, perhaps more than we realised.' They were interrupted by a shout from Adrian Seymour, 'Are you coming Mike?' Charlie was cut off from pursuing a certain line of thought which was probably just as well, he thought on reflection, for Michael had not appeared to link this latest death with the others. 'Are you sure you can cope with us all at the wake?' 'No, you must come,' replied Michael as he hurried away, 'you've been very loyal to us'. Before following, Charlie went over to look at the floral tributes. One had a familiar look about it. There was one word inscribed on the card: 'Goodbye,' followed by the 'K' symbol and the squiggle.

The gathering in The Cow's Corner was a very restrained affair. Even the young members of the Carter family with a pronounced taste for vodka looked and sounded withdrawn. The four Outcasts felt slightly more comfortable talking to the cricketers who they knew from the circuit. None of them seemed to have thought that there was anything peculiar about the succession of deaths in Middle Daychurch. They went no further than commenting on the bad luck of the Carter family. Charlie decided to keep his thoughts to himself. He noticed that Brian Stagden and Martin Norwell were both present, suggesting that the ice between the Daychurch villages had begun to melt. 'It's a terrible thing,' said Brian. 'Joseph was a good bloke at heart. He may have struggled a bit to relax the iron rule of his father, but he'd made a start. He's a real loss. Yet I reckon this'll force them to widen the net for players. So you still won't beat us.' That was about the only note of levity in the entire proceedings. The Outcasts and the other non-family attendees were inclined to an early retreat.

On the way back home Greg told his companions of a conversation with Richard Love. Unlike other members of his family Richard seemed to have imbibed rather heavily, a process which Greg deduced had begun comfortably in advance of the funeral. It had become quickly apparent that the sorrows being drowned by Richard may not have been exclusively connected with his uncle's demise. Nor did his pain relate to the injury he had sustained in the recent match. Greg admitted that he was not sure he had picked up a wholly coherent story. Richard had talked of his life being ruined. It seemed that this had more to do with a woman or women than with poor Joseph. At first Richard had been maudlin, but as he drank he lapsed into vituperation. 'Bitch,' he said, slamming his fist on the only surface available which had been Greg's right knee. 'How could she do this to me?' Greg had tried to elicit some clue as to what this might be about, but Richard went quiet and filled their glasses from a conveniently handy bottle. Then he said 'bitch' again with extra emphasis. As his raised fist came down Greg in anticipation had spread his legs. Meeting no immediate resistance, its owner fell forward burying his head in Greg's stomach. 'And just when I'd found my true love.' Greg said he thought that those were the words he had heard before he had revived the doleful Richard by sharply pinching his cheek. What he held back from his description of the encounter because he was less sure he had heard correctly were the words 'I'll kill her'.

There had been no further sensations and so it was in early October that the planned outing took place. The watering hole selected was semi-countrified, close to the river and conveniently reachable by the Underground. Charlie, Greg, Jon and Stewart were supplemented by Rashid Ali ('we need his legal mind,' Charlie had said). For all its macabre name 'The Grim Reaper' was a fine establishment. The day was just warm enough to allow enjoyment of a well-appointed beer garden. After the first pint (Wild Oats Bitter) had disappeared in quiet appreciation, Jon turned to Charlie and said, 'OK, spit it out,' adding swiftly as Charlie spluttered, 'not the beer, stupid. What's bothering you?' 'Well,' said Charlie, 'I can do coincidence in moderation, but with what's happening to the Carter family I can't help feeling there's more to it.' 'You sure you haven't read too much Agatha Christie, my friend?' asked Rash. There was more banter and a third round before Charlie was allowed much of a hearing.

He admitted straightaway that it was the sheer number of deaths that had set him wondering. That there was an explanation for each one, he admitted, but he asked his friends to consider the implausible. What if the deaths had all been deliberate? 'Just do some free thinking about this,' Charlie implored. Three pints of good ale encouraged flights of fancy. 'All right,' said Rash, 'let's go through them in order. The old man, Edwin, he died at the wheel of his car. It was a heart attack, wasn't it, that caused him to crash? There was no reason to think otherwise.' 'Not at the time, no,' said Charlie, 'but five fatalities later there's room for speculation. What if the car's steering or brakes had been fixed?' 'But he still had a heart attack, that's definite,' said Stewart. Charlie persisted. 'He could have had the heart attack when he realised he was going to crash. I wonder what happened to the wreck. I bet no-one bothered to examine it.' His companions remained visibly sceptical.

'OK,' said Charlie, 'unbelievable maybe, but then let's take Douglas Carter. The family seemed all too ready to believe that he took his own life.' He paused. 'But do you really top yourself because you weren't made captain of the cricket club? That explanation was just accepted as a given. What if there was something else? Douglas was unmarried. Could he have had a private life that he didn't want revealed?' This produced snorts of laughter. 'Oh, come on,' said Greg, shaking his head. However, Charlie could not be deflected. 'Let's just suppose that someone wanted to get Douglas out of the way and confronted him with evidence that he could not face being published. That someone could even have persuaded, even helped him to escape the shame and humiliation. Did anyone ever ask where the rope came from? If the family suspected something about Douglas, wouldn't it have been natural to cover up his death with the cricket excuse?' 'That's just one guess after another,' said Stewart, 'you should try your hand at writing novels.'

'As you've set me going,' retorted Charlie, 'let me finish. It's important to paint the whole picture.' 'Not half so important as getting in another round,' said Jon heading towards the bar. Whilst he was gone Stewart questioned Charlie. 'How're you going to fit Philip Carter into this pattern? After all they dug him up and proved it was a natural death.' 'I agree that's an oddity, but do wait till I'm through. Then you might see Philip's death in a different light.' The beer arrived. 'I'm going to miss out Philip Carter for the moment,' Charlie announced. 'Who was next? Oh yes, Paul.' 'That was food poisoning,' interrupted Stewart. 'Everyone was caught out with that even Alan and Tim. Paul just had a violent reaction.' 'That's absolutely right,' said Charlie, 'but you might equally say that it was perfect cover for poisoning someone.' The others looked at him with incredulity. Before they could challenge him, Charlie ploughed on. 'Suppose the oysters that night were not bad, but adulterated. Mild adulteration in every case but one, enough to cause violent stomach pain or vomiting, but in that one case a massive dose deliberately served to Paul.'

Charlie could see by the looks on their faces that his friends were not impressed by this wild theory. To forestall a chorus of criticism he went quickly on to the case of George Carter. Falling masonry could be just an accident. Then again someone might have been lying in wait for the poor man. 'But there's no evidence either way,' protested Jon. Charlie ignored him. 'We've been told Joseph Carter was a scrupulously careful man. So it's really hard to believe that he would not have sealed off a gas cylinder he had used. Someone could have got into his hut and laid the trap. All I'm saying is that these deaths might all seem innocent, but they could be explained in a totally different way. Six deaths all in the same family. What do the dead have in common?' Giving the others no time to venture an answer, Charlie supplied his own. 'After Edwin himself they're all his male heirs. If I was Michael, I'd be feeling very uncomfortable right now.'

There was a short silence broken by Rash. 'But we come back to Philip Carter. There is no way you can pass that off as a deliberate killing.' 'Even if I suspend belief,' Stewart chipped in, 'I'd want to know who and why. Have you worked that out, Charlie?' 'I don't know,' admitted Charlie, 'I was hoping you guys might have some ideas. For me I'm just not convinced all the deaths in Middle Daychurch can be put down to coincidence. You can't say in every case – well, perhaps one – that the cause of death was proved beyond all doubt. There is a sort of pattern. If something happens to Michael Carter, perhaps you'll start taking me seriously.' Seeing that Charlie was getting a little upset, Jon spoke up. 'It only starts to become a credible theory if you can spot a motive and, if you can do that, you might be able to work out who might want to attack this family.' No-one had any suggestions beyond Rash remarking, 'It's greed as often as not.' The conversation petered out. Charlie felt rebuffed. Another pint improved his spirits. Some roast beef baguettes complemented the beer. The five friends turned to the prospects for England's forthcoming overseas tour. This discussion turned out to be more animated than the last.

It was during the following week that Charlie took a call from Greg. 'Sorry you got a bit of a roasting on Sunday. Hope the beer made up for it. Wild Oats wasn't a half bad brew.' Charlie said that he had got over it, but it hadn't stopped him thinking. 'I'd never put you down as the amateur detective type, but you've got to admit it's a bit of an outlandish theory you've dreamt up.' Charlie interrupted, 'You haven't just rung up to turn the screw, have you?' 'No way, mate. I've actually been mulling over what you said. I talked to Colin about it. He reminded me of something we'd seen outside that restaurant. I don't suppose it's important, but I thought I'd mention it if only to show I'd at least given you a fair hearing.' So mention it he did, the dodgy-looking dealing. Charlie pressed him on detail, but Greg was not able to add much. 'Well, thanks anyway,' said Charlie in ending the call and congratulating himself on having suppressed any chuckles or unseemly exclamation whilst his girlfriend's hands had been wandering over him. For the rest of the evening Liz was a greater priority than Middle Daychurch.

Apart from sorting out the shotgun licence Joyce Simpson's mind continued to be troubled. There had been no response of any description from her husband Frank. Shirley too had been ignoring her. She knew she led a busy life, but she usually found time to call her mother even if it was not much more than a cheery hello and goodbye. It was also a bit strange that she had not been home for several weeks. She must have wanted to see Richard if not her mother unless . . . but Maisie Love had not said anything. Joyce did not like to over-fuss in case it alienated her daughter, but neither of the calls she had made to Shirley's mobile had been answered. It had been a relief when Maisie had asked her round to tea. 'We haven't had a chat for what seems like ages.' So it was duly arranged. They had talked about this and that until Joyce could hold out no longer. 'Has Richard been seeing much of our Shirley lately?' 'Funny you should say that. I've been thinking it a bit strange, but I didn't like to say anything. You know what young people are like.' The two mothers then pooled what they knew which they soon realised was very little. For Joyce the therapeutic value of the session was minimal. She parted from her friend in a state of profound depression.

It was a state shared by Richard Love. At first he had been thankful to have avoided contact with Shirley. Yet as the weeks ticked by he could not understand why she had not communicated with him. His mother had made a passing comment that he did not seem to have been out with Shirley lately. He had not enlightened her, but the nagging worry of a paternity order had begun to affect his relationship with Debbie. When finally he had decided that he could carry on no longer without knowing what was happening he plucked up the courage to phone. Shirley's number was out of service he was told by a disembodied voice. What was he to do? He could hardly ask Mrs Simpson or mention Shirley's name to his mother, because he was relying on both of them assuming that the friendship was still intact. He had absolutely no wish to be questioned on the subject.

This uneasy status quo for both Joyce Simpson and Richard survived another week. It was Halloween when purely by chance Richard spotted what he thought was a familiar car. In fact the car seemed more familiar than the person who emerged from it. On closer scrutiny it was undoubtedly Shirley, but Shirley looking like he had never before seen her. There had been a glamour makeover. She might have stepped straight off the catwalk. Her figure was ultra slim line. There was about her no trace of a suggestion that she was with child. Richard hurried to have words with her. She greeted him with an air of disdain as though he was a reminder of a past life from which she had detached herself. In the circumstances the commonplace 'How are you?' seemed as good an opening gambit as any. 'In the pink,' she replied. Richard thought there was a hint of a mid-Atlantic accent. 'I've been worried about you,' Richard tried next. 'Why would you be worried?' 'Your message,' said Richard with some incredulity. 'Oh that, I'd forgotten.' 'Forgotten? How could you forget something like that?' She laughed. 'It was a joke.' From that point the exchange spiralled sharply and swiftly downwards. Some very hard words were used, some very unkind remarks made. Finally with a withering and obscene put-down Shirley marched towards her mother's front door. Richard was left in the road with murderous thoughts passing through his head.

Shirley's arrival was unheralded. Joyce Simpson had been oiling the handgun when the doorbell sounded. This had to be concealed before any visitor could be admitted, not least if the friendly constable was calling again. There was double relief when she discovered her daughter on the doorstep. In this case 'How are you, darling?' came after 'What have you done with your keys?' The answer was that darling had left them in another bag, but then there was a lot more explaining to do when Joyce majored on how distraught she had become. Shirley was subjected to a rigorous inquisition such as distraught mothers are likely to inflict on neglectful daughters. She chose her answers carefully, having been advised to be as sparing as possible with the passage of information. She was also as loving and tender towards her mother as of old whilst she looked for the right moment to ask the big question, which was the real purpose of her mission.

After Shirley had turned her heels on him Richard had stood in the road paralysed with shock, confusion and anger. He had barely moved when a voice hailed him. 'Fancy a pint?' It was cousin Michael, whose cheerfulness was in marked contrast to Richard's despondency. Having had no immediate response, Michael said, 'Come on, I'll buy you a pint'. 'I think,' said Richard deliberately 'I shall need a lot more than just one.' That seemed to be indication enough and so without waiting for prevarication Michael steered Richard firmly to The Cow's Corner. Michael, once two pints were in front of them, was not slow to recognise that Richard had something on his mind. His mood seemed to alternate between gloom and gladness, but it took until the third round before Richard was ready to explain himself.

In real time it took Shirley longer than that to find the point in the mother-daughter catch-up when she could broach the subject which had brought her back home. They had talked about her father. Joyce covered her worries by saying that she thought he was in Cyprus. Shirley hoped that her expression gave nothing away, but grabbed the opening. 'I was going to ask you about that. I wanted to know if there was any possibility that I could go there for a couple of weeks. With someone. Dad wouldn't mind, would he?' Whether Frank would mind or not was far from being the first thought on Joyce's mind. She had fastened on the 'with someone' part of what Shirley had said. Her daughter had to disabuse her of the idea that her companion would be Richard Love. No escalation of that relationship, sighed Joyce, before entering interrogative mode as to the identity of her daughter's new beau. She was supplied with the minimum of information: businessman, tall, sort of dark and definitely gorgeous. Not all of this was true, but Shirley did not feel that mattered too much. She burbled on about how she wanted to impress Carlo. They could have a wonderful holiday. What she was after were the keys. In the end, although she felt she was suffering from an information deficiency, Joyce succumbed. She could see that her daughter was happy, excited even. She wondered what Frank would think if he actually was in Cyprus. Perhaps she had better try and get a message to him. Then she changed her mind. Why should she? He had not bothered to keep her in the picture. It might wake him up if Shirley and this Carlo were to turn up on his doorstep. What Joyce did not know was just how completely in the dark she was.

By the time the third pint had been sunk in the Snug bar of The Cow's Corner the word 'bitch' had been spat out of Richard's mouth several times and with increasing venom. When he looked back on it Michael thought that he had handled the situation quite well. He had steered Richard into recognition that he was not after all faced with being the father of a child by a woman who no longer loved him. He had needed to be careful about this because he was not entirely sure how Richard had felt about impending fatherhood. Things had become clearer during the course of the fourth pint when Richard had revealed that he too had moved on. This emboldened Michael to turn Richard away from the anger over Shirley's deceit and think more about the new beginning on which he had very obviously begun. Now he was unencumbered. Gradually this realisation of freedom began to dawn on Richard. He enunciated 'bitch' one more time and then told Michael that they must drink to freedom 'and the future'. Michael had been looking forward to dinner, but felt he had to settle for one more pint.

Reconnaissance

DURING THE WINTER WANDERINGS of the Outcasts (*Accidentally Cricket* 2009) Middle Daychurch had been largely forgotten. Charlie Colson himself in harness with his most dedicated drinking partner, David Pelham, had been absorbed in his Australian adventure still reeling from girlfriend Liz's news that she was expecting his baby. It was not until he was back in England and giving an account of himself in The Sink and Plumber that Colin Banks dropped a minor bombshell into the conversation. 'You know that Carter family in Middle Whatsit. Well, one of them had a skiing accident a few weeks ago.' The reaction from Charlie was delayed. He was well into reacquainting himself with proper ale after the appalling beverages he had been obliged to drink in Australia for what he regarded as purely diplomatic reasons. Finally what Colin had said sank in. 'What, which, when, who, how?' Charlie slurped. These staccato questions were too much for Colin, who was himself by then several notches short of acuity. Nor were other members of the assembled company on this occasion able to supply much enlightenment. 'What I want to know,' said Charlie, trying to concentrate on the essential, 'was whether he was killed'. 'I can't remember,' said Colin disconsolately. And nor could anyone else. 'It was Jon who told me,' added Colin eventually after a desperate attempt at recall.

Charlie was well into the next day before out of the mists Colin's announcement of the previous evening came back to him. But it was not until the evening that he was able to reach Jon Palmer. 'It wasn't me,' said Jon, 'but I did hear it from John Furness. He'd seen it in *The Guardian*. You'd do better talking to him. It was Michael Carter, but he's OK. It was just bad luck. A broken ski. I can see what you're thinking, but there seems to be no doubt it was an accident. Not even the tabloids seemed interested.' This assessment was confirmed when Charlie spoke to John Furness. 'You mean no-one thought there was anything odd about it?' exclaimed Charlie with

incredulity. 'Oh, come on, Charlie, I know about your wild theories, but no-one saw this as other than a piece of bad luck. If you don't believe this, talk to the man himself.' So after a day or two of contemplation Charlie did. He found Michael to be in good, bordering on exuberant form.

After an initial exchange of pleasantries during which Charlie had given a very restricted account of his adventures in Australia, he drew attention to Michael's winter escapade. Michael was very dismissive. 'This kind of thing happens,' he said, 'even when it's your own skis.' 'You mean it wasn't, wherever you were?' queried Charlie. 'God, no,' replied Michael. 'I can't afford my own, I hire.' 'And were the skis you were using the same ones each day?' 'Yes, I think so,' said Michael, 'but no, come to think of it, the pair I'd been using had to be replaced, because they had to re-treat them or something.' 'Hang on a minute,' said Charlie, 'are you saying that on the day of the accident the skis you were using were not the same as you'd used on the previous days?' 'You could be right,' said Michael with what Charlie regarded as an irritating lack of certainty. He concluded their conversation by telling Michael that he had huge respect for him. However, he added the warning, 'Do be careful'.

A similar admonition had been conveyed by Brian Carter to his brother James when they had been together in the gents at a hostelry in a nearby village where they had reckoned that it would be easier to pass off James as being of legitimate drinking age. They had succeeded, James' false moustache seemingly having tilted the balance in his favour. In reality the publican had not been fooled, but trade was not good in remote country establishments such as his. If these two young lads had money to spend, he was pleased to get it. After serving two pints of his best bitter (they had thought vodka would be pushing it too far) he discreetly took down the RU18 notice and placed it under the bar counter.

The Horse's Shoe, despite being a compact building, nevertheless had two bars. Brian and James had chosen the public bar where there was a darts board and a bar billiards table. They had both facilities to themselves. An hour had passed before they were aware that there were any other customers on the premises. Even then it had taken raised voices to draw attention to the fact that the saloon bar had occupants. James was buying unaware that his moustache had acquired an unnatural angle. The landlord affected not to notice. James was tall for his age and a mistake in serving him would have been excused for that reason if anyone had been around to challenge. Fortunately, thought the landlord as he excused himself to change the barrel, there was not. As it happened he was mistaken.

James, waiting at the bar whilst Brian tried to see how many times he could hit double top, was the first to appreciate the risk of exposure. With no sound other than arrows (mostly) hitting the board James found he could pick up strands of the conversation in the next door bar. There were two voices, one male the other female. With a start he realised the man's voice was familiar. If he needed any confirmation, it came a moment later when he heard the woman say, 'Face it, Brian, you messed up. It was a perfect opportunity, I grant you. But was there really a need?' James did not wait to hear more. He darted across to his brother. 'Brian Stagden's in the other bar.' 'Does that matter?' asked his elder brother. 'It could be awkward if he sees us, me especially. Word might get back to mum. I'll be grounded.' 'We'll be all right. He's in that bar and we're in this. I'm more interested in who he's with. He might not want to see us.' 'But, if he wants to use the bog, he has to come through here. Which reminds me.' Brian made a move in that direction. Turning at the door, he said with a grin, 'Didn't you want something?' 'I need some change,' said James reddening. 'I think we'd better make this just a half and then scarper.'

By now the landlord had tested the new barrel and placed two glasses of crystal clear amber liquid on the counter. Tendering a £10 note, James asked for the change in coins, took the beer to a table near the darts board and shot into the loo. To his further embarrassment the false moustache fell into the urinal. Now thoroughly discomfited, his brother's smile not helping, James said, 'Let's sink it quickly and get out while the going's good.' They could still hear conversation in the lounge whilst they emptied their glasses and returned them to the bar, wishing goodnight to the landlord. He was unable to resist saying, 'A close shave, was it, sir?' It might well have been, thought James, missing the point.

Once outside Brian said, 'Hang on a minute. I'm going to take a peep'. Pulling the hood of his fleecy top over his head, he went quietly back inside The Horse's Shoe. He was gone not more than a minute. 'He must like older women' was his bulletin on return. 'She looks old enough to be his mother.' Laughing they pedalled off into the night.

The shake-up in Charlie Colson's personal life gave him something else to think about other than Middle Daychurch and the welfare of the Carter family. When he had time to drink with fellow Outcasts he disciplined himself to avoid raising the subject. However, he had fallen into the habit of ringing Michael Carter at periodic intervals ostensibly to compare notes about how their seasons were progressing, but hoping to pick up gossip which might or might not feed his theories. He also liked to be assured that Michael himself was keeping clear of 'accidents'. It seemed that despite the convulsions which had rocked Middle Daychurch in recent years their cricket had remained of high standard. Some of their young players had 'come on' very well, but their studies meant that they were not always available. 'Now I'm in charge,' said Michael, 'I'm prepared to call on alternative talent. We've even discovered that Pierre – I mean Pete – from the restaurant is quite handy. It was a surprise when he appeared at our nets session. So he's been turning out for us occasionally. All in all I think we're proving a hard side to beat.' Charlie knew this was true from what he had heard from other teams. It crossed his mind that it might be useful on a day when the Outcasts had no match, to go and have a look at Middle Daychurch in action. He was unable to conceal from himself the desire to see the folk there again and try to sense what was going on. Having established the right combination of circumstances, he persuaded David Pelham to go with him by heavy reference to The Cow's Corner.

If the delights of The Cow's Corner were to be enjoyed, the question of transport arose. The Outcasts had by now acquired the services of Arthur. What a find he had been for them! Arthur was a man of independent means and a love of cricket. On acquaintance he had taken to the Outcasts as a bunch even to the extent of tolerating their sometimes riotous behaviour. More pertinently still he owned a coach which he was prepared to drive for the Outcasts' convenience. It had proved even within a short time to be a happy marriage. It had made Bill Blimp seem like a disgustingly bad dream. Arthur was a shrewd and resourceful asset. It had not taken long for him to pick up the lively topic in Outcasts' circles, namely the dark or otherwise doings at Middle Daychurch. Whilst not wishing to rush prematurely into taking a side in the argument Arthur's own hunch was to share Charlie's doubts about coincidence. On the way back from their match against West Durling Charlie had let it be known what he had in mind. There was a chorus of derision. The Outcasts were in ebullient form having won the game and disposed of the contents of a barrel of the guest bitter at The Priest and Piecrust in record time. At the journey's end, however, Arthur had said to Charlie, 'I'll drive you there. I'm curious.' He smiled. 'And let's face it, it's just a scouting mission.' 'Absolutely,' said Charlie, except that the word came out less clearly than that.

The appointed day did not begin in promising fashion. In south-west London it was drizzling. Charlie's phone rang at nine o'clock. It was David. 'I don't think I'm going to be able to make it,' sounded a strangulated voice. 'Ridiculous,' retorted Charlie, 'are you man or mouse?' 'Man, I'm ill.' 'Ridiculous,' repeated Charlie. David complained, 'It was a hell of a party.' 'I know,' said Charlie, 'I was there, remember?' There was a groan from the other end. Charlie pressed home the advantage. 'Make sure you're at The Sink and Plumber by 12 o'clock. Don't forget, Arthur's doing us a big favour.' The next complaint was from Liz, who said the baby had been in match practice for Wembley all night. Charlie took time out to console. So it transpired that when Charlie got to The Sink and Plumber David was already in occupation of the bar smiling broadly with what looked suspiciously like the second pint of the day in his hand. Remarking that his friend had made a miraculous recovery, Charlie settled for a quick pint himself before Arthur arrived. As they had not so far seen Arthur behind the wheel of other than a coach they were quite surprised by the bright orange supercharged Ford Focus in which he was intending to convey them to Middle Daychurch. During the journey Arthur showed himself to be a sporty driver, a skill he had not hitherto displayed. A mercy, thought Charlie, considering his other vehicle was a bus.

It was their fastest journey to date. They reached Middle Daychurch comfortably ahead of the start-time for the match – something not always achieved when they themselves were playing. It was also comfortably in time for a leisurely pint or two accompanied perhaps by one of the landlord's tasty pies. The weather had cleared; in fact there was no sign of recent rain in the village. The pub's new facility was up and running, but Charlie and David preferred the Snug. Arthur excused himself saying that he might take a look at the French restaurant. He would see them at the match. The pub was quite busy. Mostly visitors Charlie and David reckoned. Apart from the landlord and one of his staff there was no face which they recognised until a young man appeared in the main bar. 'It's Brian, isn't it?' The young man responded to Charlie's greeting with a stare and came towards them. It was evident that he was nursing some kind of injury as he was walking stiffly. 'You're from the Outcasts, aren't you? I didn't think you were playing here today.' David was about to explain when the newcomer dropped his voice to a whisper. 'Did you think I was Brian?' he said. 'Actually I'm James, but people say we're quite alike. I'm trying to look more like him.' He fingered the facial hair he had sprouted since the last time they had seen him. 'I'm not 18 yet. It would be convenient if this place mistook me for my elder brother.'

Arthur meanwhile had reached Le Rêve Royal. The Saturday offer in the main restaurant was still proving popular, but Arthur was informed by a smart young man wearing a white t-shirt and faded blue jeans that there were spare tables in the Garden Room where light lunches were available. He spoke in English with a fake French accent which was obvious to all and embarrassing to the young receptionist himself. Jake Bell, the youngest of that family, had long ago recognised that an aspiring, but struggling, artist had to grab income by any means however cringe-making. There had been, however, one line he had been compelled to draw whilst working in the restaurant environment. He led Arthur into the Garden Room, the name given to a conservatory-style extension, and indicated a particular table. Halfway towards his seat Arthur stopped short as a voice hailed him. Initial surprise overcome he settled down into the spare seat at the table otherwise occupied by an old acquaintance.

The hopes of James Carter had not been fulfilled. The landlord was too canny to be deceived by someone he had known since his short-trouser days. 'It'll be an orange juice then, will it?' James was asked as he approached the bar, 'assuming you're with these two gentlemen.' David nodded. A crestfallen James rejoined them. 'Is that a limp you've got there?' queried Charlie. He thought he detected a blush as James answered. 'It's a bit of a groin strain. But I don't suppose I'd have been picked in any case. It's still bloody hard for some of us to make the team.' 'But I thought your cousin Michael had opened things up a bit,' questioned Charlie. 'Right, I suppose he has in some ways,' replied James, 'but he's been chasing talent from outside the family circle. My grandfather must be turning in his grave.' Charlie pondered this for a moment before saying, 'Yeah, but isn't this good for the club in the long run?' James sniffed. And then pushing his glass forward he said,

'Do us a favour and pop a vodka in that, will you?' Noticing the look which passed across Charlie's face, he quickly added, 'My round next.'

There had been two more postcards. Both had carried the same picture of the Simpson villa. The message on the first had been twice as long as its mysterious predecessor, being 'going, going'. On the next one, a few months later, the word 'gone' had been added. None of this had made any sense to Joyce Simpson, but having had assurances from Shirley that the villa was fine she had done her best to quell her unease. Not that her daughter's continued absence made her happy. Nor the fact that there had been no sign of Frank. The original couple of weeks' holiday had extended to a month before an obviously excited Shirley had rung her mother to say that she had got herself a job in a clinic. Carlo had been very helpful. She was being paid three times as much as she had earned in the UK and was loving the lifestyle. Carlo was being super. No, her father had not appeared. She was told that he had been there, but had gone again. Then there was more about Carlo and how terrific he was. Shirley seemed besotted to a point at which Joyce began to grit her teeth. She looked back at that spasm of irritation with reproach after several weeks had passed without further word from Cyprus. She had agreed with Frank not to ring the villa, but worry finally forced her into it. She was greeted by a babble of words which she assumed to be Turkish, but then the line went dead. She tried this three times without getting anywhere. She knew Shirley would not be pleased, but she next rang her mobile number. This time the response was in English telling her that this cell phone was out of service. Then Joyce really did begin to fret. She wondered if she should go to Cyprus, but Frank had always insisted that she should never venture out there except with him. But she had not heard from him for an exceptionally long time. And now Shirley had cut herself off. Joyce began to fear that something was terribly wrong.

'It's been a long time,' said Arthur after all the 'What on earth are you doing here?' questions had been answered. The gaps were filled in and the new connection revealed. 'Your life sounds a lot more leisured than mine,' laughed Roy Groves. 'I guess you must find those Outcast boys light relief.' 'It keeps me young,' replied Arthur, 'and village cricket is the real essence of the game. I haven't been with the Outcasts long, as I said, but the fixture in this village seems to be the one with the biggest story attached to it.' Roy Groves laughed again, 'Oh you mean the village of the damned stories which have come out?' Without trying to look too eager Arthur indicated that that was what he meant. 'I suppose I could point out,' said Roy with a mischievous glint in his eye, 'the deaths didn't start until after your team had visited! No, OK, I agree it looks suspicious, but I really think that's the most you can say.' 'But wasn't there a near-death experience involving another member of the family?' 'Oh come on, Arthur, accidents happen on skiing holidays. We all know that.'

Arthur let it go for a while as they consumed with mutual pleasure a culinary creation around breast of guinea fowl. And then he tried another tack. 'Have you had many dealings with the family?' 'Which family?' Roy started to say before recovering. 'Oh, sorry, the Carters. Well, no, not really. I mostly look after the affairs of the club. Old Edwin did once ask my opinion about some investments, but otherwise I've not been involved in their individual financial arrangements. But, if you were to ask me – and it can't be more than pure speculation – I'd say there must be a fair amount of money swilling around the Carters. Now, do you fancy some cheese?'

Along the road James' round had been surreptitiously bought. Two pints, an orange juice and two vodka chasers. Another round had followed by which time James had been ready to talk more freely in updating his companions with the latest team news at Middle Daychurch. The Carters were still the backbone of the team, but some extras had been acquired. A young couple had moved into the village from London. They were the Norringtons. Clive Norrington looked at first sight as if he could be a fast bowler. It turned out that he was, having had a season or two in Carshalton. Michael Carter had been commensurately fast in engaging his services. Martin Norwell volunteered the news that a cousin of his had arrived in the area. He gathered that he was a useful bat, had suggested that he come to nets and was gratified when the twenty-three year old had shown some flair. In the course of the season this had been borne out in match conditions. So now Keith Kirkham had established himself in the team. Middle Daychurch had also obtained the occasional services of Pete (Pierre) from Le Rêve Royal. 'So that's what's made it hard for some of the rest of us,' said James gloomily as he pushed his empty glass across the table towards David with his right hand whilst his left stretched under the table in the same direction with a banknote.

With another round set up Charlie tried to broaden the conversation. He was not really sure what he was trying to find out. He knew he had to tread warily. It was not so long ago that James had lost his father. Airing his theory that Paul Carter might have been poisoned might not be the most tactful or productive ploy. A general question about how the family was bearing up produced the answer 'All right, I suppose'. Quizzed as to whether 'anything funny' had happened in the village of late, James looked blank although he seemed to be considering it. 'Not unless you count the vicar falling off his bike and into the pond,' was his eventual pronouncement. 'That was a laugh. Claimed after that someone must have tampered with it. Can't think why anyone would do that. Don't suppose it's anything to do with the village curse.' Charlie did not suppose so either as their companion had not been able to conceal a smirk.

Seeing that they were not going to pick up anything useful from James, Charlie returned to the subject of cricket. 'Perhaps one more pint and then we'd better stroll along to the match.' David got up to do the honours. Reverting to the composition of the Middle Daychurch team, Charlie remarked that as many as half of them might now be from outside the family. James grunted. 'When they choose to play. They're not reliable, not like the Carters.' Charlie momentarily considered the fairness of that in light of the family's attrition rate, but let the thought pass unspoken. James swallowed the remains of his 'orange juice', put the glass somewhat heavily on the table and added, 'I wouldn't be surprised if that Brian Stagden's missing again.' Looking for a reaction and not getting one, James said, 'He's got a woman.' Then he giggled. 'Not exactly a goer.'

During the consumption of another highly fortified drink it was not difficult to get James to explain himself. 'So you didn't actually see this woman yourself?' asked Charlie. 'No, it was my brother who told me, but they seemed quite close.' Charlie soon realised there was no more to be learned. In any case it was probably no more than a piece of salacious gossip. Nevertheless he was curious to see if Brian Stagden was playing that afternoon. They finished their drinks. James rose unsteadily and went off to the gents. Charlie and David went out towards the ground. The scene was not what they had anticipated.

The cheese trolley had been and gone. The varieties on offer had been entirely French. Not a single concession to any English cheese soft or hard. Considering this was a French restaurant in the English countryside owned and run by two Englishmen, Arthur thought this was needless conformity to the image. It had not stopped him enjoying his selection. He had declined the suggestion of a glass of port and had opted for coffee to round off his meal. Roy Groves did take some port in what Arthur thought to be a generous measure. He let him savour it before asking a question which had been puzzling him. 'Did old man Carter favour anyone in particular in his will?' 'Why do you ask?' countered Roy. 'Surely' said Arthur, 'there must have been some sort of money trail and I should think that all these deaths could have played a bit of havoc with it.' Roy subjected him to a hard stare before saying, 'It was none of my business. So it's not for me to say.' He said it in such a way that Arthur's senses were immediately alerted. This was a line of enquiry that ought to be pursued. They shortly thereafter went their separate ways although not without sharing telephone numbers. Yet Arthur was left with the feeling that the initial cordiality of their chance meeting had waned by its end.

A small number of spectators had so far turned up to watch Middle Daychurch play Nudgworth, but their only companions were two sets of stumps. The match had evidently not started and there was no sign that a start was imminent. One or two players could be seen in the pavilion. Charlie recognised Bert Love in an umpire's coat consulting his watch. Charlie felt sufficiently intimate with the home team that he could approach the pavilion to find out what was happening. As he did so there was a screech of brakes in the adjoining parking area where a mud-bespattered saloon car arrived at speed. The disturbance brought Michael Carter from the interior. The man whom Charlie supposed to be the visiting captain practically fell into Michael's arms in his hurry and gasped his apologies. 'Very sorry. Terrible jam on the road. Then we got behind a tractor. Must have left your number at home. Anyway here we are. Sorry.' At that moment the 'we' seemed to embrace only four people, but then two more vehicles trundled sedately into view. In response Michael diplomatically suppressed a reproach, gave a word of welcome, smiled at faces he recognised and suggested in a voice which brooked no contradiction that play would begin in fifteen minutes. As the visitors disappeared upstairs into the changing room it struck Michael that they were light on numbers. He had not consciously been counting, but he doubted that he had seen twelve players pass him.

It was when he was in conversation with Charlie and David, having been surprised to see them, that he discovered he was right. The Nudgworth captain reappeared in his whites with commendable speed and a frown on his face. 'I'm afraid there is one other problem. We've only got ten men. Have you got a spare player you could lend us?' ''Fraid not,' said Michael, 'but,' turning to Charlie and David, 'perhaps one of those gentlemen could help out.' Charlie looked at David, who stared back at Charlie. Both turned towards Michael. Charlie said, 'We weren't planning to stay all day.' David said, 'Well, I wouldn't have minded, but we've got no kit.' 'I'm sure we could fix that,' said Michael with a gleam in his eye. David suddenly realised that he had used the wrong excuse. He was completely undermined when Charlie said, 'I promised Liz I wouldn't be late back, but you know what, I think it'd be a great idea if you could stay on.' The Nudgworth captain chipped in: 'We'll get you a ride back into town.' David realised he was cornered. 'Great,' said Michael as he suggested to his opposite number that they should toss. 'Wonderful,' added the Nudgworth captain as he set off for the middle with Michael. 'We really owe you.' 'Look at it this way,' said Charlie, 'you may pick up something useful – always provided you manage to remain upright, I'm proud of you.' David was hauled off by Charles Bell to locate some kit before he could utter an appropriate withering response.

The Nudgworth team might have been light in numbers, but its members were not light in years. Apart from the captain and a couple of others the rest, reckoned David as he looked around the changing room, must have been over fifty. And in one or two cases he was probably being over-polite. 'Very good of you to help us out, young man,' said the man next to him who already seemed half-exhausted after tying the laces of his boots. 'My name's Vincent, by the way, Vincent Bailey.' Feeling a little more might be needed, he added, 'I usually open the bowling.' By appearance this had not struck David as likely. Perhaps he failed to suppress a doubting expression, because Vincent said, 'I notched up eight in our last game.' David must have shown surprise, for he went on, 'I reckon I could get to ten before the end of the season even though there aren't many games left to go.' David felt the need for a rapid change of subject. 'Who are your missing guys today? Not nursing hangovers, are they?' 'Nothing like that,' said Vincent, suddenly very stern. 'It was a double blow. We lost George – he's one of our best bats – last night. He rang the skipper. His lumbago had come back and he was apparently in agony. He's been a martyr to it for years. But then we had a terrible shock this morning. Graham's wife rang to say he'd suffered a heart attack and he'd been taken to hospital in the middle of the night. People are being struck down younger and younger these days.' 'I'm very sorry,' said David. 'How old was he?' 'Sixty-seven, but he could still bowl some crafty off spin.' 'Well, you know,' came the reply, 'that could be a sign.'

It was then time to take the field, the Nudgworth captain, Humphrey Hutton, having announced that he had won the toss. 'We're putting them in. I've had a look at the pitch. I think we might get something out of it.' David studied his leader for the afternoon. He was perfectly attired in what was pre-modern kit: cream shirt and flannels, which had a knife-edge crease. He had a knotted cravat around his neck and wore a loudly coloured quartered cap which despite appearances did not denote any club, famous or otherwise. As they clattered down the steps, some more circumspectly than others, David found his captain's arm around his shoulder. 'I think I'll open with you, David, at the opposite end to Vincent. That'll give 'em something to think about. I bet you don't always get to bowl when the ball is hard and new, well nearly new.' Humphrey must have suddenly remembered that Edwin Carter's parsimony had survived other changes which had taken place at the club since his death. Nearly new meant third time out, second if you were lucky.

The umpires were already in position with Bert Love appearing by age to be the junior partner. His opposite number turned out to be Vincent Bailey's uncle, Walter Evans. He had an upright military air about him and gave the impression of a man who enjoyed being in charge. As he had anticipated, Vincent Bailey was given the first over. The opening batsmen for Middle Daychurch were Charles Bell and the Martin Norwell cousin, Keith Kirkham. From their different vantage points both David and Charlie were interested to observe the newcomer. Although Charles was the first to take strike it was not long before Keith was part of the action. David's changing-room doubts as to Vincent Bailey matching the profile of a fast bowler were soon borne out. His approach to the wicket was ponderous, but culminated in a whippy arm action which propelled the ball at a quickish speed. What he lacked was any awareness of where the ball might most profitably pitch after its propulsion. The effort devoted to despatching it caused his head to fall away so that his gaze was directed at a 90-degree angle from the batsman. The contortion was not an asset to the control of direction. What was to follow was not foretold by his first delivery.

Charles Bell may have had the advantage of seeing Vincent Bailey in action on previous occasions and become used to the idiosyncratic action. What he was not expecting was a fast yorker which hit him full on the toe. Whether or not it struck him in line to uphold an lbw appeal was beside the point. By the time Vincent was looking in the right direction all he could see was the batsman on the ground. His team mates were as surprised as Charles had been by the deadly accuracy of his first ball and concerned as much for the victim as for their side's advantage. In any case it rapidly became clear that Charles was not fit to continue his innings. He was helped off the field (and later taken to hospital for an x-ray). It was only at that point that the ball's whereabouts were called into question. It had gone via Charles' toe direct to the boundary. Four leg byes proved to be the only compensation for the home side.

From the point-of-view of the bowler that was the high point of the over. Interspersed between three wide balls were five hittable deliveries which between them Martin Norwell and Keith Kirkham duly hit for a yield of 15 runs. In total Middle Daychurch had 22 runs on the board. As he prepared to bowl David was unsure what to make of the Nudgworth captain slapping Vincent on the back and saying, 'Stick to it, Vince'. After that performance he hoped he himself might seem miserly, but at their last encounter he remembered being punished by Martin Norwell. Yet with a newish ball and his captain's naive faith in him David felt obliged to make the extra effort. On the whole to give away only eight seemed not too bad and he was sure that he had got one ball to spin and bounce. It was a surprise therefore to be told by Humphrey Hutton, 'Thank you, David. That was very good. I think I'm going to hold you back and put you on later at the pavilion end.'

What seemed odd at the time became mystifying in view of the carnage which followed. In the course of five overs the score had leapt to over a hundred. Keith Kirkham had passed his own personal fifty. The bowling had come from two elderly gentlemen. What they bowled defied classification except in impolite language. David could not fathom why he had been removed from the attack in favour of these two. His mood was no more cheerful for being made to field on the boundary where a great deal of chasing had to be done. He felt uncomfortable. The kit that had been found for him must have been lying at the bottom of someone's bag. It was creased and musty. The trousers were tight across his midriff, slightly too long in the leg and, to make matters worse, flared. The footwear was his size, but the right boot pinched. He had disdained the proffered jockstrap. He should never have allowed himself to become involved in what was increasingly becoming a farcical game. If only he had stayed in The Cow's Corner for another pint. And suddenly with the thought of the beer he had so pleasurably consumed and the exercise he had subsequently taken came a pressing desire to go to the loo.

Charlie Colson had presumed on old acquaintance to watch the match from the pavilion sitting alongside Michael Carter. The Middle Daychurch captain was not padded up. He explained to Charlie once the drama involving Charles Bell had been overcome that he expected Martin and Keith 'to be there a while yet'. As the game proceeded Charlie could see that he might be right. When the fifth six of the innings had been struck Charlie turned to Michael and asked if Nudgworth were always as bad as they appeared on this occasion. 'That's a difficult one to judge,' said Michael with a wry smile. 'OK, so there's something more to it,' said Charlie, 'otherwise why play them?' 'Tradition in part. My grandfather was always very strong on tradition. He had connections in Nudgworth.' Michael smiled causing Charlie to persist. 'But there's something else?' 'You're going to think this very silly,' said Michael. 'You see that guy over there fielding at third man. Well, he's Trevor Kenyon, actually the Hon. Trevor Kenyon. His father's Lord Coverdrive. That name must mean something to you.' 'Oh yes, that's the man who's responsible for . . .' 'Yes, you've got it. There was a time in the past – before he was Lord Coverdrive – when he had a little difficulty and my grandfather helped him out. He never forgot and when we had a bit of a financial crisis in the club a few years ago he came to the rescue. Another thing. Whenever we go there he gives us a magnificent after-match dinner at Coverdrive Hall. So what does it matter that the team he sponsors is crap? We grin and enjoy it.'

There was a call from the boundary edge. It was David enquiring as to a twelfth man so that he could leave the field. 'Oh God, yes, I said I'd find someone for them.' Michael called across to Andrew Carter, who was lounging a few feet away. 'Did you get hold of James?' 'Yep, think he's in the bog. Didn't look in a great state to me.' 'He'll have to do. Get him out here, will you?' James, as Charlie might have guessed, did not look a pretty sight. The half-smile imprinted on his face did not boost confidence in his readiness to take the field. Nevertheless despatched he was and there followed an interesting passage of play.

There seemed no end to the diversity of talentless bowlers at the disposal of the Nudgworth captain. After one more (calamitous) over from Fergus Edrich he made a double switch. Trevor Kenyon replaced Bernard Lock at the pavilion end. 'This is obligatory,' whispered Michael to Charlie. The new bowler affected to bowl leg spinners. They came out of his hand in a variety of trajectories. This did have the effect, albeit temporary, of staunching the flow of runs as the batsmen had difficulty sighting the ball. The total yield from Trevor Kenyon's first over was four byes and a leg bye. It should have been greater, but the umpires seemed to pay no great heed to regulations covering height and even in a couple of instances width. The bowler was lucky to be credited with a maiden over. There would be no repeat.

The sixth bowler called on by Humphrey Hutton was Roy Brown. He again was not someone in the first flush of youth. His speciality seemed to be to bowl full tosses with remarkable consistency although with some subtle variations of pace. His first offering was struck majestically by Keith Kirkham for six, but in attempting to repeat the shot the batsman was deceived. Instead of a straight drive off the full face of the bat the ball took an edge and flew high to deep third man where a fielder was strategically placed. The fielder was James Carter whose engagement with the contest was so tenuous that his attention had to be drawn to the approaching missile. The warning had little effect as James wandered as if in a daze ending further from where the ball landed than he had been before the alert. He seemed to have difficulty even in retrieving the ball after it had crossed the boundary. His return throw was a further embarrassment.

Keith Kirkham evidently decided that third man was a profitable area to exploit. Two reverse sweeps eluded James and a false shot which saw the ball go wide of a slip fielder comfortably avoided any other form of resistance as James was being violently sick at the time. He had to be helped from the field. Michael's concern for his young cousin was more than matched by anger over the exhibition he had made of himself. Charlie maintained a discreet silence before realising that David had not reappeared. He felt he should investigate. Bounding into the visitors' changing room, he could see no sign of his friend. The shower and lavatory area was deserted. Where the hell had David got to? A puzzled Charlie put his head round the door of the home changing room. The only occupants appeared to be Lee Lingrove and Brian Carter. Asked if they had seen David, they pointed. 'He's round the corner, in the bog.' Not obviously so when Charlie looked, but the door of the W.C. was closed. Charlie hammered on it. 'Quick, you're needed. Young James has just spewed his guts up. Why've you been so long?' 'I'll tell you later,' finally came David's voice. 'I think you're going to be interested. Tell them I'll be down in two ticks.' Charlie went to report. For the remainder of the Middle Daychurch innings he was left to speculate about what possible meaning David's words could have. In the average lavatory cubicle in a sports club you would not expect to find anything other than graffiti – and a toilet roll if you were lucky.

Trevor Kenyon and Roy Brown were allowed another couple of overs each. Trevor's variations, to give his eccentric style a respectable name, were the less expensive if only because gymnastic skills were needed by the batsmen to get their bat in contact with the ball. Nevertheless the scoring rate did not flag. Two air shots and the concession of four byes had passed before Martin Norwell by virtue of a paddle shot had reached his 50. He then managed to put away Trevor Kenyon for two further boundaries before the end of the over. It took only two further strokes to give Keith Kirkham his century. At this point Roy Brown displayed a degree of savvy by choosing to bowl from round the wicket and directing his full tosses wide of off stump. When it became clear to the batsman that this was no aberration he employed the reverse sweep and added another boundary. After two more overs the Middle Daychurch total had advanced beyond the 200 mark.

Charlie Colson turned to Michael Carter. 'This is embarrassing, isn't it?' 'The crowd's enjoying it,' said Michael with a smile, 'but what can I do? I can hardly declare. Nudgworth would see that as an insult.' 'But at this rate you'll top 500,' insisted Charlie, 'or is that what you always get against this lot?' Michael rubbed his chin. 'Well, no, 300 maybe, but, as you know, Martin's quite useful and I don't want to discourage Keith. This is helping him back to form after two low scores in a row.' 'I can see your dilemma,' replied Charlie, 'but I think you need to do something. One of them could feign an injury.'

As it happened, pretence did not have to enter into it. Humphrey Hutton decided to recall Vincent Bailey to replace Trevor Kenyon at the pavilion end. However, being reminded that Vincent's last over had cost over 20 runs, Michael Carter had a bright idea. Stepping back inside the pavilion, he told Clive Norrington, Pete Simmonds, Adrian Seymour and David Carter to get padded up. Seeing Lee Lingrove at the top of the stairs, he shouted to Lee that he would be in next. 'I'm changing the order,' he announced in general to his team and then to Richard Love, 'You and I will go in last.'

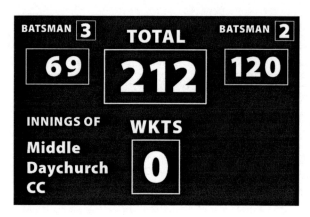

BATSMAN 3	TOTAL	BATSMAN 2
69	212	120
INNINGS OF Middle Daychurch CC	WKTS 0	

Out in the middle there had been much touching of gloves as the boundaries had accrued. Said Keith to Martin, 'It's a bit like taking toffee off kids.' 'Look at it this way,' replied Martin, 'it works wonders for your average.' Noticing the change of bowling about to take place, he added, 'I should be able to get a few sixes off this guy. I'll be catching you up.' 'Dream on, mate.' Their scores were then 51 runs apart. Vincent Bailey meanwhile had been undertaking loosening-up exercises of an idiosyncratic nature which had caused amusement to spectators whilst there was a lull in play. Public pleasure seemed to be the sole benefit from this preparation, for Vincent's first ball was called wide. So too was the second. Sensing a reaction from onlookers, Vincent steadied himself. This time the delivery was on line, but that was the most that could be said for it. Short of a length and safely wide of off stump it asked to be cut. In his enthusiasm Martin Norwell tried to hit it too square and slammed it forcibly into the ground from where it rebounded into the ample chest of Henry Simpson. The fielder, who had been retreating steadily with each ball bowled, showed anger more than judgement in flinging the ball back in the direction of the stumps. He then promptly keeled over, groaning and massaging his chest before wondering why no-one was giving him attention. Eyes were instead focused first on the wicket which had been shattered by a direct hit, secondly on the batsman who had incautiously advanced out of his crease and, thirdly, on the umpire who had to decide whether Martin Norwell had recovered his ground. In reality Bert Love could give no other decision and Martin was sent on his way. Much like the footballer who has dived in vain, a disconsolate Henry Simpson regained his feet and recovered sufficiently to accept the plaudits of the rest of the team.

Lee Lingrove had responded with alacrity to his captain's call. On the occasions when he was available (and selected) to play he had only rarely been given the chance to bat, because usually Middle Daychurch had not needed to rely on its very low order batsmen. In any case Lee's ambitions were higher than that. In practice he took his batting seriously. So this was a rare opportunity. He was ready just in time and secretly pleased that a wicket conveniently fell. His first delivery from Vincent Bailey was similar to its predecessor and so Lee aimed a mighty blow against it. He missed. Another ball, another miss. At the other end Keith Kirkham, thinking what he might have done to those two balls, reckoned it might be wise to pinch the bowling to give his partner a chance to get his bearings. Vincent's next delivery had the virtue of being straight, but the fault of being a full toss. Lee redeemed himself with a firmly struck and stylishly impeccable forward defensive stroke. The bowler managed an acrobatic dive to intercept the ball and succeeded in diverting it into the stumps with Keith injudiciously a step too far down the wicket in anticipation of a quick single. Walter Evans, who had moved from behind the stumps, raised his finger with an indecent display of enthusiasm in response to the appeal. As so often in cricket after a big stand the fall of one wicket can lead to another albeit in this instance with a generous dose of contributory negligence.

Michael Carter greeted the double reversal with equanimity. 'We're not exactly in trouble,' he remarked to Charlie Colson, 'and anyway the tail enders can do with a bit of time in the middle.' 'So who else have you got to come?' enquired Charlie innocently. Michael rattled through the names. 'No Brian Stagden today?' Michael looked at Charlie with surprise. 'As it happens, no. He cried off. Any reason for asking?' 'No, not really,' said Charlie relapsing into silence and transferring his gaze towards the action. This was his first sight of Clive Norrington, who was to provide early proof that his primary skill was more likely to lie in bowling. Vincent Bailey's over had been completed with no more incident than another wide ball. The newly formed partnership met in conference. 'This's a bit of a turn-up, Lee. Didn't expect to get a bat today. Let's have some fun.' 'I'm up for it,' said Lee and they punched gloves. Neither was yet off the mark.

No-one had reacted faster following Michael's decision to change the batting order than Richard Love. Suddenly a window of opportunity had opened. He knew that Debbie was at home. He sent her a one word text and set off towards Cricketers Close, masking his purpose by entering The Cow's Corner from one side and emerging at the other. He was well received at number 8, the more so for their encounter being unexpected. Lost in Debbie's arms, he was totally detached from the unfolding events on the cricket field.

Roy Brown's three overs had cost 51 runs. His captain thanked him for his efforts and said that he deserved a rest. David Pelham was beckoned. 'I'm going to give you a long spell from the river end if you feel up to it,' said Humphrey Hutton. David was unsure how to interpret the term 'long' after his opening spell had consisted of only one over, but he thanked Humphrey for his confidence and silently thanked God that Keith Kirkham and Martin Norwell were no longer batting. The surprise change in the batting order, he reckoned, moved the odds in his favour. The first over of his new spell did nothing to diminish his confidence. Clive Norrington was either playing himself in or simply not handy with a bat. He played and missed twice and otherwise prodded and poked acquiring no more than a single off the last ball of the over.

Against the more erratic and unpredictable Vincent Bailey there were clear signs of Clive Norrington wanting to have a go. However, his aggression was thwarted and the pattern was different from the previous over only to the extent of another wide to be added to the single off Clive's bat. It was not too difficult for David to bowl a tight over to him.

However, there were equally clear signs that the batsman was getting his eye in. At least a couple of runs were saved by some tidy fielding, but a leg bye from the last ball of the over meant that Clive had kept the strike again. Lee Lingrove's face wore the frown of a frustrated man. As the run rate had dried up Humphrey Hutton's mood had brightened. 'Are you up to another over, Vincent?' Indignantly his opening bowler assured him he was fine. That may have been how he felt; how he could perform was another matter. Avoiding wides and aiming mostly in line might of themselves made this the best of his five overs. Unfortunately for Vincent his length let him down and Clive was able to employ the slog sweep very effectively. He collected three fours and a six from the first five deliveries and appeared to have gained the psychological ascendancy. The bowler by contrast looked less fine than he had asserted two or three minutes earlier. But Vincent was a stubborn and proud man. Fearing that he would be imminently removed from the attack he summoned up his remaining energy and tore in once again. He managed the equivalent of the ball which had caused the retirement of Charles Bell. The only difference was that Clive Norrington saw it coming. Mindful of the integrity of his toes and not wanting his contribution to the match to be confined to twenty runs with the bat, he jumped to one side and watched his middle stump being flattened. The Middle Daychurch halfway score was 237–3.

The fall of the wicket interrupted an intriguing conversation in which Charlie Colson had been engaged with Pierre from Le Rêve Royal. The real-life Pete Simmonds was next man in. Charlie told himself that it could be in the interests of the Outcasts to know how well the chef could perform with a bat as opposed to a stirring spoon in his hand. Nevertheless a fascinating discussion had been disturbed. When Pete flopped down beside him Charlie had brought to mind the rather odd tale he had been told by Greg Roberts about what he and Colin Banks had witnessed outside the restaurant on the day of the food poisoning. Before mentioning the incident to Pete he asked him whether they had ever pinned down the cause of what had happened. 'Nah, mate, we never did. We made enquiries like. No-one in the kitchen could throw any light on it. They all swore blind there was nuffin wrong. Oysters was always on the menu. We knew what we was doing with 'em. We tried our supplier. We'd quite a battle with 'im. Really got on 'is 'igh 'orse, he did. I thought at one point 'e might sue us. But I will say this for 'im. 'E told us 'e'd talked to all 'is staff. None of 'em 'ad left their vans unlocked. They couldn't see 'ow any interference could've taken place. The boss man even rang us back cos one of 'is drivers was off sick. Turned out it was the one who'd come to us on the day in question. When 'e told us it were Ted we knew it couldn't be 'im. We knew 'im well. Still do. Salt of the earth. So in the end, you see, we just 'ad to accept it were bad luck. All we could do was work our backsides off to get our reputation back. In the end you could say we've been bloody lucky to survive and oh, Jesus, it looks like I'm in.' Charlie was left with two thoughts. For want of any other explanation the money-changing incident witnessed by Greg and Colin was as good a clue as existed to the possibility of foul play. Secondly, he wondered how someone who spoke such rough English could be so impeccably fluent in French.

David Pelham's task in bowling to Lee Lingrove had been eased by the young man's bottled-up impatience. Lee was revved up for glory. He opened his account with two glorious straight sixes; he closed his account when David tossed up his next delivery and bowled him neck and crop. The expletive forming in Lee's mind remained unspoken, but it was evident in the manner of his leaving the field how cross he was with himself. When Michael patted him on the shoulder as he came off and said 'well done' he was not referring to the strokes. Adrian Seymour was Lee's replacement. David's assessment was twice the age (probably) and half the ability (possibly). He fancied his chances, but Adrian dealt with the rest of the over with a solid bat.

Despite the wicket he obtained at the end of his previous over Vincent Bailey was asked to give way to Bernard Lock. There was no obvious reason for this move. It appeared that Humphrey Hutton was using his bowlers by rotation. Bernard Lock did not appear to have anything different or better to offer second time round. However, he was helped by having a less accomplished batsman at the other end. Pete was neat and unobtrusive in his play. He looked in no trouble and his two scoring strokes realised a couple of runs each. They took the home team past 250. David Pelham seemed to have won the confidence of Humphrey Hutton, because he was asked to 'continue the good work' at the river end. Adrian Seymour seemed in no hurry, preferring to play himself in. The over yielded no more than a single to him and another to Pete. The latter seemed to pick up the pace of things faster than his partner. Bernard Lock's next over was twice as expensive as its predecessor with Pete finding the boundary twice.

With one wicket for twenty-three runs off five overs David Pelham was feeling good and increasingly sure that he could pick up another wicket or two. He embarked on some variations in an attempt to tease Adrian Seymour. Twice he passed the bat, but then he dropped short. Adrian went on to the back foot and lashed him powerfully through the covers for four. The next one was a floater. Adrian was bold enough to use his feet. The ball dipped. He missed and frantically slid his foot back towards the crease. Douglas Compton took the ball neatly, had the bails off and roared an appeal in the direction of square leg umpire, Walter Evans, who up that that point had had a quiet match. 'Out,' he yelled at about the same decibel level as the keeper. It was a poor decision, but Adrian stoically contained his disappointment. There was no equivalent suppression of pleasure on David Pelham's part, but there seemed to be few other members of his side who were accustomed to high fives. He was still in celebratory conversation with the captain and a couple of others when David Carter had completed his preparation and was waiting for the field to settle and the next ball to be bowled. He eased himself off the mark with a single to a deeply-placed mid off and Pete Simmonds blocked the last ball of the Pelham over.

Michael Carter, now kitted up, rejoined Charlie Colson and looked around him. He could see his cousin Andrew similarly equipped for action, but that left Richard to be accounted for. 'Anyone seen Richard?' he called out. But no-one after a quick check upstairs had seen Richard. 'If he's playing tricks again ...' muttered Michael to Charlie. 'What's going on?' said David Pelham, who had just taken up his fielding position close to the boundary in front of the pavilion. 'Richard's missing, that's all,' said Charlie with a degree of levity which did not amuse Michael. He was even less amused by David's reply. 'I think I saw him a while back heading in the direction of the pub, but I could have been mistaken.' With a groan

Michael turned to Martin Norwell. 'Go and dig him out of there, do you mind, Martin?' But after careful inspection of the premises Martin had to report that there was no Richard to be dug out. Matters were not improved and Michael's mood was darkened when another wicket fell.

Bernard Lock had once again started to leak runs, twelve being scored off the third over of his spell. Most of these were to the credit of Pete Simmonds who was becoming increasingly fluent. He narrowly missed a boundary off the second ball of David Pelham's next over, but he had the satisfaction of running five before one of the more portly members of the Nudgworth team could get his foot to the ball. This left the fielder in question out of puff and out of position. So he was standing where he should not have been when David Carter lofted the next ball directly to him. There appeared to be nothing wrong with his hands, because the catch was safely taken before the momentum caused him to sit down rather heavily still clutching the ball. David Pelham in his excitement ran over as much to check his health as to congratulate him.

Andrew Carter was due in next in the revised order. Seeing how tense his cousin was, he told him not to worry. '285 against this lot should be plenty.' 'Yes, but if we get bowled out inside 30 overs, that's pretty undignified for us. We don't want other clubs to think we're becoming easy meat.' 'Oh, come on,' said Andrew, 'there are not too many of our opponents who would fancy getting that many against us.' Michael could see the force of that, but was still not happy. 'And anyway tea is nowhere near ready.' That was true. The squad of helpers had arrived later than usual. 'Just slow things down out there,' was Michael's parting instruction. Andrew passed on the news to Pete, who said that he was disappointed. 'I was just beginning to enjoy myself. You'll 'ave to work 'ard not to score off these characters, except 'im perhaps.' He pointed at David, who was eager to continue. Having met mid-pitch, Pete realised that he was the one on strike as he and David Carter had crossed while the ball was in the air. With David Pelham performing better with each wicket taken Pete was not just obeying orders in playing out the rest of the over in defensive mode.

Richard Love was woken from a misty reverie by a loud noise which he could not at first identify. He lay still, momentarily disorientated. Then reality kicked in. Stretching out an arm, he knew exactly where he was. The next question was how long he had been there. He tried to read his watch. No watch. Of course, it was in the pocket of his jeans in the changing room. Oh Christ, the match. Then there was a repeat of the noise that had woken him. It was a car horn and whoever was sounding it must have been impatient. The noise was out of place in an otherwise quiet village on a summer's day, although as he was later to remind himself it had saved his bacon. He tiptoed to the window and parted the curtains – carefully as he realised his state of undress. He was taken aback. Half-in and half-out of a pale blue sports car was an impossibly handsome man who looked as though he had stepped straight off the catwalk. He was staring impatiently towards the next-door house from which at that moment emerged a glamorous woman, who was undoubtedly Richard's former girlfriend. She ran towards the man, gave him a quick kiss, climbed into the passenger seat and they rode off with a roar of acceleration. None of this had caused Debbie to stir, but Richard knew that he must. He blew her a kiss, dressed himself downstairs and set out to check that he had not been missed.

It had been another whirlwind visit. A call from Shirley had caused Joyce Simpson to put aside thoughts of a trip to Cyprus. No, of course, nothing was wrong, Shirley had said. She had just been so busy and it was so exciting. Carlo was such a dear. He monopolised her every spare moment. Her mother must have thought her very selfish, but 'you must be happy for me'. When Joyce had complained that a phone call would have been nice Shirley had simply said that her phone had been broken, but Carlo had bought her a beautiful new one. Joyce had been about to ask for the number when Shirley broke in with the news that she was coming over again very soon. 'We can catch up properly then.' Joyce was in the act of trying to pin down exactly when and with whom when her daughter said, 'Must go now. Carlo's waiting.' The call ended abruptly without Joyce obtaining the number for Shirley's new phone. It was clearly not the previous number and BT's call checking service drew a blank as well.

Joyce was appeased to some extent. Yet there was so much more she needed to know. Her anxiety could not be entirely quelled. She put aside the thought of going to Cyprus, but whilst she had been thankful to hear from Shirley what she really wanted was a heart-to-heart. It was by now a very long time since she had seen or heard from Frank. It was not entirely unusual. She knew there were times when he was involved in some scheme or another and also when he had to keep on the move. He distrusted telephones. 'You never know who's tuned in,' he had said to her more than once. She knew that she had to endure his long absences. It would not be forever and she was acutely aware of the upside there would be to it in the end. Yet it had been a long time. The only longer period was when he had been banged up, but that had been when Shirley was too young to understand. 'Better not to visit,' was Frank's advice, 'we don't want young Shirl having any bad memories.' But Frank had learned his lesson and become much cannier since then. And more successful, she reminded herself.

The heart-to-heart she craved with Frank she found herself having with her friend, Maisie Love. It happened by chance on a day when, as she explained, she was feeling more down than up. She had decided to treat herself to a snack in the new buffet bar at The Cow's Corner. A menu had just been placed before her at the same time as the gin and tonic she had ordered immediately on entry when she heard her name being called. Maisie advanced and stood meaningfully by the table. 'I thought it was you I saw coming into the pub, but then I couldn't find you. I didn't expect you to be having a meal.' Pause. 'Especially not on your own. Are you expecting someone?' Joyce sighed inwardly. 'No, there's no-one else. I just popped in for a snack to save bothering at home. You know how it is sometimes. Why don't you join me?' 'Well, I'm not sure if I've got time really,' but she had sat down before completing the sentence. Making the best of this unexpected situation, Joyce said, 'To tell the truth I'm very pleased to see you. I could do with a good chat.'

And that was what they had. Maisie was easily persuaded to share the consumption but not the cost ('my treat,' Joyce had said) of a bottle of claret. It accompanied shepherd's pie and a venison casserole. The generous portions did not deter Maisie from saying that she'd heard there was a sherry trifle to die for. On the whole Joyce felt better for the encounter. They had talked a lot about Shirley. 'I was sorry that she split from your Richard.' Maisie seemed surprised. 'Oh I didn't know it was final.' So out came the story of Carlo which Maisie listened to agog. Whether out of loyalty to her son or just prejudice her judgement was, 'You never know where you are with foreigners. That's what I've always said.' That apart, the rest of her comments were of a more comforting nature. Before the conversation moved on to village gossip, Maisie put her hand on Joyce's arm and said, 'Never mind, dear, I'm sure it'll all work out in the end. Maybe sooner than you think.' With those sentiments she had spoken with unknowing prescience. Joyce walked home going over the conversation in her mind to reassure herself that she had not said anything indiscreet. Even to her best friend there were some things she could never reveal.

'We've just left London and we're on our way to see you.' This call from Shirley was better notice than a knock on the door, Joyce thought. She noticed the 'we' which suggested that she might be meeting Carlo for the first time. What Shirley had not said was whether she (or they) would be staying. Maybe it would be another of her flying visits. Beyond turning on the radiators in her daughter's room and the guest bedroom Joyce settled down to write a list of the questions to which she wanted answers. On arrival Shirley looked radiant, so radiant in fact that Joyce thought there was another question she needed to add to her list. On first acquaintance Carlo impressed. Very good-looking, very polite, very charming. However, they were not stopping. They had to keep an important appointment. 'After that we're booked into The Abbey Grange and we want you to come to dinner.' Joyce brightened, but further questions flitted through her mind. 'Give us a moment, sweetheart,' said Shirley. The words were addressed to Carlo, but Joyce mentally added another question to her list. Carlo went out to wait by the car ('Don't be long, my dear') and Shirley set out to persuade a doubting Joyce that she must come to dinner. 'Carlo's arranged for a car to pick you up and bring you back here. We've got such a lot to talk about.' Those words were artful bait and Shirley knew it. 'Please say you'll come.' There was a blast on the car horn. 'Please, I've got to go now.' Joyce would have wanted things to be different, but she felt she had no alternative. 'All right,' she said, 'I'll see if I can find something to wear which won't let you down.' 'Great,' said her daughter, 'pick-up will be 6.30 p.m.' and then as the horn sounded again she was gone.

Richard Love was unsure how to manage his reappearance, but thought that the safest approach would once again be to go through The Cow's Corner. Before anyone spotted him he should be able to squint at the scoreboard and check on how far the innings had progressed. However, what he saw first was Michael Carter on his way out to bat. With the batting order reversed it meant that Michael should have been last man in. Richard knew then that he was in trouble. He sprinted across to the pavilion, burst through various versions of 'Where the hell have you been?' and tore up to the changing room praying that another wicket would not fall before he was ready. He had been in too much of a hurry to take account of the actual score, but he was not kept long in ignorance. Andrew Carter, the recently dismissed batsman, made an entrance, flinging his bat down and making a scathing comment about the umpire. He then chose to notice Richard. After a barbed comment about his disappearance he provided Richard with a pithy summary of the match situation. He had barely finished when noises off suggested that another wicket had fallen. Richard grabbed his bat and ran.

As he emerged on to the field applause was greeting Pete Simmonds, who had scored his first half century for Middle Daychurch. He was as sore as Andrew Carter over his dismissal. Both had been sent on their way by Umpire Walter Evans upholding wildly optimistic appeals for lbw by Fergus Edrich. Nevertheless despite the fall of wickets the score had increased to 324. As Charles Bell had not returned from hospital Middle Daychurch's remaining ambulant players were at the crease. There appeared to be no gratitude on Michael Carter's part that there was scope for further addition to the score. Richard was greeted by 'Where the hell have you been?' He smiled and said simply, 'Well, I'm here now. What's the problem? Let's bat'. The problem quickly identified itself in the shape of Umpire Evans, who now seemed to have hit his stride. Fergus Edrich, having been entrusted with a fourth over, pushed his luck. When his first ball to Richard struck the batsman's pad albeit well outside leg stump, Fergus raised his arms in the air and yelled an appeal. It was enough for Walter Evans, who raised just one arm and bagged his fourth wicket. The innings closed at 324–9.

Charlie Colson was impatient to have a further word with Pete Simmonds. He also wanted to know what his mate David had discovered. However, he was under time pressure, a point reinforced by the approach of Arthur, who was tapping his watch. Charlie and Liz had planned their first big night out together since the birth of their daughter Helena. A babysitter was arranged and a table booked. He would not be forgiven if he was late back; nor would he forgive himself, despite the growing feeling that he might be on the brink of discovering more evidence for his dark theory. It was impossible to get David to one side at that moment and so he just said, 'We must talk,' to which David had replied, 'Yes, we must,' and that added to his excitement. To Pete he said, 'Can I call you? There's something I want to pass on to you.' Pete gave him his mobile number scribbled on the back of a table napkin. Then it was into Arthur's car for the return home during which they were able to have an interesting catch-up – and it was not about the match.

About the rest of the match there was little that could be said. David Pelham was one of only three people, excepting Umpire Evans, who emerged with any feeling of satisfaction. There had been no rush to restart the game. The tea interval was an extended affair conducted with great cordiality. Michael Carter allowed himself to overlook Richard's misdemeanour, possibly recognising that he needed one of his opening bowlers to be in the right frame of mind. Another unusual feature was a short speech by Michael in which he spoke in glowing and affectionate terms about Nudgworth, their team and their distinguished patron, Lord Coverdrive. Humphrey Hutton replied for the visitors and then the teams dispersed in readiness for the second innings of the match. The two umpires had sat at a separate table. Walter Evans was not only still eating, but also storing food in the ample pockets of his umpire's coat. David Pelham, who was due to bat in seventh position, was waiting downstairs for the action to begin. He was surprised when one of the Nudgworth players came up to Walter Evans saying, 'Now then, Walter, time to start again. Let me guide you down the steps.' Seeing David's reaction, he added, 'He'll be all right once he's out in the daylight.' Roy Brown discreetly forbore to explain that his uncle had left his glasses at home.

It soon became apparent why Michael Carter had been in no hurry to take the field. Demolition of Nudgworth's batting looked unlikely to be a long drawn-out affair. Even so Michael could not have been sure in advance of the penetrative contribution to be made by his nephew. Whether fired up by his earlier frustration or because he was facing the below par line-up of Nudgworth for the first time Lee Lingrove was on fire. Henry Simpson, who seemed fully recovered from his heroic but painful piece of fielding, lasted five balls sketchily before Lee spread-eagled his stumps. In the next over Clive Norrington had Roy Brown taken at second slip. Trevor Kenyon, who had come in first wicket down, gave every impression that Lee's pace was not to his liking. His instinctive first movement was towards leg. Lee's counter was to follow him at yorker length. After four deliveries Michael Carter intervened with a word to his bowler. Lee appeared not to have noticed that his bombardment of Trevor had led to all three stumps being visible. One further delivery pitched straight settled the matter. It could be sensed that the batsman departed without too much regret. The score stood at 0–3. Had he been a keen cricket historian thoughts of Trueman against India at Headingley might have crossed Aidan Watson's mind as he made his way out to join his captain. Such thoughts might have been made real when Lee's first ball nearly took his head off.

Humphrey Hutton remained remarkably composed throughout a fiery over from Clive Norrington even scoring a couple of runs from a firm push into a gap between cover and mid off. Having competently dealt with two fast well pitched-up deliveries from Lee Lingrove, Aidan Watson in his turn gave a hint that he knew how to hold a bat. Nor could he be faulted for edging the third to the wicketkeeper. It was a brute of a ball which could have got anyone out. He, however, survived, because the catch was spilled by Adrian Seymour, who had taken over as gloveman for Middle Daychurch. This had not been a willing switch of function, but it had been decided that Adrian's contribution to the side as a bowler would not be difficult to surpass in another role. As to whether he had fulfilled expectations the jury was still out. His record of catches was modest and he had yet to achieve a stumping. But he could not be faulted for effort even though he was a reluctant recruit. Aidan had acquired four fortuitous runs. Lee had glared at his uncle. Born of frustration his next ball was wild. Aidan let it go by and so unfortunately did uncle. Lee got himself back under control and Aidan needed maximum concentration to see out the over unscathed. The score had risen to ten.

The following three overs were a tense battle between bat and ball. There was good bowling and plucky batting. Cricket at its best. Michael Carter thought about bringing Richard Love into the attack, but it was obvious from the way they were enjoying themselves that neither of his opening bowlers wanted the ball taken from them. He rationalised their continuance on the basis that it might do them good to bowl a lengthy spell whilst they were excelling themselves. It could, he thought, bear fruit in the future when they were up against more testing opposition. His decision was amply rewarded. Lee was still bowling at speed and the first two deliveries of his fifth over required Humphrey Hutton's unflinching attention. Then to everyone's surprise, not least the batsman's, Lee produced an excellent slower ball. Whether this was through design or luck Humphrey was totally deceived and Michael found himself pouching the easiest of catches at mid off.

No flicker of enthusiasm could be detected on Leslie Wardle's face as he approached the crease. He went through all the motions, but his heart did not look to be in the task. He appeared to be wearing every form of protective gear known to man. Quick singles could not have been part of his game plan. If he saw Lee's first ball, he was too slow in getting his bat near it. However, there was plenty of pad in front of the wicket and Lee was not sparing in his appeal. It received a firm refusal from Walter Evans. The next ball produced an almost exact replay and the same outcome. Lee's face was a picture, but he kept his mouth shut. Leslie Wardle would probably have been happy to give himself out, because he had intelligence enough to guess what might happen next with the bowler in this form. And indeed it did happen. Faced with a ball that was straight, fast and rising steeply Leslie could not get his bat out of the way. An easy catch presented itself to a fielder sprinting in from backward square leg. The batsman's departure was swiftly conducted.

The situation provided Michael Carter with an altogether contrasting concern. What had happened so far amply supported his earlier conviction that Middle Daychurch would record a handsome victory over Nudgworth. This was in line with previous experience. A humiliating victory was another matter. His previous decision to give a minimum of six overs to Lee and Clive might at this rate be sufficient to end the match. So now his thinking went into rapid reverse. To a disappointed Clive he said it was necessary to take the foot off the accelerator. He then beckoned David Carter. The first need was to persuade David that it would be politic 'to give them a few'. There was understanding on David's part, but he could not resist saying that it might be harder to keep them in than get them out. 'Your young Clare might be able to bowl this lot out.' Meanwhile David Pelham had joined Aidan Watson, who greeted him with a wan smile. 'I bet you didn't reckon on having to face this when you left home this morning. I hope you're well protected.' This was a sore point with David who was almost completely in borrowed gear including in the end out of sheer necessity an abdominal protector which felt distinctly uncomfortable in more senses than one. For the moment the change in bowling brightened the mood of both batsmen.

What in retrospect might have been described as the purple patch of the innings occupied the next six overs. Aidan Watson with some deft strokes and David Pelham relying on a more agricultural method took – or were allowed – liberties with the bowling of David Carter and Andrew Carter. At first Lee Lingrove had resisted his replacement by the latter. 'But I could get four more,' he protested. It took an arm round the shoulder and a quiet lecture by Michael to smooth the ruffled feathers. Only when he said that Lee's performance would stand him in good stead for future selection did Lee acquiesce. Aidan and David raised the score to 79. Then at the start of the sixteenth over after an elegant on drive for four off David Carter, Aidan in attempting to repeat the stroke misjudged the length and put the ball down the throat of the fielder in the deep who had failed to get near the previous stroke. Douglas Compton, the wicketkeeper, was next man in. He was the third member of the Nudgworth minority who could reasonably

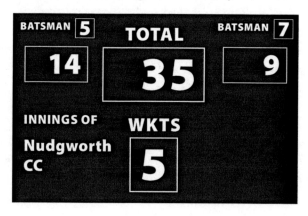

BATSMAN **5** TOTAL BATSMAN **7**

14 **35** **9**

INNINGS OF WKTS

Nudgworth CC **5**

be classified as young and fit, although not on immediate evidence able. After an edged four and a two David Carter lost patience, bowled his faster ball and hit Douglas's pads near enough in line with the stumps for Bert Love to give him out lbw.

Michael Carter thought he would let his spinners continue so that Nudgworth might take their score into three figures and so gain faint respectability. What he could not know was that control of the game had passed from his hands. David Pelham, who had hit five boundaries, decided to go into ultra-defensive mode. By complete contrast Nudgworth's remaining batsmen Edrich, Lock and Bailey, were intent on using the long handle. In Andrew Carter's next over Fergus Edrich hit three enormous sixes and was then bowled neck and crop. After David Pelham had played out a maiden from David Carter it seemed that Bernard Lock was determined to outdo Fergus Edrich. Dropped twice he managed to amass ten runs off four balls before finally holing out in the deep. Vincent Bailey edged his first ball to third man for a single. David Carter proved to be a different proposition from his brother. He was no longer in give-away mode. He was nevertheless swung away twice by Vincent to the boundary without either shot going in the intended direction. There were two swings and misses as well before David used his faster ball. Past Vincent's flailing bat it went and took off stump. Middle Daychurch had won by 201 runs. There were handshakes all round. Before he removed his borrowed clothing and took a shower David Pelham had something important to settle. He had been promised a lift back to London. The question was before or after a visit to The Cow's Corner.

Charlie Colson had Arthur to himself on the journey back to London. He began by telling him about his conversation with Pete (Pierre). 'Unfortunately I didn't get to report my bit – you know, about what Greg reckons he saw at the back of the restaurant. Pete had to go out to bat and we never had time for a further chat. But it fits, doesn't it, with what he had to say about the chef who let them down?' 'Yes, you could interpret it that way, I suppose,' said Arthur, 'but young men do come and go in the catering trade. It could be no more than coincidence.' When he glanced at Charlie and saw how crestfallen he was Arthur added, 'But it's probably worth your giving Pete a ring to ask him what he thinks when you've told him about that. Now you said there was something else.' Charlie described the meeting with James Carter. Arthur was amused. 'So you think this Brian Stagden could be up to something, is that it?' 'Well,' said Charlie, 'it was definitely him and the fragment of conversation might mean something.' Arthur laughed. 'It might just mean he has a penchant for older women. He might also be shy of anyone knowing.' 'Yes, I know these are all fragments and I might be making more of them than is justified. It's just that when you question all these deaths you tend to regard anything you hear as potentially suspicious. I'd just like to satisfy myself about this mystery woman. I must remember to ask Brian Carter when we come here next what he thought. He was the one who actually saw her.' Charlie sank back into thought, but then it was Arthur's turn.

'You met Roy Groves, didn't you?' 'Yes, he was my first point of contact with Middle Daychurch Cricket Club.' This was not 100 per cent accurate, but Charlie saw no need to mention the paints seminar. Arthur continued: 'I had lunch with him today' and as Charlie showed surprise continued 'in Le Rêve Royal. I knew him several years ago. It was pure coincidence finding him in Middle Daychurch. We'd completely lost touch. What did you make of him?' Charlie did not have much of an answer. There had been nothing he had found out of the ordinary from his contacts. 'A pleasant enough bloke. He struck me as well-to-do. I suppose I thought he was a bit big for a small place like Middle Daychurch, but then again with such things as broadband and wi-fi you can do business from almost anywhere these days.' 'I got the impression,' said Arthur, 'that he was holding something back from me. I was probing what he knew of the Carter family, but he refused to open up. I tried him out on Edwin Carter's will. That did not get me anywhere. Yet I'm sure he had some views. We need to know what that will said. If there has been some funny business going on here – and I'm not promising you I'm convinced about that – there might be a clue in how the old man distributed his estate.' Charlie wrinkled his brow as he tried to wrestle with the implications of that. It was still wrinkled when Arthur dropped him off at his flat. Reunion with wife and daughter was needed to expel these thoughts from his mind.

It was about the time that Charlie reached home that David Pelham left The Cow's Corner. The post-match drinks session had been more restrained than was David's usual experience. The camaraderie was muted. Not every member of the home team attended and only the young ones stayed any length of time. The senior Nudgworth players participated in just one round before making their excuses. Michael Carter out of politeness hung on until being genially told by Humphrey Hutton that he should feel free to get back home to his wife as he would be shepherding the remainder of his flock away from the village very soon as otherwise they would be left behind. To anyone who knew David Pelham that was not the most powerful of threats. Arising from their sterling partnership David had found a kindred spirit in Aidan Watson. They had managed to be one round ahead of the rest. However, the goodwill of the car driver had to be maintained, especially as he was the captain. Aidan and David piled into the back seats whilst Douglas Compton sat alongside Humphrey. David was in luck, because Humphrey actually lived in London. They went via Nudgworth and on the way David struck up an interesting conversation with Aidan.

It began with a comparison of their experiences in playing Middle Daychurch. Aidan had agreed that it was a strange set-up, but things had changed since old man Edwin had died. Not the results though, he had added. 'Maybe we need our own clear-out.' 'What, kill them off?' David impulsively interjected. 'No, nothing like that,' laughed Aidan. Then he stopped and turned to David and said 'Did you mean something in particular by that?' David was silent for a moment wondering whether he had somehow overstepped the mark – or was about to. In the end he said somewhat weakly, 'Well, they have been bloody unlucky with all those deaths.' 'No,' argued Aidan. 'You used the word "kill". Did you mean that?' David felt that he was now in it deeper than he intended. Either he had to find a quick exit-line or he'd be forced to plough on. He'd had a few drinks. Impetuosity led him on. 'There's this friend of mine who's got a theory . . .'

David was not even sure that he had recalled all Charlie's theories correctly. When he had finished Aidan whistled pensively. 'I hadn't looked at it that way,' he said. He then trotted out the same sort of questions that had been directed at Charlie by his Outcast friends. David was not in a position to answer, because he had to admit that Charlie's suspicions were outlandish. Unexpectedly Aidan pointed out that, if the deceased members of the Carter family against all probability were to be regarded as victims, there had to be a villain. Who was it and why? Again, David was not the best suited to nominate a suspect. 'The exact relationship between those who died is interesting,' said Aidan, 'when you think about it. If you reckon that a person or persons unknown bumped them off, you need to know why these particular family members were chosen. Is there a theory which links them? Edwin Carter being killed deliberately as opposed to just having a car crash seems the least likely possibility. But, say for a minute he was killed. Who would benefit? Until you know the contents of any will he may have left you can't begin to guess. The people you might suppose would benefit from his death are themselves dead. It doesn't make any sense.' Put like that, David was disposed to agree. So finally the subject changed and they talked instead about England's prospects on their winter tour until they parted company at Nudgworth. David took the front passenger seat and he and Humphrey talked cars for the rest of the journey.

The arrangements had gone smoothly, superbly indeed. A car, more a limousine, had called for Joyce on the dot of 6.30 p.m. The chauffeur was stiff (not the chatty type), but ultra-polite. She was delivered in style to the Abbey Grange. She had been there once before. It was a few years ago. Frank had wanted her to meet a new business associate. That had been unusual, because Frank was normally quite strict about keeping business and pleasure apart. She remembered him saying afterwards that this was someone on whom she could rely, but she was not aware that she had ever seen him again. She knew her way to the panelled dining-room. Carlo rose to meet her. Although he was in the same sharp suit he had been wearing earlier, Shirley had changed into an expensive-looking green cocktail dress. She looked elegant, but Joyce was not sure the colour suited her.

Carlo had insisted on starting with champagne. In answer to Joyce's questions he gave an account of his background, painting a picture of a lowly start, hard work, a slice of luck, some good deals and clever part-ners. It sounded impressive, but Joyce was no wiser as to what he actually did. She began to quiz Shirley about Cyprus. Had she seen her father? No, she had not seen him, but he had left various messages. One month he had been in Africa. Another time she thought it was North America or it might have been South. 'You know what my geography's like!' He had decided to sell the villa. Joyce's knife and fork stopped in mid-air when this piece of news emerged. 'But he loves it there.' 'I know,' said Shirley, 'but he now thinks Northern Cyprus is a bit dodgy. I don't really understand.' 'Do you, Carlo?' said Joyce turning to him. 'Oh no, lady' – Carlo flashed her a wide smile – 'I am just helping to carry out your husband's instructions. The matter is being handled by his agent.' 'Well, I never,' said Joyce with thoughts of those postcards reappearing, but she kept quiet.

It was not until the dessert trolley had been plundered and Joyce had given in to the temptation of a glass of Château d'Yquem that the favour was asked. Joyce had felt there had to be something. 'Carlo's got to do some business in the States. Do you think we could borrow the apartment?' 'But that's in Florida,' was Joyce's first response. 'Is that where you're doing busi-ness, Carlo?' It was Shirley who answered. 'He's got to go all over the place. Some big deal or other, isn't it darling?' Carlo obligingly nodded. 'So,' said

Shirley, 'I'll have somewhere nice to sit and wait.' Joyce wanted to know why her daughter now seemed able to give up work for so long, but felt it would spoil the atmosphere if she asked. It was apparent that Carlo was supplying her every need. 'Oh well I suppose so,' said Joyce. 'I'll give you the contact for the keys. I suppose it will be good to have someone living there for a while. When are you planning to go?' 'Next week.' 'Next week? That's a bit quick, isn't it? Don't you need visas?' 'Got them already,' smiled Shirley. 'Carlo knows how to fix things.' Yes, thought Joyce, why doesn't that surprise me? Her world was unravelling. She would be glad to go home. Having an evening with her much-loved daughter in the company of a rich man to whom she seemed devoted over a wonderful meal, it might have been the most perfect evening. Why then the next morning did she think that maybe it had been a little too perfect?

Before turning in on Saturday night David Pelham sent a text to Charlie Colson asking to see him the next day. The reply awaiting him on Sunday morning was to come round to the flat. Further messages established that eleven o'clock would be fine. That left David five minutes to swallow a piece of toast, wash, dress and forget about shaving before setting out for Charlie's place. He noticed how after the arrival of baby Helena the flat had been restored to something akin to the shambles which had existed prior to Liz moving in and achieving almost perfect order. After initial pleasantries and acceptance of the offer of coffee, David brandished a plastic pouch. 'You need to see this.' Charlie opened the pouch and extracted a few sheets of paper. He studied the typed words. Each message was brief and menacing. For whomsoever they were intended the threat was unambiguous. Finally Charlie said, 'Where did you get hold of these?' He almost dropped the package when David replied, 'In the lavatory.' He explained that he could not get the lavatory to flush when he pressed the handle. He removed the lid of the cistern and found the pouch was snagging the ballcock. It looked as though it had come loose from where it had been attached to the side of the cistern.

After being told the indelicate reason why David although playing for the visitors had been in the home team's facilities, Charlie said that the discovery backed up his theory about the death of Douglas Carter. 'Strictly speaking,' said David, 'there's no proof that these anonymous messages were intended for Douglas.' Seeing the look on Charlie's face, he hurriedly went on, 'OK I know it looks likely, because it fits with Douglas topping himself, but that doesn't mean it was other than suicide. And, if these messages were sent to Douglas, why did he keep them and why did he hide them where they might be found? What we don't know is how long they've been there, nor when they were sent. They can't all have been sent at once. Whoever wrote them must have been tormenting Douglas, if it was him, over a period of time. Was it weeks, months, years even?' 'Quite a speech,' said Charlie. 'You seem to be taking me a little bit more seriously now.' 'Don't be too sure,' his friend replied, 'but I agree there's food for thought. If Douglas – OK let's say for a minute it was him – if he put this stuff where he did, do you suppose he wanted it to be found and, if so, wouldn't he have put a note of his own with it? Was it put there because he was contemplating death or was it just a hiding place? There's a helluva lot of unanswered questions.' Charlie started to speak, but David interrupted him. 'Hang on a minute. I've just thought of something. There is one other person who could be connected to vile rubbish of this kind and who now seems to have access to that changing room. Pete.'

Matters were not much clearer after a meeting a few days later between Charlie, David, Rash and Arthur. Match and post-match conversations were aired. The package of anonymous letters was tabled. Arthur rather quickly dismissed the idea that their target was Pete Simmonds, pointing out that his lifestyle was not a secret. He produced an altogether different theory. In appearance as opposed to content the letters looked similar. 'I don't get the impression looking at them,' explained Arthur, 'that they were all composed at different times. They seem like a job lot. Same paper, same printer, same font. It wouldn't surprise me if they were prepared after Douglas's death.' This exposition clearly did surprise Charlie, David and Rash. It took a moment or two for Charlie to work it out. 'So, if they were put in the lavatory cistern after Douglas died, what you're saying is that the person responsible must have had a reason and . . . and that could only be the someone who might have had a hand in his death? But why do it? Putting the letters in the loo, I mean.' 'It's pure guesswork,' admitted Arthur, 'a bit like yours, Charlie. Perhaps it depends on when it was done. If it was soon after Douglas's death, this mysterious third party could not have known when they would have been discovered. In any case it would have been simpler to have left them in Douglas's house. However, it wasn't necessary, because the general conclusion was that his death was cricket-related. That leads me to believe that the anonymous package was an afterthought, maybe even a recent afterthought. If you allow yourself to believe that this mysterious third party exists and he is getting worried that the number of deaths may at last be giving rise to suspicion, might he not think that double-banking the suicide theory would be useful insurance?

I doubt whether that pouch would have remained undiscovered for long.' Three heads were locked on Arthur. 'Wow,' they said in one voice.

Further refreshment was felt to be imperative at this juncture. When the discussion was resumed it was Charlie's turn to shock. He felt that he had slipped to second place in the detection stakes behind Arthur. What Arthur had just said sparked another idea in Charlie's fertile imagination. 'What you're suggesting, Arthur, is that a potential murderer may be providing extra cover for his tracks to sort of bolster the pure coincidence theory?' 'You've got to admit it's vaguely possible,' Arthur replied. 'Yes,' said Charlie looking at each of his companions in turn, 'but it could just as easily be cover not for what has happened, but for something yet to come. Someone else is going to die.' Suddenly all eyes were locked on him. Mention of Michael Carter's narrow escape when on his skiing holiday was immediately prompted. Was it an accident or was he targeted? Was he at risk again and, if they thought he was, could they do anything about it? He had laughed it off when previously tackled about it. Talk spread to the other deaths and was in danger of becoming improbably far-fetched when Rash cut in with a dash of reality. 'The will,' he said, 'I will obtain a copy. That may help us to inject some order into our minds.' That was agreed. They all relaxed. Some more ale was purchased. Before they departed it was decided that nothing more could be done until they had heard from Rash.

Rash was in fact a little lax in dealing with this assignment. This was largely because he was immersed in a complex case in his practice. New evidence had come to light and he was working extra hours to deal with it. Part of him still believed that his friends were getting excited over nothing. It was an amusing brain-teaser, but he did not see it as much more than that. When Charlie rang him to find out what was happening, Rash made his excuses. It was while the Outcasts were in France that Rash finally got round to making enquiries about the last will and testament of Edwin Carter. Such had been the events in France and the turmoil engendered by the clash of fixtures involving Fluxworth and Avery St. Agnes that Middle Daychurch had taken a back seat. When asked by Arthur whether he had acquired the information, Rash confirmed that he had and thought that it was worth sharing with the Outcasts as a whole before their next match with the village. A special meeting at The Sink and Plumber was called for the Thursday night ahead of the Saturday fixture. Bruised and battered though by then he was (*Unusually Cricket* 2010), Charlie Colson could barely contain his curiosity.

There was a good turnout on that Thursday evening. Winston Jenkins, being still detained by the French police, was an obvious absentee, but most of the others were there whether to mock if Charlie's wild ideas were to be knocked down or to lap up any possible scandal. Adopting his most professional manner, Rash settled everyone down and began his report. Edwin Carter's will was unusual, perhaps reflecting the strange character of the man. Ethel Daniels, a name previously known only to Charlie, was given a handsome cash legacy. There were annuities for his children for a fixed period after which his whole estate would be split equally between those of his male heirs who were still living at an appointed date. The really strange feature was that, if none of his male children had survived at that point, the whole estate would be vested in his grandson, Michael, who he considered the most likely to ensure that cricket would continue to flourish in Middle Daychurch. In that eventuality Michael was further mandated to maintain an annuity to benefit his Aunty Maisie. 'And that essentially is it,' said Rash following which a babble of voices broke out. 'No, sorry, there is one more thing.' Rash had to shout to make himself heard. 'There was a trust set up to handle the situation when the time limit is up. The three trustees Edwin chose were this Ethel Daniels, George Carter and a certain man called Roy Groves.'

When glasses had been refilled it was quickly agreed that in the interests of orderly discussion Rash should be allowed to take the chair. Toby Lederwood caught Rash's eye first. Up until then he had not taken much interest in the speculation he had heard about possible dark doings at Middle Daychurch. Being a more recent recruit to the ranks of the Outcasts, he had not even visited the village. So his was very much a fresh voice on the subject. 'If this was detective fiction, the first thing the sleuth should consider is who stands most to gain from the death or in this case deaths. And from what Rash has just told us the answer has to be this guy Michael Carter. It looks like he stands to scoop the lot.' This telling verdict was too much for some of the others and several hands went up.

Rash chose Charlie next. 'I feel I'm in a strange position here. I know I'm the one most ready to believe that something sinister was happening to the Carter family whilst pretty well everyone else – except you, Arthur – just saw it as a series of accidents. None of us could see any actual reason why it might be something else. I don't know why we didn't think of looking up Edwin Carter's will before now. But now we have a possible motive staring us in the face, I don't believe it.' The others remained silent whilst he took a long swig from his glass. 'I've been closer to Michael Carter than any of

180

us, going back a few years now. I would lay heavy odds he's not a killer.' He stopped again and looked around him. 'Sorry, but it's just a gut feeling.' He looked so solemn that his friends held back from any uncomplimentary remarks about what his gut had been responsible for on a number of occasions in the course of their association.

Others then spoke. Stewart Thorogood: 'If what Toby says is right, what about the deaths of George and Philip? They don't seem to fit the pattern. Why would Michael want them out of the way?' Dean Faulds: 'Wasn't it proved beyond doubt that Philip Carter died from natural causes. After all they dug him up and took another look.' Jon Palmer: 'Might it have anything to do with George Carter being on this trust thing?' Nigel Redman: 'Is there any relevance in this Ethel Daniels woman? What do we know about her?' David Pelham: 'We ought to remind ourselves that Michael Carter himself came close to death on the ski slopes.' John Furness: 'That could have been staged, I suppose, to draw suspicion from himself if anyone other than us had taken an interest. A solicitor or someone could be asked to look into it if Michael were to inherit.' Basil Smith: 'Let's get back to the old patriarch. Do we believe he was killed?' Rash intervened at that point. 'It was from his death that the clock started ticking, because the will prescribed an end date for when the estate would be distributed.' 'Well, when is that?' demanded Basil. 'Six weeks from now,' replied Rash, who let Basil speak again. 'So from the point of view of anyone with a malign motive, the sooner Edwin was out of the way the better. That does lend weight to the assisted accident theory.'

This jumble of thoughts was thirst-inducing. The discussion when resumed became in part repetitive and increasingly argumentative. It could not be said that any one view prevailed. Some took Michael Carter's side; others felt he could be the culprit; and there were still those who remained hard-line sceptics who refused to accept that any sinister plot was involved. Arthur had sat silent throughout the proceedings. Eventually when he concluded that nothing sensible was any longer being said, he signalled to Rash and was given the floor. 'If the police had felt any reason to begin an investigation, one of the first things they would have done would be to check the movements and whereabouts of anyone they thought might have a motive for killing any one of, for want of a better word, the victims. The only person we've pointed the finger at is Michael Carter. For all we know he might have an alibi. Only two of the deaths, as far as I can tell, would have involved the actual physical presence of another person. There seems no doubt that Douglas Carter took his own life however much he may have been goaded into it. However, there was no post mortem examination. What if he had been physically 'helped' on the night in question? Can Michael account for his movements that night? If that sounds fanciful, the masonry falling on George Carter was either accidental or someone was up on the roof or wherever aiming it. The time it happened is known. So it would be useful to know where Michael was then. So we need a few of us to do some very focused detective work when we go there on Saturday. It would help if those of you who aren't playing would come along for the ride.' To minds which in some cases were now clouded unlike the ale they had been drinking, this sounded like a good plan and relieved them of any further intellectual effort for the time being. They were now able to turn their attention to the landlord's guest ale which he pronounced to be exactly ready for consumption. The opinion of his most exacting patrons was important to him. Before he left them to it Arthur had a quiet word with Rash, Charlie and Dean Faulds (whose turn it was to captain the side against Middle Daychurch) to explain how he thought the investigation should be conducted.

There was, however, a hitch. The Outcasts were denied a trip to Middle Daychurch on Saturday. Still off work Charlie received a phone call from Michael Carter on the Friday preceding the match to say that it would have to be called off. 'I really am sorry to be doing this at such short notice. I left it as late as possible to see if it would stop raining, but it's kept going. I reckon we've had a month's rain in two days. The pitch is sodden and the forecast is for more rain. Once it stops it's going to take a few days before it's fit to play.' Charlie made sympathetic comments. 'I feel really bad about this,' continued Michael. 'You and the Outcasts have been very supportive. We could stretch our season, if you're not playing anywhere else four weeks from now. Obviously it would depend on having a fine day. And anyway it'll mean we finish our season on a winning note.' Charlie had been checking the Outcasts' fixtures. They could do that date. They had to do that date in view of what they'd been planning. And that final barb of Michael's added some extra spice to the encounter. 'Done,' he said and reported immediately to Arthur that they were now much closer up against Edwin's deadline.

Ten days after the session in The Sink and Plumber Ray Burrill was sitting in his dentist's waiting room. He had not been able to join the other Outcasts that night. To some extent he thought it a waste of time. If there had been anything wrong in Middle Daychurch, it was a matter for the police to investigate. What point was there in complete amateurs like the Outcasts messing about in something none of them properly understood? They were cricketers not investigators. Anyway he had had something much more important to do that night. He had got tickets for a show in the West End which he knew his girlfriend badly wanted to see. Andrea had taken a couple of days off work for the trip to London. Ray had planned a romantic dinner afterwards at a top-class restaurant and then he had something else in mind. The whole evening had gone like a dream and he was now engaged to be married. Stuck as he had been in the waiting room already for half an hour, Ray felt he had very much been brought down to earth.

He was wishing that he had brought a book with him. There was still one patient ahead of him. Whoever was with the dentist must have been there ages. He had gone back to the receptionist to query the delay. 'It's a difficult case, an emergency which Mr Barnes felt he had to fit in.' She said it in an utterly convincing way. She had become well practised in covering for her boss. The emergency, an overwhelming desire to see his mistress, was entirely his. Some emergency the receptionist was thinking to herself. He usually took only twenty minutes. She smiled at Ray. 'He won't be long, I'm sure.' She saw Ray glance at the other patient. 'Mrs Caldwell's here just for an x-ray. He won't be more than a minute or two with her.' No, she thought, aged sixty and weighing about eighteen stone, he would not be long with her.

Ray stepped disconsolately back into the waiting area and riffled through the magazines a second time. The selection was eclectic. The only thing to be said was that they appeared to be up-to-date. Pushing to one side *Dental Engineering Monthly*, he came upon a hitherto concealed journal *The Rural Clerical Examiner*. Adorning the front was a pencil drawing of a church which looked familiar. He had to look at the inside of the cover to see that it was St. Stephen's Church in Little Stubworth where the Outcasts had played a match earlier in the season. But for that he might never have bothered to flick through the pages of the slim publication. As he did so the words Middle Daychurch caught his eye. He found the page. It contained advertisements of vacancies. In the box headed Middle Daychurch applications were invited for the combined living of Near, Far and Middle Daychurch. It did not at first seem of special significance to him, but at the back of his mind there was a recollection that Middle Daychurch had acquired a young, dynamic vicar not so long ago. Perhaps he was so dynamic that he had moved on to greater things. There proved to be some truth in that.

When Ray next spoke to Charlie, which was when a few of the Outcasts got their first chance to congratulate Ray on his engagement to Andrea, he remembered to mention that Middle Daychurch was looking for a new vicar. The following morning Charlie in his turn remembered this innocent piece of news. The more he thought about it the more he felt he needed to know the story of Garry's departure. He held back from ringing his usual contact, Michael, for a reason he could not quite explain. He then decided that Pete at Le Rêve Royal might be able to throw some light on the situation. He had called him after the Nudgworth match to fill him in about the supposedly dodgy chef. Pete had said it fitted, but he and Marty were no nearer getting a lead on someone who seemed to have vanished. He was surprised to hear again from Charlie. 'Oh yes,' he said, 'that Garry 'e were a right one. You knew 'e had a bit of a thing about skinny dipping?' Charlie did not. 'Well it seems 'e dipped too far, know what I mean?' Charlie was not sure he did. ''E went and drowned, mate, that's what 'e did.' Charlie felt himself shiver. What was it he had said such a short while ago about cover for another death?

The facts were gradually established. The Reverend Garry had a secret passion for bathing in the nude. In a village like Middle Daychurch once discovered it had soon become an open secret. Nevertheless Garry had maintained a clandestine approach to indulging his pleasure. His grotto, as he liked to think it, was at a bend in the river which was accessed by a rough track leading from the main road between Near and Middle Daychurch. It was a secluded spot curtained by bushes. Garry's chosen spot for bathing was a secret which unbeknown to him he shared with Clarissa Maxwell whose interests had turned (temporarily) to fishing. One day she had approached the curtain of bushes and was about to penetrate them to reach the river bank when she suddenly saw the wheel of a bicycle protruding from the foliage. If that in itself had been insufficient to identify the rider, Clarissa was left in no doubt when a reedy tenor voice broke into an uneven rendering of 'A wand'ring minstrel, I' from 'The Mikado'. She had heard that voice too often at church and at school. She knew as most residents of the village would have known what lay beyond. Showing a sensitivity quite out of character, she chose not to look. However, her sensitivity was not coupled with discretion and anyone in the village who might have found such a sight irresistible would have known where to go. There was one further fact relating to Garry which was no secret at all. He was a very poor swimmer. This had been discovered when he had been the victim of that mischievous prank which had led to his being deposited in the village pond. It was not terribly deep, but he was out of his comfort zone and panicked. It had taken two men to effect his rescue. Taking all

these points together it was as clear as daylight to everyone what must have happened at the shady nook.

Charlie Colson was disposed to be less clear. Another death coming on top of six others was unbelievable. Even so he could see no connection with the theory that members of the Carter family had died by design. Yet he supposed that when the Outcasts' visit to the village took place added to the list of enquiries would have to be the whereabouts of Michael Carter on the day the Reverend Garry Woodworth's 'accident' had occurred. The young girl, who had almost witnessed his pastime, should be asked whether she had gone fishing again between the day of her discovery and the day when it was thought that the vicar had died. It was just possible that she might have seen someone near the scene.

Joyce Simpson had cheered up a little. She remained worried about Frank, but persuaded herself that he must be in to something big. He was such an operator. Perhaps, if he pulled off whatever he was doing, it would be his final coup. Then they could enjoy a luxury retirement. This dream apart, what had improved her outlook was Shirley's apparent eagerness to keep in touch. This was in total and welcome contrast to the way in which she had treated her mother after disappearing to the villa in Northern Cyprus. In fact her daughter had become quite chatty although there was one early surprise. She had moved to an apartment in Sarasota to live for a week or two with Carlo's sister. Carlo had been so considerate, because whilst he was travelling across the States she would have company. His sister, Lucia, was a sweetie and they were getting on just fine. And so for a while that is how it seemed to be.

It was not too long before a mother's ear caught a different note. The words were much the same. Everything was super, but Joyce began to doubt it. She pressed her daughter gently, but the verbal facade stayed intact. When the next call came Joyce could sense the anxiety. Shirley's words were more brittle and less enthusiastic than those which had characterised her since Carlo had come into her life. Eventually there was no pretence. Joyce picked up the phone and at first all she heard were sobs. There was no doubting it was Shirley. The first words which Joyce made out sent a chill through her. 'I'm frightened, mum.'

After hearing the news from Charlie that yet another person had died in Middle Daychurch Arthur was pensive. He wondered what role Garry Woodworth may have had in the life of the Carters during his short incumbency. He thought what vicars did: baptisms, confirmations, weddings and funerals. Garry had had more than his fair share of funerals, but had that been his only interaction with the Carters? Once again his had been another death that had been readily accepted for what it had appeared to be. The indelicacy of the vicar's activity and his well-known weakness as a swimmer had said it all. No questions had been asked except at a pub in south-west London. A thought suddenly popped up in Arthur's mind. The vicar had been a single man. What would have happened to his possessions? Who were his next-of-kin? He was not sure why, but Arthur had a strong feeling that he would like to see what Garry had left behind.

In his office Rash returned the phone to its cradle. He had no appointments that morning and he called out to his secretary that for the next hour or so he did not wish to be disturbed. Arthur had been very insistent. The tasks he wanted done could be more easily carried out by a solicitor. Rash had protested that he might very well be put in breach of his professional ethics. Arthur had sought to cast this doubt from his mind by stressing what he thought was the urgency of the situation. 'One of the things,' he said, 'is perfectly straightforward, but in the case of the other two enquiries I think a solicitor would get more attention. Anyway I simply have to be away for the next two days and you really would be doing me a favour, assuming you're not too busy.' Rash succumbed uneasily. He could see that he might have to tell at least one lie if he was to be successful in completing this unexpected, but intriguing, assignment.

Fourth encounter

THE DATE OF THE POSTPONED FIXTURE with Middle Daychurch arrived. It had been preceded by a fine spell. Michael Carter had confirmed that there was no problem at their end. The pitch had dried out and should play well. The forecast had been good and as the Outcasts gathered at their departure point the sun was shining brightly. They were a large assembly for this trip. Those not picked to play had been encouraged to come along. Curiosity ensured that they did. Their other halves came too. A sense of subdued excitement was shared amongst them although there were no solid grounds for supposing that the mystery of which they were all conscious would be cleared up.

Unusually Arthur with his coach was the last to arrive. Often expressionless, he had the appearance on this occasion of suppressing some inner excitement. Everyone piled on the coach apart from the Crossleys and Syd Breakwell. Simon and Sophie had acquired a capacious four-wheel drive vehicle into which they could comfortably fit their two young boys, Brian Sachin and Michael Ricky, and all their paraphernalia. There was room for Syd as well. He had developed a good relationship with the boys and they treated him as an elderly uncle who told them funny stories.

Dean Faulds had retained the captaincy for this match. As everyone, bar Winston (still not released from custody in France) and Charlie (still not fully recovered from his injuries), (*Unusually Cricket* 2010), was available for selection more thought than usual had gone into the composition of the team. 'Let's remember,' Stewart Thorogood had said at their meeting two nights earlier in The Sink and Plumber, 'we're going there first and foremost to play a game of cricket.' He fixed his eyes on Charlie while saying that. 'And to win it,' chipped in Jon Palmer. 'We've still not beaten them and if anything they've become a better side since losing some of their older players.' This provoked Kevin Newton into exclaiming, 'You're not suggesting they were killed for cricket reasons, are you?' This had produced a gale of laughter, but then they concentrated on the task in hand. It was agreed that they would have a playing squad of thirteen. Dean had said, 'Then we can play an extra batsman or bowler according to the conditions.' This brought a riposte from Colin Banks, 'We're not a ruddy test team.' Cue more laughter. So in the end they settled for a first choice eleven with a twelfth and thirteenth man.

Colin Banks was right. Choosing the supposedly best Outcasts team owed nothing to science. Neither was form a reliable guide. Gaps between matches and between appearances for the most part do not allow form to be a measurable factor. Too much ale or other indulgences frequently affected performance or even last minute availability. With a full complement (minus Winston and Charlie) from which to pick, justifying one player over another might have been cloaked in cricket jargon, but it was largely a matter of hope fortified by the (sometimes distant) memory of the odd good innings or spell of bowling. The eleven on which the meeting settled was:

Palmer
Thorogood
Faulds (c)
Rashid Ali (w)
Lederwood
Burrill
Furness R.
Pelham
Smith
Redman N.
Banks

In no particular order Phil Cole and Harry Northwood were nominated as the extras, who might take the place of one of the others if the state of the pitch prompted a change in the balance of the team. Following up his previous remark, Colin Banks muttered that the state of someone's gut might be the more decisive factor. This left Greg Roberts, Tom Redman, John Furness, Kevin Newton and Charlie Colson as the team cheerleaders. Amanda Sutton (Stewart's partner), Adrienne Palmer, Joan Smith, Andrea Firbrook, Liz Colson and even Gloria Lockwood (Kevin's girlfriend) made up the female contingent.

The journey to Middle Daychurch was without incident and without refreshment. Establishments were passed on the way which on another occasion would have been considered a compulsory stopping point. However, this visit had been treated with sufficient gravity, even among the sceptics, that no-one had consumed more than four pints on the previous evening. There was equal resolve by those down to play in the match to hold off a visit to The Cow's Corner until close of play. The private thoughts of the Outcasts were unlike any others they might have had in travelling to a game of cricket. They had never previously faced a team captained by someone who might have committed multiple murders. Even if that theory was rejected, it was just possible that somebody in the Middle Daychurch team or connected with the club could be a killer. Charlie Colson was the Outcast with the richest imagination in this direction. He was suspicious of Brian Stagden without really knowing why. He had also remembered mutterings he had heard from some of the youngest of the Carters. Although it seemed improbable, Charlie could think of notorious cases where a seemingly normal young man had been discovered too late to be mentally unhinged. Other Outcasts, whilst not seriously harbouring thoughts about any particular member of the Middle Daychurch team, had the unsettled feeling that this would be no ordinary contest. Toby Lederwood and Richard Furness, neither of whom had been to the village before, were thinking exclusively of cricket and ale.

Despite the forebodings of some of the visitors nothing could have appeared more normal than the scene which greeted them on arrival in Middle Daychurch. It was a beautiful late summer day. The ground looked in tip-top condition having obviously recovered well from the heavy rainfall which had so recently plagued the area. The Crossleys had arrived, as evidenced by the sight of Syd Breakwell, already white-coated in conversation with his opposite number, Bert Love. Some spectators had come into the ground early bringing picnics or taking advantage of a barbecue service mounted by the landlord of The Cow's Corner. The ice cream van was also doing business. The home team had changed and was engaged in fielding practice which some Outcasts would have thought to be taking unfair advantage.

Michael Carter broke away from the group and trotted across to welcome the visitors as they stepped down from Arthur's coach. He extended a warm welcome and could not have been more charming. 'It's really good to see you. I'm very pleased we were able to fix another date. You Outcasts seem to have woven yourselves into the fabric of this village. But we're still keen to beat you when you get out there.' He jerked his thumb towards the pitch were the stumps were already in place. 'Shall we toss now or when you've changed?' Dean Faulds said, 'Let's do it.' They did. After a cursory glance at the pitch and a prod with his flat key Dean, not entirely sure what he had learned from that, called 'Heads'. And heads it was. Without hesitation and as cover for his uncertainty, Dean announced that the Outcasts would bat. All in all normality prevailed.

The same could not be said of 10 Cricketers Close. Shirley Simpson, after the resolution of some difficulties, had returned home. This was not the Shirley whom her mother had last seen in the sophisticated surroundings of the Abbey Grange. No longer did she look a million dollars. The girl who had come through the front door was a mess. Joyce quickly became aware that it was not just the decline in her physical appearance. Shirley gave every indication of being on the brink of a nervous breakdown. She was a punctured balloon. Slowly and gently Joyce gleaned the story from her. At first everything had gone well, but then Carlo had taken a call from one of his associates. He told her that he had to go to an urgent meeting in Chicago and that would lead on to the other business which he had to do. To try to overcome her disappointment he suggested she might find it more fun to stay with his sister to whom he had already introduced her. She had been fine with that. Carlo had called her every day. Lucia had been a really friendly companion – at the start, but as the days passed she felt her becoming more distant. The blow when it came was completely unexpected.

One morning Lucia said that she was suffering from a migraine and would not be able to do the trip with Shirley that they had planned. She insisted that despite Shirley's protestations that she should stay with her she should go out and enjoy herself. So without further thought Shirley had obeyed. She did in fact have quite a good day and she was looking forward to relating it to Lucia on her return. At first she was merely bewildered when the key she had would not open the door of the apartment. She rang the bell. There was no response. After five minutes or so it became clear that there was not going to be a response.

Her first concern was for the stricken Lucia, but that did not explain the key. Moving on from Lucia's possible needs, she was forced to think about her own. The police were disinterested. With no more than she was carrying with her that day her only recourse was to return to the apartment on the Bay coast. There she was to find the rest of the belongings which she had brought from home. What she also found was a place which looked as though it had been taken apart. Not, as far as she could tell, a burglary, because everything seemed to be there, but not in place. She had repeated the attempt she had made in Sarasota to ring Carlo. He had not answered and when she tried a second time a mechanical voice told her that the cell phone was no longer in service. At that she had broken down and called her mother. And Joyce had taken over from there.

After observing her daughter's condition she had insisted on calling the doctor. Dr Gibbons told her that Shirley might have suffered psychological damage, but it was too early to tell. She asked Joyce what had happened to her daughter. Joyce confessed to not knowing much of what Shirley might have experienced since she had been swept off her feet by Carlo. It was what Shirley might be holding back that worried her. Yet Shirley seemed in no condition to be cross-examined, however slowly and gently her mother might try. The big question was what was behind it all. Frank had been away too long. With increasing certainty Joyce felt that these disturbing happenings were somehow connected to Frank's activities. How and why she had no idea. Frank, she was sure, would know what to do. Frank would have all the answers. Of these assumptions she was soon to be cruelly deprived.

Several days passed during which Joyce devoted herself to Shirley's care. The girl herself was reluctant to leave her bed and when she was persuaded to do that she preferred to stay in her room. She cried a lot and ate very little. There was no word from Carlo and nor did Joyce expect it. She herself was beginning to adapt to a gloomy scenario. Something sinister had to account for the sequence of events which had shaken up her family life. She had never regarded herself as naive. She knew she had lived with risk, but as year had followed year she had come to discount it. Now she was having to undertake a reality check. She knew she had to prepare, but for what she could not tell.

Maisie Love had phoned. Joyce updated her only with the simplest facts, keeping speculation out of it. The conversation had then turned to familiar topics. It was all totally inconsequential, but Joyce drew some comfort from it. She declined Maisie's suggestion that they might have a spot of lunch, explaining that she was unwilling to leave Shirley alone. A few minutes after returning the phone to its stand a thought struck her and she returned Maisie's call. 'I don't suppose your Richard would come round to see Shirley. They used to be such good friends. A familiar face might cheer her up.' 'Oh, I don't know, dear. I got the impression that it ended badly between them. I'd heard he'd taken up with someone else.' 'Sorry,' said Joyce, 'perhaps I shouldn't have asked.' 'No, no, dear, I'll ask him of course. He's a good lad at heart even if I do say it myself.' And there it was left.

First innings

Jon Palmer and Stewart Thorogood ran out on to the field, bats whirling. Whether this was a loosening exercise or to indicate that they meant business was unclear. When they had similarly opened the batting two seasons ago they had put on ninety-two for the first wicket. That had been in very different circumstances. Then they had been facing Philip Carter and Adrian Seymour. The former was now dead and the latter had become the Middle Daychurch wicketkeeper. On this occasion the home team had a trio of rather better quick bowlers at their disposal. They had not faced Clive Norrington on any previous occasion, but Charlie Colson and David Pelham had both reported that he was a powerful addition to the Middle Daychurch armoury. Lee Lingrove had come on in leaps and bounds if the evidence of the Nudgworth match was anything to go by. It was assumed that Tom Carter might also have come on a bit since last year. So whilst opening the batting on this occasion was likely to be more testing it soon became apparent that the pitch itself held no terrors.

Arthur watched Jon and Stewart navigate the first few overs without any sign of difficulty. He then had a word with Rash after which he mentioned to Dean Faulds that he needed to slip away for perhaps an hour or so. There was nothing unusual about that. Arthur seemed to have many interests and many contacts wherever the Outcasts went. They were quite used to his disappearing from time to time although it was never out of disinterest in cricket. Some of his absences were connected with matters of benefit to the Outcasts. Dean thought this to be highly likely in view of their being at Middle Daychurch and he did not question Arthur as to the exact purpose. What was different this time was that Arthur walked not to his coach, but to the score box. After collecting the key from Simon, temporary insurance cover having been prearranged, he took the Crossley's four-wheel drive and swept out of the club car park. For the mission on which he was embarked the coach would never have done.

Jon and Stewart were in mid-pitch discussion as Arthur left the ground. They were unsurprised. They had noticed how formally he had been dressed in contrast to the casual clothing he would usually wear when behind the wheel of his coach. However, their words were about the business in hand. They readily concurred with the pre-match assessment that Clive Norrington and Lee Lingrove were a trickier proposition than the home team's previous opening bowlers. Runs had had to be earned, but all in all the two batsmen were satisfied with the start they had made. The satisfaction was short-lived. Perhaps Lee Lingrove was getting into his stride. The pitch did not appear to be offering him any help. Yet having seen Stewart reach for a delivery outside off stump which got him two runs past extra cover Lee tempted him again with a ball just a little wider and was rewarded with an inside edge which was safely gathered by Adrian Seymour. The opening partnership was broken with the score at nineteen.

In the next over there were two leg byes before Clive Norrington conceded another boundary to Jon Palmer. Then trying another square cut to a shortish ball which did not get up as much as Jon expected he succeeded only in slicing it into his stumps. With both openers gone the score stood at twenty-five. Dean Faulds and Rashid Ali, a right-hand left-hand combination set about repairing the damage at first cautiously, but later in more buccaneering style. Lee Lingrove was rested after six overs, Clive after five.

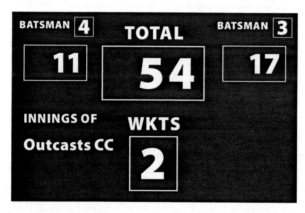

Tom Carter had been third into the attack and it was soon clear that he was an improved bowler. After two overs in which speed and accuracy had achieved no breakthrough he adopted a different approach with emphasis on the short-pitched ball. On such a true wicket and with their eye in, the two batsmen took full advantage. Their cause was further boosted by what appeared to be an out-of-sorts Richard Love. He was pedestrian at best and wore a distraught look. On previous occasions the reasons for Richard's distractions had been known to be the onset of amorous pursuits. This time it did not seem like that at all.

Those Outcasts close enough to make this judgement were right. Richard was not himself. He was in shock. The previous evening he had finally bowed to his mother's persuasion, or nagging as he had seen it, and walked round to the Simpsons' house to see Shirley. After her cruel trick he had felt very angry with her. Then to see her with an almost unbelievable style make-over prancing round some rich Italian playboy disgusted him. From what his mother had told him Shirley had evidently had her comeuppance big-time. He could not help feeling pleased. She deserved all she had got by being brought down to earth. He did not know what he would say to her. Before actually seeing her he would not have imagined speaking the words, 'Oh my good God'. But that was his instant reaction on seeing her tear-stained face, hollow eyes and lank hair. She was the very picture of misery, a picture made more poignant when a fresh round of sobs erupted when she saw Richard. Afterwards he could not remember whether she had moved towards him or he had stepped towards her, but there was no doubt they had hugged. There were therefore understandable reasons why on the following day Richard was finding it difficult to concentrate on his cricket. He had much on his mind.

Michael Carter was also having to do some thinking. His pace attack was starting to cost runs. It was too early to think of bringing back his opening bowlers although he could do with their economy rate. The Outcasts were gathering momentum. He doubted whether on this pitch his spinners would be able to stall it, but he had to try something. His cousins David and Andrew made up the remainder of his bowling armoury. He had a hurried consultation with them resulting in a decision to give Tom a talking-to about short-pitched bowling and one more over, possibly two. David's off spinners would then be employed at the pavilion end. Pace at one end, spin at the other. Michael hoped that might change the tempo. It did, but not to his liking. Tom reverted to length bowling, but lost a little accuracy. David's problem was over-pitching. For their part Dean and Rash felt they were well set and beginning to enjoy themselves. The crowd loved it, because it was always good to see stroke-play and it meant that Middle Daychurch were set a good challenge. At the twenty over halfway mark the Outcasts had reached 104–2. Two balls later with fierce strikes off David Carter, Rash posted his half-century. Three overs later Michael was forced to make another change. The Outcasts were then 135–2.

Arthur was another that day with much to ponder. What he had to ponder was in stark contrast to the brightness all around him. He sped through leafy lanes as yet untouched by autumn. His destination was a residential care home. On the basis of what Rash had been able to find out for him Arthur could see the shapings of a very dark plot. If Roy Groves had any connection with it Arthur would have no difficulty in suspecting nefarious activity. What he recollected about him was sufficient to arouse his distrust. Those memories had been revived by the chance meeting at Le Rêve Royal. Roy Groves in the locality and unexplained deaths were surely not just another coincidence. And he was one of the trustees tasked with implementing Edwin Carter's will. Rash had found out that after George Carter's death his place as trustee had been taken by the vicar. That had a strange feel about it. George Carter was dead and now too was Garry Woodworth. The other trustee was Ethel Daniels. Her name had hardly been mentioned in all the speculation which he had heard since he had been with the Outcasts. Yet the more he had thought about it the more he could see that she had to be a key component of the plot – if there was one.

Arthur also gave some thought to the Reverend Garry Woodworth. No next-of-kin for the drowned vicar had yet been identified. Enquiries were still being made. The infant Garry had been found in a box laid inside the

porch of the Church of All Saints in the East End of London. The day-old baby survived this indignity and was brought up as a foster child, but not before the Vicar of All Saints had given him the name Garry after Sir Garfield Sobers, who was a hero of his. No trace could be found of his foster parents, although someone came forward who could say no more than the man was a bad lot. Neither of the natural parents were ever identified. The Bishop of the Diocese covering the Daychurches could not be said to have had the finances of the church to the fore in his mind when he expressed his determination to hang on to the vicarage for a little longer in case some distant relative of the deceased might yet come forward. It had been Rash's task to provide some substance to that hope.

Armed with a totally bogus business card representing himself as Mr B. J. Chagunde, Rash had been successful in obtaining a meeting with the Bishop. The card had cost £10 and the other 299 had been shredded. The cost was justified, because the card was of such professional appearance that the Bishop was easily persuaded of the fiction that Rash and Arthur had concocted. Mr B. J. Chagunde had a brother in Rajkot ('Yes, it is a lovely cricket ground, isn't it?' said Rash hurriedly as he saw the Bishop's eyes light up at the mention of the name.) 'Well you see, he is a holy man who regularly visits hospitals to comfort the sick – no, I haven't been to the ground myself. I have only seen it on TV – and last week he saw this woman. She is possibly dying, but she talks of a long lost son in the UK. My brother, Mr L. K. Chagunde, says the circumstances seem similar to what I told him in my last email. We are always emailing each other. It is such a wonderful invention.' Rash sensed that the Bishop was keen to explore further the delights of Rajkot and so forestalled him. 'My brother, Mr L. K. Chagunde, wondered if in the house of your late priest there might be a photograph or some other artefact which could help to stir the memory of this poor unfortunate woman. I would truly appreciate being allowed to look at what is in the house. I would not, of course, borrow anything without your express permission.' Rash could see doubt written across the Bishop's face. 'If it would help to assure you I can get my brother, Mr L. K. Chagunde, to ring you himself this evening.' The doubt disappeared. The Bishop had experienced his fair share of calls to his credit card company in India and knew how difficult communication could be. 'Well, I suppose it's all right if it is the only lead we've got.'

Once inside the vicarage Rash had been surprised to find no sign that anyone before him had thought to go through Garry's papers with a view to tracing the elusive next-of-kin. Loose papers and files had been gathered in cardboard boxes. The scene did not suggest that there had been any systematic search. What Rash hoped to find was, of course, quite different from what might have satisfied a genuine searcher. Then again Rash himself was not absolutely certain what he was after. Bank statements possibly, maybe a safe although that would be locked. Ditto a filing cabinet. Secrets these days were probably embedded in a laptop. He could not think of any pretext under which he could remove a laptop, at least not without further stretching credulity.

Suddenly a thought came to him. What had Garry Woodworth been doing when he met his end? How many personal items would you take with you if you were popping out for some nude bathing? Rash checked the study and the vicar's bedroom. He found a laptop, but not much else. He could find nowhere a list of pass codes. It would need a professional to have any hope of getting the laptop to reveal its secrets. The desk in the study was a roll-top model. Rash vaguely remembered watching some mystery drama on television in which a desk of this type had featured. He thought there had been a secret compartment which had led to the discovery of a vital clue. He fiddled around with the desk. He pushed, he pressed, he squeezed and was about to give up when he heard a click. A small drawer came forward revealing a space behind in which lay some papers. They would do nothing to assist the memory of the fictitious lady in the hospital in Rajkot, but they would certainly assist the Outcasts with their enquiries. Rash put the evidence in his jacket pocket and returned to the Bishop's house clutching a cheap and nasty, small and garishly painted vase. 'This'll do,' he announced. 'It may be at least a fortnight before I can let you know. Please on no account dispose of the house contents before I (he nearly added 'or the police') return.'

In the match Andrew Carter had been introduced into the attack more in hope than expectation. Andrew had not had a particularly good season. His 2–59 from five overs against Nudgworth had been an analysis too common for comfort, but he did add variety to the attack. It was the variety in his own bowling which caused concern to his captain. Michael spent some time with him setting the field and it was disappointing that Andrew's first delivery was hit out of the ground by Rashid Ali. It does not matter where you put your fielders if the batsman is set on big hitting. However, fielders had something to do when Rash worked the second ball for a single on the leg side. Thinking perhaps that he should be taking his cue from Rash, Dean swung at the second ball. He mis-hit it and it went vertical. Wicket-keeper's job. Adrian Seymour had time to position himself and safely took the catch. Andrew Carter's reaction showed that he was not displeased. Dean was disappointed with himself, but a score of 51 and a partnership of over 100 were distinctly creditworthy.

Ray Burrill was next man in. If appearance was any guide, Ray looked to be brimming with confidence, a state of affairs to which his private life might be contributing. Putting Ray in ahead of Toby Lederwood maintained a left-hand right-hand partnership which complicated things for a captain if his bowlers were having difficulty controlling their line. The dismissive way in which Ray drove Andrew's next ball past mid on for four did not augur well for the fielding side. Rashid Ali was also looking good. The new partnership flourished.

It got off to a bright start by virtue of a calamitous over from Andrew Carter which cost twenty runs. At the other end David Carter was improving, but on average he was costing eight runs an over. Michael Carter brought back Clive Norrington, but his first over was loose. In five overs the Outcasts had added fifty rapid runs. Just when it looked that nothing could stop Rash reaching an elegant century something did. Having hit Clive for a superbly driven four off a slower ball, he was deceived by a very much quicker one and was unarguably lbw. A left-hand right-hand combination was maintained with the arrival of Toby Lederwood, who was facing Middle Daychurch bowlers for the first time. Clive Norrington had worked up a good pace and Toby's first scoring shot was a streaky single. Facing David Carter, he found a gap for an easy single and then Ray Burrill thumped David for a four and a massive six. Clive was fully in the groove for his last over. Toby took a single early on which was followed by a leg bye. Back on strike Toby fenced fatally at one of Clive's faster balls. He did not think he had touched it, but the Middle Daychurch team went up as one. Crucially Bert Love agreed with them.

In the pavilion Dean Faulds doubted whether they had sufficient runs. On previous outings they had failed to defend a total of 250 and not managed to overcome a village total of 220. He therefore opted for aggression in choosing to send in Richard Furness rather than David Pelham. One of the younger members of the side, Richard had developed into a very useful all-rounder. His success as a cricketer may have been helped by a curb on his social profligacy since he had formed a relationship with Suzy Waterbeach (*Accidentally Cricket* 2009). Faithful to her in her absence on a luxury break, his undiluted concentration on cricket seemed to have paid good dividends. Richard conveyed instructions to Ray. 'Skipper says I'm to have a go and you should anchor. If I don't get many, David's in next and then it'll be you to hit out while he farms out the strike.' Seeing that Ray's look was disbelieving, he added, 'Simple.' Both of them laughed.

There had been no laughing in the Simpson household. Joyce had been sure that her daughter's homecoming was not the end of the matter. Even though Shirley had withdrawn into herself and was taking time to recover, it was clear to Joyce that she had either been blind to what might have been going on or kept completely apart from it. She had been unable to say anything which gave her mother any clue as to what to expect. But Joyce was certain there would be a contact. She had prayed it might be Frank, although by now she was almost on the point of giving up on him. The call came before 8 a.m. on what was the Saturday of the Outcasts' visit to the village, not that her life was calibrated any longer by Middle Daychurch Cricket Club since Richard and Shirley had split. The voice was somehow familiar and the familiarity was soon explained.

'How are you, Mrs Simpson, or may I call you Joyce?' Joyce let that go. 'You may remember' – she did – 'we met at the Abbey Grange a while back, for dinner.' He nevertheless introduced himself, but wasted no time getting down to business. 'I'm sorry to ring you so early, but I thought you might be going out and I didn't want to miss you. As one of his business associates Frank wanted me to pop by to get some important papers signed.' Anticipating what must have been an inevitable question from Joyce he went on, 'He's terribly sorry not to be back in the UK himself, but we've got something really rather big on and he's got to be on the spot. You know Frank, very hands on'. Joyce could have believed that, if she had not got to the state of dreadful doubt about her husband's well-being and whereabouts. The voice was in her ear again. 'Would ten o'clock be all right?' Joyce agreed and then sat down to think very hard about what she should do.

Promptly at ten a car had drawn up outside. Joyce could see that his face was familiar. So too could Shirley from her upstairs window. Joyce had told her that she was expecting a visitor. As the man got to the gate Shirley called out to her mother. 'I know him, I know him. He visited the house in Cyprus and I'm sure he came to see Carlo in Florida.' And as the doorbell rang, Shirley said he was called Dick Grant. 'Was he indeed?' Joyce said under her breath and then to Shirley, 'Keep out of sight and don't make a noise.' Then as the bell rang again she moved slowly towards the door. 'I'm sorry,' she said to her visitor, 'I'm not as lively as I used to be. I can't rush around. I was just making some tea. I find I need a good cuppa more often these days. I'm sure you'll have one with me.' The man seemed less sure about that, but he needed to keep the woman sweet. Resignedly he took the chair to which she pointed him and she made her laboured way into the kitchen, pleased that her performance seemed to have had the right effect. Her years in amateur dramatics had taught her a few things.

When she returned with the tea and some biscuits the man was sitting at the living room table with a file of documents in front of him. He had placed his briefcase against the side of a bookcase. Joyce embarked on an elaborate charade, first of all explaining that she 'really needed' her cup of tea. The man had little choice but to drink his whilst she asked him questions about Frank to which he was careful to give unilluminating answers. Trying to get down to business, he pulled a sheet of paper from the file and held it out to her. She took time to put her cup down before accepting the document. She held it up almost to the end of her nose before declaring, 'It's no good, I'll have to get my glasses. I wonder where I put them'. She got up from her seat still clutching the paper and began her search. Of necessity this would take some time, because Joyce did not wear glasses. Saying 'Perhaps I left them in the kitchen,' she went back in there.

The man did not seem to notice that when she emerged she was not carrying the piece of paper. In fact any impatience he might previously have shown had been replaced by an appearance of discomfort. As Joyce knew the potency of the substance she had put in his tea, she felt only pleasure that it was working as soon as she had hoped. She continued to look around her for her non-existent spectacles when the man emitted a strangulated moan and shifted in his chair. Five seconds later he was on his feet demanding to know the direction of the lavatory. He disappeared through the door at speed, grabbing the file as he went. A terrible sound came from the direction of the downstairs lavatory. Joyce smiled grimly and retrieved the sheet of paper she had taken into the kitchen.

The document told only part of the story, but it seemed that Joyce's signature was required to authorise disposal of the property in Cyprus. That she had expected. The shocks came when she transferred her attention to the briefcase, confident that she would not be interrupted as she examined its contents. It took her less than five minutes to learn some terrible facts. Frank, her husband, was dead. There was even a copy of his death certificate in the briefcase. It told her that he had been a long time dead. Her daughter had been groomed by Carlo to achieve simple access to the Simpson properties. As neither of them had yielded what Frank's erstwhile associates had been seeking, Shirley's usefulness had been considered to be at an end. A copy of an email telling Carlo what he was to do was also lurking in the briefcase together with another message from someone unknown beyond the name Roberto saying that 'the hunt' would now have to concentrate on the only remaining Simpson property. To this end the wife 'would have to be removed'. The anger welled up in Joyce, but she managed to remain icy calm. She knew with certainty what she had to do.

She knocked on the door of the downstairs loo and asked, 'Are you all right?' 'I'm afraid I'm in some difficulty, Joyce. I had this terrible pain and, well, I just didn't make it. You must allow me to clean things up, but my biggest embarrassment is my clothing. There wouldn't be a spare pair of Frank's trousers I could borrow, would there?' Although disgusting, Joyce took satisfaction from imagining the scene within. It was no compensation for the horrors she had learned, but there was some pleasure to be derived from the man's acute discomfort. In no hurry she selected from Frank's wardrobe a pair of stained gardening trousers which she had threatened to throw out. This would be as good an exit for them as any. She left them outside the lavatory door and waited for the man to rejoin her.

He needed a bucket and mop and then he asked for a bag in which to place his soiled clothing. 'I really need a bath,' he said, but there was no hint on Joyce's part that he was likely to get one in her house. No, she told him she had not been able to find her glasses, 'what with all the fuss'. He would have to come back. Would he leave the rest of the papers in his file, which had left the loo in a less than pristine condition, so that she could read them at her leisure? That was something he did not wish to do. If she was going to be at home, he would return later in the afternoon. He had another appointment in the meantime. With as much dignity as he had left he gathered his case and apologised once again. 'I do not know what came over me. Rather exceptionally I had a full breakfast this morning. It included two pieces of black pudding. I'm wondering if that is what led to my problem.' No good reason to impugn black pudding, thought Joyce, but she did not enlighten him.

She knew she needed Shirley out of the way. The only person likely to persuade her to leave the house would be Richard. Would he cooperate? More importantly, would Shirley? It was Joyce's sole option. She didn't want her out on her own, but since her return from America she had not been outside the house at all. She achieved her purpose with surprising ease. Richard himself had answered the telephone. He had reacted cautiously, but willingly. He named a time. Joyce pretended to Shirley that the initiative had come from Richard. Perhaps this little white lie made a difference, for Shirley, having shunned outdoors ever since her return home, seemed to welcome the prospect of Richard's company. And so it had turned out. With the Outcasts batting and Richard on the field of play, Shirley had parked herself close to the score box where she was able to have intermittent chat with Maisie Love.

Shirley was not particularly into cricket and so she could not have understood the calculations behind the installation of the Furness/Burrill partnership, which was later to allow Dean Faulds to lay claim to cricketing nous. 'First time for everything,' as Jon Palmer observed. Richard was a forthright cricketer, who knew how to strike the ball. As any batsman might claim, when you're going well the luck often keeps you company. Ray Burrill was not by nature a blocker, the role to which Richard had cheekily assigned him. He already had 39 runs to his name. He felt well set. Even a partisan crowd could take pleasure from what they were to witness.

The innings had only eight overs and two balls left to run. Richard signalled his intention by hitting the two balls, which completed Clive Norrington's allocation, for four apiece. He claimed that the first of his two boundaries was a deliberate steer between first and second slip. Other opinions were heard. However, there could be no doubting that the second came from a resounding blow to leg when the bowler pitched short. Michael Carter had worked it out that the final eight overs of the Outcasts' innings – if it lasted that long – would be bowled by Lee Lingrove, Tom Carter and Richard Love. He was unsure what caused him to change his mind. It might have been a renewed suspicion that Richard was off colour, but he decided to keep going with David Carter at the pavilion end.

It proved to be a costly mistake. The punishment meted out by Ray Burrill at the end of David's previous over should have been a warning. David began his seventh over with two full tosses; Ray began the over by taking two straight-driven boundaries. David corrected his length, but only temporarily. He then dropped short and was pulled for six to bring up Ray's 50. The batsman acknowledged the applause and then in a show of provocation asked for a new guard from Umpire Breakwell. David Carter was stung by this kind of treatment and his mood was not helped when Ray jumped down the pitch to the next ball, missed and Adrian Seymour fumbled and lost the stumping opportunity. The final insult came when David lost his line, allowing Ray to pick up the ball cleanly off his hip and deposit it over deep mid wicket. It was thrown back by a customer outside The Cow's Corner whilst Richard strolled up to Ray and said 'some blocking'. David's seven overs had cost seventy-one runs and as he had not taken a wicket it was easily his worst performance for his team.

Michael Carter then made his second mistake. Deciding that he wanted Lee and Tom to bowl their remaining two overs consecutively, he chose Richard to bowl his next over from the river end leaving him to bowl his last over, if needed, from the opposite end. Unfortunately for his captain Richard's

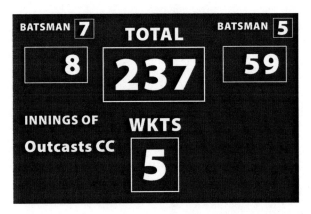

BATSMAN 7	TOTAL	BATSMAN 5
8	**237**	59

INNINGS OF **WKTS**

Outcasts CC **5**

brain was not fully in tune with his cricket that afternoon. He found himself increasingly glancing in Shirley's direction. His bowling had none of its more usual zip and nip. It was his bad luck that what he might have got away with lightly on another occasion was not going to happen when the batsman on strike was eager to take liberties. Richard got a two and a three with ease, Ray obligingly ran a single and then Richard let rip. He flicked the ball over the wicketkeeper's head, cut a wide ball square for another boundary and was almost run out in going for a second run which at best should have been no more than a cheeky single. The home crowd may not have liked seeing sixteen taken off the over, but Richard's desperate dive for the crease gave them great amusement. From neck to foot he was streaked with green and brown, but he had put the Outcasts past the 250 mark. Six overs remained.

Arthur would doubtless have enjoyed this whole spectacle if he had not been engaged on a clandestine mission. In his piece of subterfuge with the bishop Rashid Ali had actually been a solicitor. Arthur drew up at the Sunnyrest Residential Care Home with no veneer of authenticity at all. When he had rung up to make an appointment he had represented himself as Edward Lambourn of Lambourn, Smith and Payne, solicitors specialising in financial matters. He had been unable to say anything by way of detail, because he was engaged on a matter of the utmost confidentiality. It was possible that one of the residents at Sunnyrest could be a substantial beneficiary in a matter which had been placed in his firm's hands. Before he could confirm this there were one or two delicate points which had to be checked. This could only be done in direct enquiry with the person in question. 'I stress,' Arthur had said, 'extreme delicacy.' The care home owner to whom he had been speaking was called Mrs Foxwell. 'I don't know, really, it's a bit unorthodox. We do have our reputation to think of. Don't you

think you ought to talk to his wife first? I mean, I wouldn't want to find I'd let him be bothered by some cruel hoax. You do hear about that sort of thing, but, if his wife says it's OK, then I suppose it would be all right.' The last person Arthur wanted anything to do with was the man's wife. 'You are, of course, quite right, Mrs Foxwell. I can tell you are a lady of great discretion. Indeed, when I established that the person I was seeking was in the care of Sunnyrest I heard some excellent reports of your establishment. Your reputation, you know, has gone a long way before you.' Then Arthur changed his tone. 'And I hope that the same can be said for Lambourn, Smith and Payne. I can assure you that my firm does not deal in scams. I am a very busy man, Mrs Foxwell, I would not be giving up my precious time on a Saturday to drive out into the countryside if I did not think this was an extremely important matter' – and then to bait the hook he added – 'involving, and I shouldn't say this, but I see you can be trusted with a confidence, a seriously large sum of money.' Arthur could sense the cogs turning in Mrs Foxwell's mind. Large sum of money, elderly resident, legacy, a wife who wouldn't have the same gratitude. When she broke the silence she said, 'What time did you say?'

On appearance neither Sunnyrest nor Mrs Foxwell lived up to the flattery which Arthur had mendaciously used. That would not have mattered. What did matter was being met by the owner with the words, 'We've got the bug. I'm afraid you've had a wasted journey. I can't let you in to see him or for that matter any other patient. I did try phoning you, but I must have taken the number down wrong. It just rang out'. That last piece of

204

information surprised – and relieved – Arthur, because it was a number he had invented. Seemingly she had not troubled further than that.

Arthur was forced to think fast. This was an unexpected blow. It was obvious that Mrs Foxwell herself was disappointed by the turn of events. She enquired if she could ask the necessary questions of her resident or, she wondered, was it some form of physical mark that needed to be identified. After all, she had added with a little laugh, 'There's not a lot we don't know about them in here, you know. Not when you have to bath them and other things which I'm sure a gentleman like you would not want me to specify'. By this time Arthur's mind was working in another direction. 'I can see you are a very resourceful lady, Mrs Foxwell, but it's not really as easy as that. It does rather look as though I shall have to come back another day when you've got over this outbreak. I compliment you on the strict standards which you are observing. Others in lesser establishments might not be so scrupulous.' Arthur could see that these words were having a good effect. There was just one last chance.

'Tell me, Mrs Foxwell, is that a very attractive sun lounge I noticed when I was coming up the drive?' 'Yes, it is one of our outstanding features.' 'May I take a look – from the outside obviously?' 'I'm sure I can spare a few minutes to show you. When you come next time you might like to see some of our other top-class facilities. Do you have an aged loved one who may soon be requiring superior care facilities?' 'No,' said Arthur, 'but I do have clients who may have an interest.' That seemed to cheer her up and to encourage further sales patter. 'Of course, all our residents' rooms have large windows with garden views.' Arthur had hoped this might be the case. 'The ones who've gone down with this bug are confined to their rooms at the moment. If any resident gets really ill, we have a small, well-equipped sanatorium which often saves them having to go to hospital. Oh, there he is now,' she said breaking off from her list of Sunnyrest's virtues. 'He must be feeling a bit brighter. He's in his chair by the window.' She waved. The man did not wave back. 'Do you know, Mrs Foxwell, this is very lucky?' Arthur took a step or two closer to the window and extracted a photograph from his document case appearing to compare its likeness to the face in the window on which he was really focusing. The photograph was actually one of the great Trevor Bailey, but it sufficed as a prop. Arthur had discovered all he needed to know. The Sunnyrest resident he had come to see bore the unmistakable family likeness he had hoped to find.

In reality his interest in Sunnyrest Residential Care Home ended at that point, but Arthur felt it was necessary to go through the motions of arranging another visit. It was agreed that Mrs Foxwell would call him when the virus had been expelled. To that end Arthur this time gave her his real mobile number and said how much he looked forward to her call. She pressed a couple of her brochures on him – 'Just in case,' she said. 'We prefer a certain quality of resident here. I'm sure you know what I mean.' Arthur immediately regretted giving her a reliable way of contacting him. Later he would be glad that he had. He waved her farewell and began his return journey at about the time the Outcasts' innings was coming to its end.

After the punishment handed out to Richard Love Michael Carter invested a lot of hope in the return of Lee Lingrove. 'Keep it tight, Lee,' he advised. Lee had kept it tight to date. His six overs at the start of the innings had cost only eighteen runs and he had taken the wicket of Stewart Thorogood. He felt he had more chance against Richard Furness, who seemed happy to take risks. Ray Burrill seemed ominously well settled and it was Ray who was due to receive from him. Lee was lucky that his loosener escaped punishment and his next two deliveries kept Ray quiet. Then Ray got a routine single which enabled Lee to glare fiercely at Richard before turning towards his bowling mark. Richard had returned the stare and reckoned he might be getting a short-pitched ball. He was prepared and he was right. He rocked back and hooked lustily. The two fielders who had been positioned for the catch had no chance. The ball soared clear of them. Stares were exchanged again between batsman and bowler. Lee ran in again determined not to be rattled. This time he had the better of the contest. Richard flashed and missed. 'I'll get him next time,' vowed Lee to himself.

Tom Carter was returned to the attack as well, but this was not Tom's best day. He lacked consistency and the batsmen were able to score freely without hitting a boundary. Lee wanted his final over to live up to his captain's expectations. He was given two slips and told to pitch the ball up. His first was a beauty and should have taken a wicket. Richard went to drive, but Lee had achieved some slight outswing. The ball went fast, but at catchable height to Andrew Carter, who spilled it. Almost inevitably Richard got a full bat on the next and sent it wide of mid off for four. Lee beat him again with his third ball. Richard took a single off the fourth. Then Lee bowled a rank bad ball. He cursed himself. Ray Burrill swung hard, but high. Keith Kirkham pulled off a magnificent running catch. The partnership was broken. It had been thoroughly entertaining. The one that followed was less so in that it was stillborn. For his finale Lee produced a straight ball of no great speed to Richard (the batsmen having crossed) who missed it. He had aimed to cut, but after pitching the ball kept low and hit off stump with sufficient force to dislodge the bail.

In view of this double disaster Dean Faulds shuffled the batting order again. With three overs left Colin Banks was promoted above Basil Smith with the instruction 'to have a mow'. This was something of which Colin in the right mood and in the right circumstances was well capable. The record showed that the necessary conjunction was only infrequently attained. Tom Carter had one over left to bowl and David Pelham was facing. He sought to emulate the form he had shown on this ground a few weeks earlier when he had been pressed into service to help out Nudgworth. It was form which had deserted him in the interim. He felt comfortable in dealing with Tom, but his shots were going straight to fielders. Half an over had gone without him getting a run before a mis-field gave him an opportunity. Yelling 'run' in the direction of his partner, he shot up the pitch. Having made his ground, he was soon wondering whether it had been the right move. Colin seemed to have taken no more than a casual glance round the field before adopting his stance at the crease without any aid from the umpire. It did not bode well. Tom ran in smoothly scenting a wicket. It was quick, but overpitched. There was nothing in the slightest way textbook about the stroke, but it was highly productive. Colin thought it good for a laugh. Tom did not. He had one delivery left. Surely Colin could not connect twice. But Colin could and did, although not to the same effect. He swung powerfully, but the only contact was high on the bat. The ball spiralled over the keeper. Had either Adrian Seymour back-pedalled or David Carter at third man sprinted, a catch might have been taken. Colin's exertions meanwhile had caused him to collapse at the crease. When he saw what had happened to the ball it was too late to run. It was now the bowler who could afford to smile.

At this point and on the basis of the form shown Michael Carter's bowling options were a problem. If in doubt, he told himself, do the unexpected. So he chose Andrew, whose two overs thus far had cost 31 runs. On the other hand he had taken a wicket. The combination of Colin and Andrew in cricketing terms might be explosive, but first it was David Pelham at the striker's end. And it was still David at the striker's end when the over was complete. Honours were even. David had one handsome boundary to his name and another well run two. Andrew felt that he had got a bit of control back. The stage was set for a last fling by Colin against whichever of Richard Love and David Carter Michael Carter chose to use.

Despite his appalling figures Michael chose David reasoning that Colin would be more likely to have a go at the slower bowler and make an error of judgement in the process. The field was well and truly scattered. At this stage of the game ones and twos scarcely mattered. David's first ball was deliberately well wide of the crease, but just legitimate. If there was any doubt, Bert Love gave it to him. There was nothing Colin could do. David tried to repeat the manoeuvre, but pitched instead in line and with a hint of turn. The likelihood of turn had not entered Colin's reckoning. There were no fielders close to the wicket and so he carved at it. They ran two. David's third ball went wide again and might have been given as a wide, but this time Colin had a different idea. To noisy guffaws from his team mates he employed a reverse sweep. It was so unexpected and audacious that it evaded the field. Colin had visibly preened himself over the success of the stroke, making it all too probable to anyone who knew him that he would be tempted to try it again. The thought also occurred to the bowler. David tossed the ball up invitingly on a good line. Colin could have hit it anywhere with an orthodox stroke, but he was now determined to employ the reverse sweep. It was a case of user error. The stumps were scattered by a combination of the ball and Colin's foot which slid backwards as he tripped over himself.

With two balls left there was little scope for drama. Basil Smith in both his private and cricket lives was something of a new man. He might have felt that number ten in the order was a little low for him but it was to that position he had been relegated on this occasion. He took elaborate guard, examined the field as if to check that the lawful number of players was not being exceeded and then broke off to prod the pitch. To the first delivery he offered a neat forward defensive stroke. The second he drove perfectly for four through the covers. With job done he tucked his bat under his arm, collected David Pelham at the non-striker's end and said as they walked off, 'You and I could have a good bowl on this.' 'You reckon?' 'I reckon,' said Basil firmly. 'Give it a few more overs and I think we'll get some turn.' But first what they got was tea.

Tea interval

For reasons which had been only vaguely alluded to, the hosts had been a little short of help in the preparation of tea. On hearing this Liz Colson, having given her parents the joy of looking after baby Helena for the day, was an immediate volunteer. Adrienne Palmer was happy to join in as well, having made a similar arrangement with her young son. The lady in charge of the operation was Michael Carter's wife, Clarice. 'I feel I had to support Michael as he's taken so much on at the club. In any case it's team work and so I actually find it a pleasure, not a duty.' Liz, mindful of all that Charlie had said to her, threw in an occasional question as she buttered the bread. She was not sure how much of what she learned was already known to the Outcasts, even such a mundane point that Michael was a teacher and sports instructor at a sixth form college. There was plenty of family gossip of no great significance. Clarice talked of their daughters, Clare and Isabel, their different characteristics and how they were getting on at school and nursery. Liz thought it might be rather pointed to refer to the earliest deaths in the saga and so when she got round to this subject she concentrated on the latest. In view of what had happened she felt that she could refer to it in a light-hearted way. Without her having to probe, it worked.

'I know I shouldn't laugh,' said Clarice, 'but the vicar was a strange bloke. Don't get me wrong. He did wonders for the church, but the rest of the time he kept himself to himself. To be on his own in that vicarage – well, you know how people talk. He didn't strike anyone as a particularly scholarly man, although he had a way with words. Then when it came out that he splashed around in the river with no clothes on, it did set people talking. Discreetly, of course. But then so soon after, him being found dead, that was a real shock. When Michael came home he couldn't believe it.' 'Came home?' Liz found herself saying. 'You mean from school?' 'No, from Norwich,' Clarice explained. 'He'd been with the second team there. He didn't get back till gone half past seven.' When Liz found a moment to relay this piece of information to her husband Charlie knew at once from the estimated time of the vicar's death that Michael could not have been involved. However, Michael's exoneration did not mean that the drowning was after all an accident. But then who else had a motive for killing Garry? Charlie frowned in concentration. Equally if it had been an accident, it still left Michael with a motive for the other deaths.

Adrienne Palmer had been asked to cosy up to whichever of Joseph Carter's daughters might be one of the tea ladies on duty. In fact both Josephine Lingrove and Margaret Seymour had turned up. Adrienne chose Margaret, who had started to slice a pile of scones. It was a delicate task, harking back to a fatal explosion, but trying to engage in a discussion about poisoning (Paul Carter) or falling masonry (George Carter) were judged to be worse investigatory cul-de-sacs. Adrienne felt she needed a long lead-in time before she could get as far as mentioning Margaret's father's name. Adrian Seymour's wife remained composed. Yes, it had all been terrible, but they had had to move on. Adrian had been very supportive and their daughter Jennifer, who had doted on her grandfather, had come through the ordeal. Margaret had been especially worried for her, because she had sometimes gone to watch her grandfather at work. 'She might so easily have been with him when it happened.' Adrienne could see her eyes glisten and so she backed off rapidly. For a while nothing was said. It was Margaret who broke the silence. 'You see, he was such a careful man, if you like. He did everything by routine. But they said with those gas canisters you could think you'd turned them fully off, but you haven't.' Her voice dropped away. Adrienne put an arm around her. 'I'm sorry, I shouldn't have made you reminisce.' But, of course, that is precisely what she had wanted. She now felt rather badly about it and said as much to Jon afterwards. However, the point had been re-emphasised. Joseph had not by nature been a careless man.

Harry Northwood had been a little below his best form and was not unduly surprised to be picked for the visit to Middle Daychurch only as a twelfth (or thirteenth) man. Naturally he had brought his kit with him, but he thought that he might be able to grab some net practice if he was not after all included in the team. He had approached his fellow twelfth man, Phil Cole, to see if he would bowl to him. Phil, always ready to experiment with his bowling, readily agreed. Their opposite number in the Middle Daychurch side was Brian Carter. Hanging around with him was his brother James. Charlie Colson recognised this as an opportunity for Harry to engage with these two. Being of the same generation he might pick up some indiscreet comments which could be useful. 'Keep off the subject of their own dad, but see if they've anything to say about their Uncle Douglas and for that matter Brian Stagden.' It turned out that Brian and James were only too pleased to pass the time with Harry. The club's nets were in full view of the ground and Brian could be called to duty, if need be. On Charlie's advice Phil Cole left the three of them to bond. However, it was not long before the three became four.

What might be described as Harry's Gallic awakening had taken place only a short time ago (*Unusually Cricket* 2010). He had acquired a much keener eye for the fair sex and a greater appetite for the pleasures to be derived from their company. He was bowled neck and crop by Brian Carter when his attention was momentarily diverted. He remembered to say 'good one' to Brian and the term might similarly have been applied to the cause of his loss of concentration. The girl, who had strolled up to the nets, was wearing a white T-shirt and pink shorts. Whether designed to capture attention Harry could not be sure, but he was curious to find out. The girl's appearance did not seem to have the same effect on either Brian or

James. Her very presence gave rise to some scornful comment. 'Not in your league, Jenny,' said Brian. Harry was unsure whether this meant him or the activity in which they were engaged. 'Run along, cousin,' said James, 'this is men's work.' Jennifer Seymour was not put off. She told Brian and James to do something to themselves which they would have been very ill-advised to try. Harry liked her spirit and he liked more than that about her. 'Do you want a bowl?' 'Don't encourage her,' said Brian in mock horror. 'Girls do play cricket much more these days,' responded Harry, 'so why not give her a go?' James sniggered, but tossed the ball in her direction. Jennifer caught it sharply, measured out a few paces, ran in and delivered out of the back of her hand a fizzing leg break. Harry tried to convince himself afterwards that he could have played the ball, but had chosen to let it hit his stumps. No harm in a bit of flattery.

In the course of the next ten minutes she deceived him three more times before James bothered to mention that she was captain of her school side which had not been beaten all season. The brothers tired of the exercise after a while and excused themselves. Jenny seemed keen to continue and Harry was keen in his turn. Eventually he said, 'I don't suppose there's any point in asking whether you'd like to bat.' She laughed. 'No, I didn't bring my kit, did I? Anyway I'm not much of a bat. Bowling's my thing.' Harry sat down and she parked herself opposite him. She asked him his name and from that very basic start the talk flowed in a very natural way. The interruption came when Harry thought that a change of shirt and a shower might not come amiss. With a stab of guilt he realised that he had let Brian and James drift off without any attempt on his part to question them. The sense of guilt abated as he helped Jenny to her feet. 'I think I need a shower as well after all that effort,' she said with a smile. 'In fact why don't you come and use the shower in our house? It's much better than any in the clubhouse.' And Harry was certain it was. Trying not to rush out the words, he said, 'Let me just pick up my other top.' As they were walking to Cricketers Close he remembered something. 'By the way, why did they call you cousin? Aren't you more their niece?' 'It's just easier that way,' she answered. On the whole Harry felt very easy about it as well. Although why he had not unstrapped his pads and was still carrying his bat was a mystery even to him.

Generously the club had extended its tea-time hospitality to the whole Outcasts contingent. All bar one had accepted and all bar one of them partook. Arthur had excused himself, because he had some business to do and none of the players knew where Harry was. Michael Carter was a genial and attentive host. Charlie was not the only one who found it difficult to believe he could be a serial killer. Yet he realised that murderers came in all shapes and sizes. Often they turned out to be the last person you would imagine. For all that Charlie had urged his friends to ask questions he actually found it very awkward to talk about aspects of the family tragedy in the convivial atmosphere of a hearty tea in the pavilion and amidst the wider camaraderie of a cricket match. He remained keenly aware that time was running out and that Michael could soon be a wealthy man. Michael was the member of the home team to whom he felt closest. As he bit on a delicious pork pie and drank more tea he was willing himself to raise the subject very openly with Michael. If he did nothing bold in pursuit of a theory which he had been the first to promote, he would be the butt of his friends' jibes for ever more. The counterbalancing thought in his mind was that he could cause so much offence that the relationship between Middle Daychurch and the Outcasts could be ruined. It was only later that it occurred to him that, if in fact he was confronting someone who had been responsible for a half a dozen deaths, he could be the next victim.

During the afternoon Shirley Simpson had been 'adopted' by the Outcasts' female contingent. Maisie Love in the score box had introduced her to Sophie Crossley. There had been an instant rapport between the two younger women. Gradually she had met the rest of the gang as they had dropped by. Shirley had no real interest in cricket, but she paid attention whenever Richard was in action. So she was really pleased to have people to talk to about anything or everything which had nothing to do with her ordeal or its possible aftermath. She sat with them at tea. Richard had checked that she was all right and when she glanced across at him she noticed that he was looking in her direction. Each time he smiled she felt better. Her recovery gained strength. She cheerfully joined in the clearing up after tea and found herself looking forward to seeing Richard bat. It was a chance remark later in the afternoon that set her back.

Second innings

The Outcasts were obviously not privy to the Middle Daychurch team talk which preceded the start of their innings. Michael Carter was bullish. 'We're going to get these runs. We know their bowling pretty well by now. They've got that guy Banks in their team this year. You'll need to watch him, but he'll tire quickly. Be careful with Burrill. He got a few wickets last year. But the rest are pretty ordinary and the wicket's not doing much to help them. Charlie, Keith, give us a solid start and then we'll motor. Anyone got anything to say? No? OK, good luck everybody. Then we'll have ourselves a real party in The Cow's Corner tonight.'

This exhortation would have been unthinkable just a few years ago. Charlie Bell reflected on how much the club had changed since he had first been picked to play. The Carter family still predominated, but the mood and the spirit had been transformed. The club was doing so much better now the older members had gone. It was almost as if God was a cricket lover. He smiled and then suddenly he froze. What was he thinking? Like everyone else he had wondered about the succession of deaths. There had just seemed to be too many. It was eerie. Yet why suddenly had the thought flitted across his mind that some demented person had been culling those cricketers who they had regarded as a spent force. Now the opening batsman shivered, casting a glance at his fellow players and wondering. No, he told himself as he set off from the changing room with Keith Kirkham, any such ridiculous thought should be kicked into touch. Unfortunately it continued to obtrude. Perhaps he needed the insurance of a good innings.

The first over of the Middle Daychurch innings was to be bowled from the pavilion end. Remembering that his dramatic opening spell two years ago had been achieved from the river end, Colin Banks asked if Stewart Thorogood would be happy to commence operations. Stewart had no problem with that and so prepared to bowl to Charles Bell. It was an uneventful over with each batsman acquiring a single. Colin Banks and Keith Kirkham were new to each other. There was caution on both sides. The outcome was mutual dissatisfaction. Colin thought the pitch had no life in it; Keith was disgusted that he had allowed Colin to bowl a maiden over. Stewart in his next over caused Charles to play and miss twice, but accurately assessed that this was due more to the batsman's misjudgement than his own bowling skills. The only run was a leg bye. In his second over Colin worked up a better pace which induced patience on the part of the batsman. Again the only addition to the score was a leg bye. It was to be doubted whether four runs off four overs was exactly what Michael Carter had had in mind in calling for a solid start.

On Keith Kirkham's call a single was scrambled off the opening ball of Stewart's next over. The pace was then upped by Keith hitting the first boundary of the innings and insisting on a third run after carving a full toss from Stewart into the deep with less than perfect timing. It ensured that he kept the strike. Colin Banks, whilst not feeling that he was bowling at his best, had nevertheless not had a run taken off him. That was to change now that Keith Kirkham regarded himself as settled. Colin tried to dig the ball in, but Keith anticipated the tactic, got himself in position and pulled it one bounce for four behind mid wicket. Colin tried again and gained a moral victory, but at the end of the over he dropped short and he was driven square for another boundary.

Charles Bell was given further cause for concern. Part of his mind was not in the game, but the part that was began to worry that he was not fulfilling his role whilst his partner evidently was. On the edge of turmoil luck came his way in the shape of a full toss from Stewart Thorogood. He hit it hard, but not perfectly and they ran two. Charles felt slightly better. He remained cautious, but added another single to his tally. It was not ostentatious, but it was a textbook cricket stroke. It made him feel better. Unhappily for him the feeling was short-lived.

The captain and bowler conferred. Dean and Colin agreed that four overs would suffice so that Dean could keep the others in reserve for later in the innings. So Colin was released to make a last effort for the time being. He put everything into it. The first ball whistled past off stump and Charles was wise to let it pass. He was less wise in addressing the second ball, playing a false shot which saw the ball narrowly slant across the stumps without hitting them and skew off in the direction of fine leg. Charles collected a couple. He left the third, made a mess of the fourth which was short and flew past his nose and failed to recognise the slower ball that followed. He played too soon and obligingly popped it into the hands of Dean Faulds at mid off. The Outcasts had got their first wicket. Martin Norwell clipped his first ball crisply for four past extra cover. Dean Faulds clapped his hand on Colin's shoulder and said, 'Well done, but we'll still keep you for later.'

By this time Arthur had returned from his mission and assured an anxious Simon that all was well with his car. He had a few words with Charlie and then found a place on the grass in front of the pavilion next to where Brian Stagden was lounging in readiness for the fall of the next wicket. There was a perfunctory greeting between them, but Arthur seemed to indicate that he was intent on watching the cricket and no more was said.

Keith Kirkham and Martin Norwell proceeded to give a demonstration of the benefit to the club of having relaxed the family-only qualification. Despite the lack of any responsiveness from the pitch or the conditions Dean Faulds persisted with a pace attack. Stewart Thorogood bowled one more over before being rested and was replaced at the pavilion end by Ray Burrill, who was asked to bowl his cutters. Nigel Redman was called on to follow Colin Banks at the river end. In fairness to Dean his bowlers did not let him down, but at best theirs was a containment exercise. There was no sign of penetration. The batsmen looked entirely at ease even if Michael Carter might have wished for an acceleration of the scoring rate. The end of the partnership when it came was therefore entirely unexpected.

Keith Kirkham and Martin Norwell had seemed in no hurry. The scoring rate was not lifted above four an over until the fifty mark had been passed in the fourteenth over. The asking rate had risen to over nine runs an over. Martin must have been doing some mental arithmetic, because fifteen runs came off the next two overs all from his own bat. He and Keith Kirkham exchanged a word and to general surprise Ray Burrill, who to that point had bowled his first three overs for only twelve runs, was hit for two massive sixes by Keith. The first of these brought up the fifty partnership. The effect of the second was to enliven the spectators and there was a rustle of expectation around the ground.

These had been classily executed shots and so what happened next was a disappointment to supporters of the home side. Ray Burrill was an intelligent bowler. He weighed his options before trying his Bedser ball. Ray had recently read an account of the feats of the great Surrey and England bowler, A. V. Bedser. He had been especially impressed by the performance of Sir Alec (as he became) against the Australians at Nottingham in the Ashes year of 1953. His most potent weapon had been a fast leg cutter. Ray had been experimenting. His hands, although not petite, were not as large as those of the legendary Sir Alec. However, he was smarting from the indignity of being hit for successive sixes. So he thought there was not a lot to lose. He wrapped his hand round the ball and steadied himself to bowl again to the now seemingly rampant Keith Kirkham. Ray could see as he ran in what the batsman's intention clearly was. He did not change his plan. Whatever Keith had expected he did not get. He tried to swing the ball to the leg side, but its speed and turn outwitted him. Middle and off stumps were disturbed. Keith looked back with incredulity. His next action was a nod in Ray's direction as he began his walk back to the pavilion.

'Wow,' said Brian Stagden as he climbed to his feet, 'I hope he can't bowl too many like that.' Probably not, thought Arthur, but he was not going to impart any intelligence to the opposition. Keith came off to generous applause and Brian set off to take his place. Arthur waited until he had taken half a dozen steps before calling after him. 'By the way, Brian, Kenneth sends his best.' Brian stopped as if hit by a thunderbolt. He turned to look back at Arthur with his face creased in anger. But then he had little option except to move forward. 'What was that all about?' asked John Furness, who was standing nearby. 'Just making a friendly connection,' replied Arthur. 'Brian didn't seem to be taking it that way.' 'No, he didn't, did he?' said Arthur with the suspicion of a smile. He had in fact been delighted with Brian's reaction. He felt he had hit the bull's-eye. If so, he hoped that it might have a secondary effect.

Martin Norwell had not heard the exchange between his incoming partner and Arthur. He did not understand what had caused Brian to stop in his tracks and nor was there time, even if he had thought it relevant, to ask him. He and Brian had scored many runs for Middle Daychurch since being admitted to the ranks. He reckoned they worked well as a pair. Yet there was not the usual sign of recognition when Brian arrived in the middle. He walked past him and got on with the business of taking guard. With only a swift look at the field settings he signalled that he was ready to take strike. Martin noted that he wore a surly expression. He was unsure whether this was directed towards the bowler or sprang from some hidden preoccupation. Brian saw out the two remaining balls of the over like an automaton. So forbidding was his appearance that Martin avoided going up to him as the bowling changed ends.

Up to this point Dean Faulds had maintained a fairly orthodox approach to the marshalling of his bowling attack. His next ploy was therefore unexpected. Instead of one of his two off spinners and despite one of them (David Pelham) ostentatiously going through warming-up exercises Dean decided to give Richard Furness a bowl. Richard was an enthusiastic young cricketer who had often – when he had been available – enlivened Outcasts' matches with his batting and bowling. Equally often he had demonstrated that he was up with the best in terms of the off-pitch activities of members of the club. Dean was backing a hunch. Richard had not previously played against Middle Daychurch. Maybe he could turn out to be a surprise element in the game. For his part Richard was keen to complement his cameo performance with the bat. He bowled left-handed without imparting great spin on the ball, but he had variations in flight which made him a useful performer at this level of cricket. His surprise delivery was the chinaman which he used sparingly and only when he was feeling on top of his game. His first delivery to Martin Norwell was close to the bottom of his game, a rank long hop which gave the batsman all the time in the world to despatch it where he wanted. It was an inauspicious start for Richard, but he quickly bounded back forcing Martin to play defensive strokes. These were followed by a forcing single which Brian

Stagden had to hurry to complete. Richard felt already in rhythm. He gave the ball to Brian some air and was amazed when he did no more than prod forward to it. There was enough on the ball to carry back comfortably to the bowler. Brian departed with an expletive, marching back to the pavilion noticeably faster than he came to the wicket. He was not a happy man.

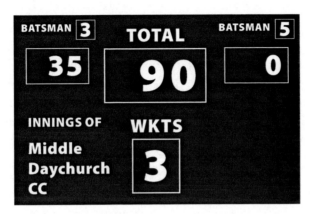

Brian's mood contrasted with that of Arthur, who had watched his performance with interest and some satisfaction. He moved from his position by the pavilion to conceal himself in a group of spectators. Brian tore into the pavilion and Arthur had a sudden inkling as to what might follow. Within minutes Brian rushed out of the pavilion still wearing his cricket top, but matched now with cord jeans. He made for the car park where Arthur was already crouching in the Crossleys' car. He wondered whether the effect of his words would cause Brian to head towards the Sunnyrest Residential Care Home, but that was not the direction he took. In fact he went no great distance, pulling up outside a cottage half a mile beyond Far Daychurch. Arthur went by, found somewhere to turn round and then went slowly past without stopping but with time to note the address. He nodded. It was no real surprise.

By the time that Arthur was back at the cricket ground the Middle Daychurch score had moved on to 119–3. Martin Norwell and Richard Love, who had begged to be given a chance to bat higher up the order, had begun to repair the damage done by the fall of two quick wickets. It was a rebuilding exercise that was progressing too well for Dean Faulds' taste. He had relied on a combination of Richard Furness, Ray Burrill and David Pelham, but was contemplating mixing things up by the reintroduction of either Colin or Stewart. He had conspicuously not used Basil Smith so far, perhaps recalling that Basil's six overs a year ago had cost 60 runs. He had first of all instructed Ray to revert to off spin. Yet there had been no evidence from the pavilion end of any irregular behaviour from the pitch to encourage either turn or lift. He told Stewart to warm up and take a turn at the river end after Richard's next over. However, before the time came he had a change of heart.

Shirley Simpson had enjoyed her afternoon in the sun with the Outcasts' ladies. It had been the nearest to normal she had felt in a long time. They had finished clearing up after tea and were sitting in a group on the grass. Shirley had positioned herself so that she could keep an eye on Richard. He seemed to be doing well, she thought, even if she did not fully understand the game of cricket. Kevin Newton's girlfriend, Gloria Lockwood, was a relative newcomer to the Outcasts' circle. Her relationship with Kevin was the deciding factor in persuading her to take a new post with a law firm in London. She had strengthened their international section specialising in her native Caribbean and the southern United States. She was being asked about some of the more sensational aspects of her caseload when she let slip the name Dick Grant.

Shirley froze, all thought of Richard and cricket forgotten. 'Did you say Dick Grant?' Gloria looked at her wondering if she might have been indiscreet in referring to a particular person, but was intrigued by Shirley's interest. She confined herself to saying that in her experience Dick Grant was a very dubious character whom she suspected of being linked to violent criminals. The colour drained from Shirley's face. 'I must go home,' she gasped. In response to questioning she did not want to elaborate. She just repeated, 'I must go.' She looked so agitated that Liz Colson called across to Charlie to tell him to escort her whilst Richard was otherwise engaged.

Greg Roberts was sorry not to see Pete Simmonds in the Middle Day-church line-up to meet the Outcasts. He was curious to know just how good Pete was as a cricketer. After tea he had decided to stroll down the road if only to say hello, but also on the off-chance of further news about the chef who had disappeared soon after the disastrous evening when Paul Carter had died. His mission was in vain. Le Rêve Royal was catering for a wedding party. Greg could see that there was no easy way of penetrating the throng let alone disturbing Pete in his kitchen where doubtless he would be working flat out. Greg took a few minutes to study out of no more than idle curiosity the gaggle of guests (the smokers) who were standing outside the restaurant. Then he began to walk back entertaining the thought that he might sneak in an early pint at The Cow's Corner. This was how he came to be involved in the high drama that was to unfold in Cricketers Close.

With hindsight Richard Furness's fifth over could be seen as a turning-point in the match. It had cost three runs, but the strokes which had led to them were all false. Suddenly the pitch had shown some response or Richard had added some devilish ingredient to his bowling. Dean had a word with Richard and David. It was agreed that the right tactic was to persevere with spin. Stewart was advised that his reintroduction to the attack was to be postponed. In the event the postponement was of short duration. Whether too much was expected of him or whether he expected too much of himself David Pelham's third over was a serious disappointment. The batsmen had also been considering their situation. To win the home side required 175 runs with 14 overs left. This was a scoring rate of over two runs a ball. Over the years many a side that had played the Outcasts would not have regarded such an equation as daunting. The evidence of one over was not sufficient to conclude that there had been a sudden deterioration in the state of the pitch, but Martin and Richard agreed to launch a pre-emptive strike. David Pelham was first in line. Without anything in the pitch to help him counteract the assault David suffered.

Martin began with a towering straight six which brought him his fifty. He followed it with another and should have added a four, but was restricted to three after a fine piece of fielding by Ray Burrill. It was then Richard's turn. He lacked the brute strength shown by his partner, but was pleased with three successive boundaries. The score leapt by 27 runs. Richard Furness had to be given another over. It was soon apparent that what had happened in his previous over had been no fluke. He should have had Martin Norwell caught at slip, but Dean had not posted one. This was immediately corrected, but Martin got off strike with a single. For Richard Love the boundaries he had enjoyed in David Pelham's over became a distant memory as he fought to keep his wicket intact. Dean Faulds then reverted to his original plan and gave the next over to Stewart, but at the pavilion end. It was during this over that the calm of the occasion was loudly disturbed.

Throughout the afternoon Joyce Simpson had grieved. She was relieved to be on her own so that Shirley could not see the agony which she was suffering. She now knew that nothing would ever be the same again. Precisely how she had come to be cast into such a dark abyss she could not comprehend. What she had gleaned from riffling through her visitor's briefcase had nevertheless revealed the terrible essentials. Frank was dead and it cannot have been a pleasant death. Shirley was at risk. Joyce herself and her home were targeted. Frank had known the whereabouts of something they wanted. Perhaps they had killed him without getting the information from him and were now trying to work it out by elimination. Cold anger surged inside her challenging the pain. Having thought long and hard, she had remembered to remove from the safe a letter which Frank had placed there to be opened only after his death. She read it as calmly as she could and then prepared.

When she saw the vehicle with its blacked-out windows approach she opened the front door and left it ajar. She took a seat opposite the living room entrance and waited for the bell to ring. 'Come in,' she called, 'it's open.' 'I'm sorry to have taken so long.' He appeared smiling in the doorway carrying his case. He was still smiling when Joyce shot him. The scream came from Shirley seeing the black vehicle, hearing the shot and putting what she thought was two and two together. She stumbled towards her home with Charlie by her side. As they got to the gate they heard a sound behind them. The car door slammed shut and stepping towards them was a brutal looking man waving a heavy pistol. 'Keep moving,' he snarled. Terrified and reluctant, Shirley and Charlie did keep moving, but as slowly as they dared. Once they had reached the threshold they and the man threatening them could see that the person lying half in and half out of the living room was male. The man with the pistol pinioned Shirley to him, told Charlie to sit on the floor and shouted an order towards the interior. 'Come out with your hands up, Mrs Simpson. I'm holding your daughter and I won't hesitate to . . .' At that point words failed him.

The cricketers had not allowed their match to be affected by noises off. Stewart Thorogood had completed his return over. It had not been particularly distinguished, leaving his captain's hopes unfulfilled. Nevertheless Dean still had reasonable grounds for believing that the match might be tilting in the Outcasts' direction. Their opponents had only 11 overs left in which to get another 137 runs. It was a big ask. Dean was all too aware that it was a challenge that had not proved beyond other sides which the Outcasts had played. True, they had been more disciplined and determined in their approach to the match on this occasion, but Martin Norwell had always seemed to display a liking for their bowling. He could see no alternative to Richard Furness using up his allocation and hopefully getting some reward for what had seemed a steadily improving spell. He had just two overs left and begged Dean to give him an attacking field. Dean was persuaded to take the risk.

Whilst to all outward appearances the disturbance had had no effect on the match Richard Love's imagination had gone to work. He had noticed that Shirley had left the ground in the company of Charlie Colson. He was very ready to accept that a gun had been fired. If it was a farmer shooting, he would have expected further shots. He persuaded himself that the sound had come from the direction of Cricketers Close. Where else would Shirley have been heading? Then there was the scream. What had that been all about? Had that swarthy Italian turned up again? Richard was torturing himself. Inevitably his concentration was being eroded. He played a false shot to his namesake's first ball and was lucky to get away with it. Momentarily reality asserted itself. His side needed runs. He wound himself up and sent the next ball soaring over mid wicket. That was the way to do it. Richard Furness kept him waiting as he had a word with Dean to be sure of maintaining his field settings. It was time enough for doubts to assail Richard Love once again. His next stroke was half-hearted. It was a quicker ball which took the edge of his bat. It sent straight to second slip where it was fumbled by Jon Palmer. Martin imperiously called for a run, sensing that he needed to get his partner off strike.

Martin Norwood recognised that the charge had to begin if Middle Daychurch were to maintain their winning record against the Outcasts. To counter the spin he came down the wicket to meet the bowler's next delivery on the full. It went straight for six. His appetite was whetted, but Richard Furness did not flinch. He read Martin's mind and defeated him in the air as he charged forward. The stumping was easy. Next in was Michael Carter. If ever there was need for a captain's innings the moment had come. The field was unchanged for the new batsman and Michael played the last ball of the over with ultra caution. On a whim Dean changed his bowling again. He felt he could not leave Basil Smith out altogether. David Pelham had achieved nothing and Stewart Thorogood's over had cost ten runs. So Dean reckoned he could afford one over from Basil without throwing the game away. Basil's expression was very much 'about time too,' but he willingly cooperated with Dean in setting the field. 'A tight over, Basil, that's all I ask.' But it was not quite what he got.

Greg Roberts was not the only witness to the crisis which erupted in Cricketers Close. To describe him as a witness was only an approximate use of the word. At the sound of the shot Greg had darted behind the large parked vehicle so that it was between him and the action. He had thought it was unoccupied and so it was a shock when he heard the passenger door

open and someone get out. He raised his head, but through the darkened windows all he could make out was a silhouette. It then occurred to him that there could be another passenger inside and so he ducked down below the window line and missed the next development in the drama.

A much better view was had by Harry Northwood from the vantage point of the front bedroom of 11 Cricketers Close. He showed a capacity for instant thinking and immediate action. Wearing socks and very little else, but crucially carrying his bat he emerged silently and speedily from the next door property. With a stroke he was apt to demonstrate whenever he had an appreciative audience he slammed his bat into the side of the head of the man with the gun.

Charlie Colson was almost as stunned as the man who had sunk to his knees and toppled to the floor. However, he had recovered his presence of mind sufficiently to take possession of the gun which had fallen from the man's grasp. He was then to suffer two further shocks. The first was to see the near naked figure of Harry Northwood, who, seemingly oblivious of the extent of the danger, was grinning from ear to ear. The second shock came later. Practical considerations prevailed. 'This guy needs tying up,' said Charlie. 'Is there a washing line or some rope in this house?' This question was addressed to Shirley, who had been rooted to the spot her eyes staring horror-struck. Charlie's words brought her to life, but her reaction was on a different plane. 'I must find Mummy.' She struggled over the man lying in the living room doorway. The force of the bullet at short-range had turned him over and he had fallen face first. The gun from which the shot had presumably come was conspicuously on the seat of a chair. Of the person who had used the gun there was no sign. Shirley flew around the house in ever-increasing panic, but her mother and for that matter anyone else was nowhere to be found.

Meanwhile Greg had emerged from where he had been lurking behind the four-wheel drive vehicle. He looked with some surprise at Harry who was on his way to the next-door house to recover his clothing. He looked remarkably cheerful, but Greg's expression told him that he would have some explaining to do at close of play. At the front door Greg found Charlie struggling with a length of rope he had found in the utility room in his efforts to render incapable a man on the floor who was starting to stir. Stirring was an activity beyond the capacity of the other person who lay prostrate half-in and half-out of the living room of 10 Cricketers Close. Greg came to Charlie's assistance and between them they bound the ankles and wrists of the man who was returning (thankfully for Harry's sake, thought Charlie) to consciousness. 'Shirley's in a terrible state,' said Charlie to Greg, but Greg had already been made aware of this by the sound of alternate wailing and sniffles coming from inside the house. They were supplemented by low moans and indications that she was missing her mother.

In these extraordinary circumstances it was Greg who had the presence of mind to understand that the house was a crime scene. He had the sense to warn against touching the body, because that was what he was sure it was. In any case an ambulance would be needed as well as the police. He realised that all three of them needed to be outside the house to avoid further contamination. They could keep an eye on the man they had tied up from the vantage point of the pathway. About to make a 999 call they were taken aback to see a police car come slowly to a halt in front of the large black vehicle. PC Eric Hillgate introduced himself with the words, 'I thought I might drop round for a cup of tea with your mother, but I see she may have visitors.' That was one way of putting it, thought Greg, but what he said was, 'Actually she's out, but I'm afraid there seems to be a bit of a situation here.' Whilst he was explaining this Charlie was trying to give sufficient care and attention to Shirley to avoid her having further hysterics or blurting out any unfortunate comments. Greg went on, 'We think someone had broken into the house. We were just coming back here. We managed to get the better of one man, but I think the other one might have been dead before we got here. We were just going to ring the police.'

Eric Hillgate just stopped himself saying, 'I'm glad you didn't.' Not much happened on his beat, if you discounted the series of deaths in the Carter family. Now he was confronted with what seemed like a major incident. If what these people were telling him was true, he would need back up, but for the moment he was the man in charge. He felt an overwhelming need to assess the situation before he put in a call to HQ. 'You say you got the better of one of the intruders. What exactly do you mean by that?' 'He's tied up,' said Greg. 'Securely?' asked the constable. 'As well as we could,' was all that Greg could say. With only that slight reassurance the officer went cautiously down the path his truncheon in hand. He could see a man writhing about and starting to find his voice, but he still seemed to be tightly bound. What he could see of the other person did suggest lifelessness, but Eric Hillgate had had no real-life experience of a dead body. He would like to have satisfied himself that there was no-one else on the premises, but he did know that he would be in trouble with the scene of crime experts if he disturbed anything. Believing that he was in command of the essentials he radioed in to HQ. He had hard work convincing the duty sergeant that this was for real.

After he had safely negotiated his first ball Michael Carter trotted up the wicket to have a word with cousin Richard. 'OK, mate?' he asked and saw immediately that Richard, despite being 37 runs to the good, was far from OK. 'What's up?' Richard said, 'I know you're going to think this sounds daft, but I'm worried for Shirley. That shot. It sounded like a gun to me. She's disappeared with Charlie. Oh look, I can't explain everything that's been going on. But she could be in danger. Can I pull a sickie and then come back later if I'm needed. Although, if you ask me, we've got a bit of a mountain to climb.' Michael could see that Richard was shot through with nerves and not exactly looking in prime condition for scaling a mountain. 'You're batting well, mate,' he tried. 'We need you.' But he could see it was not working. He called to Dean Faulds. 'Sorry to ask this, but Richard here is in pain' – that seemed true enough – 'and would like a break if you'd allow it. He thinks he'll be OK after a couple of pills.' This last was pure invention on Michael's part, but Dean was feeling fairly good about things. Two new batsmen at the crease might play to the Outcasts' advantage. 'Sure,' he said and saw Richard depart at a surprising gallop for a man wracked with pain. One cousin gave way to a more distant one in the shape of David Carter.

Finally there was play. With another new batsman in the space of two balls Dean allowed Basil another close fielder. After the space of two more balls he began to entertain doubts. The first boundary was lucky, but the second came from a very firm drive. Dean looked across at Basil, but his bowler was unperturbed. He allowed no further liberties and it was just bad luck that the last ball of the over spun sharply beating both batsman and keeper. With the four byes conceded the total cost of the over amounted to twelve runs. Middle Daychurch were by no means out of it. Michael smiled. Dean frowned. As Richard Furness came up to bowl his final over Dean felt the need to impart his thoughts. 'Hopefully no more sixes and preferably a wicket.' Richard pursed his lips. 'As long as the guys take their catches, you never know.'

Harry Northwood found himself having to make a tricky explanation to Jenny Seymour. It had been an extraordinary juxtaposition of events: an intimate afternoon and involvement in murder. Jenny had heard the shot and had seen PC Hillgate's car roll up. Harry thought he should be sparing with the details of what happened in between. 'There's a way out of here through the garden, isn't there?' 'Yes, but.' 'I think,' said Harry, 'I should get back now to watch the cricket and act normal. Better you stay here. There's no need for you to be involved. If there's anything wrong,' he quickly added seeing the expression on Jenny's face, 'I'm sure that policeman will sort it all out.' Harry did not like abandoning his friends, but could not see how they could be in any trouble. It was only a few minutes after he was back in the ground and could hear the siren of an emergency vehicle that Harry remembered abandoning something more than his friends at number 10. The thought was put out of his mind when he saw Richard Love emerge furtively from the pavilion. 'You out already,' said Harry almost too eagerly. He received no answer, because Richard wanted to know from him if he had seen Shirley. 'Yes,' said Harry, 'she's fine. She's at home.' Harry knew this was a supreme case of economy with the truth, but he could see no advantage in Richard further complicating the fraught situation in Cricketers Close.

Meanwhile another wicket had fallen. It became very clear during Richard Furness's final over that the pitch at that end was giving him considerable help. Michael Carter felt that he could not just poke and prod. That way he was more likely to get an edge, but in any case caution would not produce the runs that were badly needed. So he was going to go for it. With close fielders around the bat there were gaps to exploit. He did not get full strength behind a pull shot off the first ball of the over, but they ran three. David played and missed at his first ball, but collected two from the next. Richard had an lbw shout turned down off his fourth delivery and then had the satisfaction of bowling David with a peach of a ball. Adrian Seymour was carded to be next man in and duly arrived to take David's place. In the unexpected absence of Richard Love Michael was thinking that a big hitter such as Lee Lingrove had occasionally proved he might have been promoted. The situation was quickly corrected when Adrian edged his first ball to slip where Toby Lederwood took a neat catch. Richard Furness had done his team proud with a return of 4–39.

Before Richard Love lost patience and tried to tear himself away Harry had managed to attract the attention of Arthur, who hurried over. Harry then felt more confidence in releasing further information about what he had gathered from his bit-part performance at 10 Cricketers Close. He had to admit that Shirley was upset, but unharmed. He could tell that Richard was anxious to get to her, but he pointed out that with the police there no-one else would be allowed near. To his relief Arthur backed him up. Richard's stress level seemed to wane even though he did not know who had shot whom. In that respect Harry was in the same boat. He was aware that Shirley's mother was missing, but he reckoned that any mention of that would cause Richard to become agitated all over again. Arthur had just said, 'Let's see if we can rustle up a cup of tea' when they were made to move sharply into the pavilion by a warning shout. Lee Lingrove was on the attack.

Charlie Colson's second big shock of the afternoon since accompanying Shirley back home came when the police doctor carefully turned the body he was examining. Charlie, Greg and Shirley had been required to stand outside whilst the house was subjected to close examination. From the pathway Charlie had no difficulty in recognising the dead man once he had sight of his face. 'Good God,' he exclaimed, 'That's Roy Groves.' Shirley craned her neck. 'No, it's not,' she said, 'It's Dick Grant.'

Detective Inspector Pritchard, who was standing nearby, pricked up his ears. 'The documentation on him says he's called Groves from a firm called Turnbury, Lomax and something.' Shirley retorted indignantly, 'I've got good cause to know him as Dick Grant and he isn't, er wasn't, a very nice man.' The Inspector appeared more interested than dismissive and stepped back into the house. His interest stemmed from his awareness that the injured man, who had been carted off to hospital under police escort, was an Italian villain called Roberto Dumtani who was connected with unsolved crimes in many countries. A police officer proceeded to take statements from the two Outcasts and a female colleague spoke to Shirley. The three of them had had time to prepare. So when the Inspector came out of the house carrying a bloodied cricket bat and asked, 'Whose is this?' it was Greg who raised his hand.

226

Lee Lingrove had very cheerfully accepted instructions from his captain that he had licence to slog. The asking rate if his team was to win had risen to over thirteen runs an over. It only needed a few bad balls an over and a sufficient number of boundaries could easily come. Anyone who had played against the Outcasts would know that this was not a remote hope. The part of the pitch to which Basil Smith was bowling from the pavilion end was now starting to exhibit some inconsistency which might help a spinner. It took Michael Carter two balls to bring Lee Lingrove on strike. It took Lee two balls to hit his first six, but his second big hit bounced before crossing the boundary. Middle Daychurch passed 200. With the pitch giving help to spin David Pelham thought that he might take over from Richard Furness at the river end and was disappointed when Dean opted instead for Ray Burrill. 'Mix it up, Ray,' advised Dean knowing Ray's two different styles. And Ray did, but not quite in the way Dean had intended. The mix was of the unplayable deliveries and the rank bad. Even though he conceded 11 runs Ray consoled himself with the realisation that Middle Daychurch's task had become tougher still. It was now 14 runs an over.

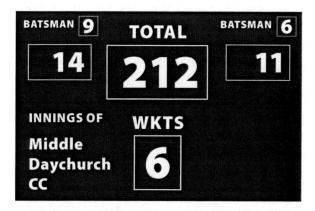

Any excitement to be derived from a closely fought cricket match approaching a climax in which either side could be victor was not being shared by Arthur. On another day he might have been absorbed by the situation, but since he had been back from tailing Brian Stagden he had been lost in his own thoughts. He wanted to share them with Charlie, David and Rash, but all were otherwise engaged. He studied Michael Carter from afar and recollected his demeanour throughout the match. Arthur believed himself to be a good judge of character. It was hard for him to accept that Michael was a killer. Yet the possibility could not be ruled out. If Michael possessed the information which Arthur had acquired, the killing might not be over or the deaths up to now would have had no purpose. However, if Michael was in ignorance of what Arthur had discovered, those other deaths could be down to him in the belief that come the deadline (now only about eighteen hours away) he would inherit the bulk of his grandfather's estate. If Michael was an innocent man and had no knowledge of the unexpected, Arthur thought that he was wearing the prospect of great wealth with impressive composure. At that point Arthur's attention was caught by the return of Brian Stagden. Arthur could not resist greeting him. 'All well?' 'Very well indeed,' came the reply. 'Why wouldn't it be?' Arthur sighed. There was still so much to work out.

Detective Inspector Pritchard had reached much the same conclusion. He had the satisfaction of knowing that two hitherto successful criminals were dead and another was in custody. However, if they had been responsible for the crimes he had them marked down for, he still had to find out where the proceeds of their operations could be located. Who had killed the man who called himself Groves or Grant? Where was the widow of Frank Simpson? She had disappeared without trace. What had brought the two crooks to her property? Was she in on the racket? The contents of the dead man's briefcase gave food for thought. Certain matters would have to be followed up, but otherwise he could see no significance in the property where the shooting had taken place. What was he to make of the three young people who had been encountered by PC Hillgate? The girl's photograph was one of the many items in the briefcase. She had given an account of how she had been weaned away from her mother towards whom she swore she had no animosity. The Inspector had a daughter Shirley's age and he judged her to be an ordinary kind of girl who had been cruelly seduced by the promise of high living. As to the young men he thought their story held up. The one guy had certainly committed a vigorous assault, but it seemed clear it had been done to save his friends. For the life of him the Inspector could see no ulterior motive. The assault would have to be reported, but he doubted there would be a charge.

The matter appeared to be sealed when one of his officers returned from knocking on doors to report that a young girl had offered a statement. She had been in her bedroom doing her nails – some euphemism – when the sound of a shot had brought her to the window. She was able to say that she had seen a man and a girl approach from one direction and a second man coming up the road from the direction of the restaurant. As the couple had gone towards the front door of number 10 a man with a gun had got out of the big black car and chased after them. Then the other man chased after him.

And that was all that she had seen till a police car arrived. Was everything all right? The officer was sent back to invite the young girl to step along to the neighbouring house. Jenny Seymour was able to identify Shirley, Charlie and Greg as the people she'd seen. The inspector thanked her for coming forward and added, 'Just for clarification, Miss, the young man coming up the road was carrying a cricket bat?' Charlie intoned a silent prayer as after no more than the slightest hesitation Jenny supplied a beautifully crafted answer. 'I suppose that's what it was.' Inspector Pritchard thought to himself much later why anyone would have taken his bat with him when going for a walk. You never knew with people who were besotted with cricket, he concluded. However, at the time he could see no need to detain the trio any longer, but warned that they might be required to give evidence at a later date. Seeing Shirley's distressed state he said, 'We'll do our very best to find your mother.' He concealed his ulterior motive, being unable to rule out Joyce Simpson as the person who had shot Roy Groves. He knew how strong her motive would have been. Charlie and Greg walked with Shirley back to the cricket ground. After disappearing into her house, Jenny took the garden route to the cricket. She was very keen to see Harry again.

Shirley's reunion with Richard was delayed. After his speedy recovery he was on his way to resume his innings as Shirley entered the ground. The match could still go either way. Basil Smith had at last got one to turn and lift. Michael Carter was caught in what Basil called his leg trap. Both he and Dean thought this was the crucial wicket. However, the remainder of the over had been a bruising experience. No sixes maybe, but a flurry of fours as Tom Carter, determined to be the equal of Lee, carved and scythed with some skill and a lot of luck. At the end of the thirty-fifth over Middle Daychurch needed 67 runs off 30 balls. Although Ray Burrill was hit for two sixes by Lee Lingrove his quicker ball accounted for him. Syd Breakwell gave the lbw shout in his favour although a keener eye might have judged that the ball would have passed over the stumps. It was at this point that Richard Love re-entered the fray. He took guard and surveyed the field. When he also surveyed Shirley he felt his heart and his spirits leap. He took up his stance at the crease and told himself to concentrate. He put bat firmly to ball and added seven runs to the total.

In the course of Basil's fourth over Dean Faulds' faith in the theory that spin would win the match began to ebb. Despite the fact that the pitch was now definitely 'doing something' the batsmen were doing a lot more, albeit by taking outrageous risks. Whether Tom Carter believed that he could be the hero and win the match for his team or whether he was keen to outgun cousin Lee was not the point. By the end of Basil's over which had seen four boundaries, a dropped catch and a near run-out Dean was well aware that if batsmen flashed hard at fast bowlers the ball could easily travel very fast to the boundary. However, Colin had seemed to be on song in his opening spell and not fretting for romance, real or imagined. He advised defensive field settings and urged his fastest bowler to 'spice it up'. The game had swung sharply in the home team's favour due to the aggression of the late-order batsmen now supplemented by a reinvigorated Richard Love. 28 runs off 18 balls were very gettable.

Perhaps advising Colin to spice it up had been encouragement too far. Colin's first ball was very fast and short-pitched. It flew far above Richard Love's head and from square leg Bert Love quite properly called it a wide. The next ball was a well-pitched-up thunderbolt which could not be stopped from crossing the boundary. Four byes accrued. Dean felt concern, but said nothing. A much better delivery followed. Richard let it pass, but fortunately for the Outcasts' cause Rashid Ali did not. A dot ball at last. Richard got his bat on the next and an easy single was taken. Tom Carter felt up for the challenge. Colin produced another express delivery. It was on a good length. A pedant might have said a little too full. However, any such nicety was not being factored in by Tom. He was just minded to hit it. It went like lightning straight back past the bowler and was not cut off. Four more runs. Dean could be seen frowning. The over had already cost ten runs. Next up Colin went for the short ball again. This time the ball flew high in the direction of third man. At first Dean feared it would go all the way for six which would have left Middle Daychurch needing only 12 runs from 13 balls. His judgement of distance proved to be false. Stewart Thorogood was on the boundary edge. It proved to be a perfect placement. Stewart possessed a reliable pair of hands and safely took the catch.

The batsmen had crossed and so Richard Love had the strike for the final ball of Colin's over. The Outcasts were aware that Clive Norrington could bat even though he was coming in at number eleven in this match. Eighteen runs off two overs was an achievable task. At least Colin ensured that only 12 balls remained available after he had produced a yorker which Richard Love could do no more than keep out of the stumps. Now Dean had to make a crucial decision. The last overs sent down by Basil Smith, David Pelham and Ray Burrill had all been extremely expensive. Richard Furness, the only spinner successfully to exploit the conditions, had used up his allocation. Even Stewart Thorogood's return over had cost ten runs.

So it was Nigel Redman, somewhat to his surprise, who was thrown the ball. 'Just keep it steady. That's all I ask,' said Dean. 'If they're going to get these runs let's make the buggers work for them.' It was not inspirational, but even so Nigel sensed the heavy burden of responsibility. He responded over and above his own expectation, let alone that of his captain. It was miserly bowling and a well-placed field complemented the bowler's efforts. Nigel gave away only three runs.

So then it came down to the last over. For Middle Daychurch the target was 15 runs away; for the Outcasts one wicket. The over began with Richard Love, his score on 46, pitted against Colin Banks. The first ball gave Richard too much width and he drove handsomely square for four. The crowd was fully engaged in the contest. Richard was cheered not just for the shot, but also for attaining a half-century. Eleven off five balls. The next ball had less width and more pace. It defeated Richard and went through to the keeper. Eleven off four balls. Now it was getting really tight. There were cries of 'Come on, Richard'. Colin came charging in again. The ball pitched on leg stump. Richard got bat on it, but without any timing. They ran two, turned for a third, but thought better of it. Nine off three. Both batsmen and bowler were feeling the pressure. Richard doubted he could hit a six off Colin unless he got a short ball. Even then he had witnessed the downfall of Tom Carter. He knew he must get a four off the next ball. He prepared himself for a forcing stroke. The ball was fast, but short and pitched just outside the line of off stump. Richard aimed to smash it square, but the ball was too close to him for the shot. All he succeeded in doing was diverting it into his stumps. The game was over. The Outcasts had finally beaten Middle Daychurch. Dean hugged Colin and the other Outcasts gathered around him. The margin may have been only eight runs, but it was worth a major celebration.

Close of play

Richard Love was a hero in one person's eyes. As he came off the field any disappointment he felt over failing to carry his team over the finishing line was swept away by the embrace of Shirley. He needed to hear from her exactly what had happened. She was only too keen to tell all. But first there had to be handshakes between the players, congratulations and consolations in the respective changing rooms and showers. There would be much to talk about in a session of indeterminate length in The Cow's Corner. The Outcasts, who had played, unlike a few of their non-playing comrades who had managed 'the odd pint' during the afternoon 'but only after tea,' would be kept waiting for their refreshment. Arthur had asked everyone to gather in the changing-room. He had spared the ladies the indignity of the Outcasts in various states of undress, but had already heard from those who had picked up anything that might have been helpful as they had mixed with the Middle Daychurch support group.

'Well done guys,' said Dean after calling for order. 'That's a first under our belt. We'll talk later, but for now Arthur's got something to say.' In his suit in the middle of changing-room chaos Arthur cut an incongruous figure. Whether he saw it as his Hercule Poirot moment was hard to say. He began. 'When you acquainted me with this strange story my instinct told me Charlie was right.' Charlie barely reacted. He was now in aftershock following what he regarded as his near-death experience in Cricketers Close. Arthur kept going. 'There was no obvious sign of a family feud consistent with multiple killings. Arguments about the cricket club maybe. Petty jealousies possibly. But, if you were prepared to kill so many people, there had to be a motive, a really powerful motive. And, if there was deliberate intent behind all those deaths, you have to recognise that a lot of careful planning was done, and maybe the odd risk taken, to make them all look accidental.' 'But what about Philip Carter?' interposed Rash. 'That was proved to be the result of heart failure.' 'I know,' said Arthur, 'but just hear me out. Let's stick with the deliberate murder theory for a moment. If you're planning to bump off three or four people and one of them accidentally dies, it not only saves you some trouble, but it gives you a devilish opportunity. As the body count increases and someone, anyone, starts to get suspicious you can arrange an anonymous call to the police alleging foul play in the one case where you know there wasn't any. So after the police have dug up one body and all suspicion of the man being poisoned or whatever has been conclusively removed, there would be less of a rush on their part to accept any fancy theory about the next victim.

'So, if these were murders, who had most to gain from them? Once we had learned the contents of Edwin Carter's will, and strange they were too, the finger pointed at Michael Carter. With all Edwin's sons dead the estate passed to Michael. Yet those of you who've got to know him best find it very difficult to see in him a cold-blooded killer. And now as a result of information picked up in the course of today it would seem that he has alibis for two of the deaths. He's a teacher and when the vicar drowned and George Carter was felled by falling stonework he was far away from here on school duties.' 'He could have had an accomplice,' said Harry. 'Yes,' said Arthur, 'but you've then got to start working out who that might be and anyway I don't think that's the answer.' 'Wait a minute,' said Tom Redman, 'Are you now saying that the vicar was bumped off as well?' 'I'll come to that in a minute,' replied Arthur. 'One other thing. Don't forget Michael's accident on the ski slopes. It was either an accident or someone was trying to cover every angle.

'If we say for the sake of argument that Michael is not the guilty party, you could come back to the conclusion that there has been a most remarkable string of accidents and misfortunes.' 'Is that it?' asked a surprised Colin. 'No, Colin, I don't actually think it is. You see, the other factor in all of this is the will. It's very unusual in the way it's constructed and so when the potential beneficiaries are departing the scene one by one, taking the two things together it's very suspicious. I'm surprised that the police never at any moment looked at it that way.' 'But still you're saying it's not Michael,' said Stewart. 'I found it difficult to believe it was Michael and now I'm sure it wasn't,' countered Arthur. 'At first it was only a gut feeling about him, but even so with Rash's help I began to pursue a new line of thought. Could Edwin have had another child?'

At that moment Arthur's performance, as it was later christened, was interrupted by a loud banging on the door. 'Are you guys coming to the pub or not? Being beaten by you lot means payback in pints. If you're not down there soon the Jugglers (the current guest beer) will be gone.' Dean answered. 'Sorry, Michael, we just had something to sort out. We shan't be long. First round's on us.' 'And some,' came the reply. 'We'll escort your ladies down there, shall we?' A sense of guilt overcame Dean. 'Yes, thank you that would be kind.' 'I don't get it,' said Michael, 'some of you haven't even been playing. Is it manicure time in there?' 'Very funny, but don't fuss yourself, Michael, it won't take us long to catch you up.' On that note the exchange ended. Dean turned to Arthur. 'It's a great tale you're telling, but I think you're going to have to speed it up. Now what's this about an Edwin Carter love-child?'

Arthur drew breath. 'Edwin had an affair before he was married. He was engaged when it happened and married when the woman found she was pregnant. She kept the fact from Edwin, fearing he would want her to have an abortion. Equally she felt she could not bring up the child in the village. Her brother, now deceased by the way, found a couple in the next village who had not been able to have any children of their own. So the child – it was a boy – was brought up by them. They were paid some money to go away from the area. Out of sight, out of mind. Years passed. Edwin's wife, Mary, produced four children for him. The mother of the child born out of wedlock was not so fecund. After she had married she was beset by miscarriages and remained childless. She outlived her husband and Edwin outlived his wife. They had kept themselves apart as far as possible, but when the woman was thinking of allowing some land to be used for a football club Edwin moved in on her. To scotch the deal he proposed marriage.

'Hang on a minute,' said Charlie Colson beginning to stir. 'That sounds familiar. I was told about that. It was purely a cynical ploy on Edwin's part. He never meant it.' 'I don't know about that,' said Arthur. 'It may have been what he hoped, but the lady proved insistent, for marry they did, although they didn't exactly broadcast it. The marriage took place in secret. The vicar who conducted it knew and that is how at a later date his successor Garry Woodworth found out. The other person who was in on the secret was Roy Groves.' This produced another response from Charlie. 'But when I first met him he was the one who said it was no more than an engagement.' Arthur smiled. 'He might just have been keeping the secret when talking to a stranger, but from what I know of the man he might also have been covering his own interests. Anyway that's by the by. The act of marriage legitimised the son born out of wedlock. In later life his mother had been overtaken by remorse in respect of her own conduct and resentment towards Edwin that her son by him was unlikely to benefit from any of his wealth. By then she had discovered that the son had married and got a son of his own, a son,' said Arthur with dramatic emphasis, 'who I think you've all met.' That announcement set the room buzzing. So did what Arthur said next.

'I think, if I keep you from your beer much longer, I'm going to be in serious trouble and I don't think we should keep our hosts, not to mention our wives and girlfriends, waiting much longer. All I've said so far is verifiable fact. You can see how it creates another scenario for someone wanting to dispose of certain members of the Carter family who were, shall we say, in the way. After that we're back to speculation about what exactly happened. I've got my theory, but before I say any more I'll leave you with some time to ponder. Now go and get some ale down you.' There were some cries of 'Unfair' and 'You can't leave it like that'. It was a question from Charlie which Arthur was prepared to answer. 'Are we likely to see this grandson of Edwin's in the pub tonight? 'Very probably.' Then the call of the ale took over. The team completed their change with speed. Their thirst was supplemented by intense curiosity as they marched towards The Cow's Corner.

After some initial pleasantries and with his third pint in his hand Charlie Colson cornered Arthur. 'Come on,' he said, 'I'm the one who started this whole thing off. I think you could spare me a few more details. It was obviously Ethel Daniels that Edwin Carter got hitched to. Where is she now? I assume she's still alive?' 'Yes, but old and living where she's always lived. Despite the marriage neither party had any thought of living together.' 'So she traced her son?' 'I'm assuming so, but I think it may have been his wife who took up the running from there. And then his son became involved. If anyone did what I might delicately refer to as the legwork, I feel sure it was him. But, Charlie, there's no real evidence.' 'All right, so who is it? The son, I mean.' 'Haven't you guessed? It had to be one of the outsiders.' 'Brian Stagden?' 'Of course. You should have seen how he reacted when I mentioned the name of his father. The fact that I knew of him must have come as a nasty shock.' Arthur went on to tell Charlie about his visit to Sunnyrest Residential Home to check for himself the person whose existence he had traced. He had been disappointed to be denied the opportunity to obtain some possibly damaging evidence from the man, but then again he was not absolutely sure that the plot would have been known to him. 'Phew,' announced Charlie, 'I need another beer. Can I get you something?' And then he made for the bar. While he waited to order he found himself standing next to none other than Brian Stagden.

In another part of the bar Richard Love was trying to console Shirley Simpson. In a strange way the acute trauma of the afternoon had driven away the lingering effects of what had happened to her whilst under the influence of the associates of her father. She was becoming more composed and ready to concentrate on the questions which really mattered. Barring the matter of where she should sleep that night, Richard had no answers. 'We can put you up at our house until the police have done all they need to at yours. I guess you might not want to be there on your own. Someone could stay with you. Me even.' He squeezed her hand. Where her mother was and whether she was the person who had shot Roy Groves no-one knew. Some other person might have shot the supposed businessman and spirited away Joyce Simpson, but Richard himself feared that Joyce had done the deed and then fled. The police had not said whether there was any evidence of her having taken clothes with her. Presumably they were trying to establish whether anyone had seen her leave the house. Jenny Seymour had not been able to assist on that point.

Charlie found it hard to make light conversation with Brian Stagden as they waited at the bar to be served. The situation was eased when Pete Simmonds put in a surprise appearance. 'Shouldn't you be in your kitchen tonight?' queried Charlie. 'I thought you had a big do on and that's why you couldn't play.' 'It's a wedding,' said Pete. 'I've done my bit by now so I thought I'd come and see 'ow you lot were doing. I 'eard it were a good game. Maybe you were lucky I weren't playing. Oh, a pint if you're asking, but I mustn't be too long.' He then addressed Brian. ''Aven't seen you at ours lately. 'Ow's that glamorous mother of yours?' Brian muttered something about her being fine and Pete would see him soon enough. Then he got the attention of the bar staff. Charlie handed Pete a pint and stepped back with the other drinks. Out of Brian's earshot he said, 'Is he one of your regulars?' 'Used to be in a lot in the past. Not as much recently, but 'e'll come from time to time with 'is mum. I ain't sure if 'e brings 'er or she brings 'im. On 'is own 'e used to like chatting to the staff. I sometimes thought 'e batted on our side, if you take my meaning.' 'Including the kitchen staff?' asked Charlie on a sudden whim. ''E didn't discriminate,' said Pete with a laugh, 'but I 'ad to warn 'im off once or twice.' Seeing the look on Charlie's face, Pete laughed, put his hand on his arm and said, ''ygiene, you mug. What were you thinking?! Now, I'm looking for Michael.' And he pushed his way through the throng, still grinning.

Charlie rejoined Arthur with apologies for delay. 'Where were we?' 'I'm not sure there's much more I can offer,' said Arthur. 'But,' Charlie insisted, 'you haven't said how the other deaths fit in. George Carter, Garry Woodworth and, I suppose, Roy Groves.' 'You're not overlooking the fact that they had one thing in common, are you? The trust.' Recognition dawned on Charlie. Arthur continued. 'There were three original members of the trust. Ethel Daniels, George and Roy. It can only be guesswork, but George might have been getting uneasy about the series of deaths. Perhaps he'd started to think like you've been thinking. He may have voiced his concerns and been seen as a risk.' 'But is that a good enough reason to kill him?' 'It has been said of some murderers that they get a taste for it. Kill one, kill two and you've got no scruples left. I agree that killing George was marginal, but the killer had lost all inhibitions by then. The prize was getting nearer. Why risk George doing something stupid? Mind you, his death could still have been an accident. That's the trouble with the whole of this business. Having said that, I feel quite sure that Garry Woodworth's drowning was no accident.'

'Go on,' said Charlie. Arthur sipped his drink. 'I was uneasy when I heard about Garry. He may not have been confident in water, but you've got to do something damned stupid to put yourself at risk. How likely was that? Anyway I've done some checking and that stretch of the river is not known for dangerous currents. It was an entirely different risk to which Garry exposed himself. Oh, sorry, no pun intended.' Charlie obligingly smirked. 'Ethel Daniels had appreciated the discretion of Garry's predecessor in the matter of the secret marriage. She assumed the same quality in the man of the cloth who followed him. So he seemed to her an obvious choice to take George's place. Alas for her and in the end alas for him not all priests are saints. After he had moved into the vicarage Garry must have read himself into his brief, so to speak, to try to assess the money-raising potential amongst his parishioners. Somehow he found out about the secret marriage. His predecessor must have left a record of some kind. It seems that Garry's great skill in raising money was helped along by blackmail.

'Rash had a stroke of luck when he talked his way into the vicarage. He got hold of copies of letters which Garry had sent to certain people. His participation in the trust led to his knowing how much money was at stake. Combined with the secret of the marriage on which so much rested the temptation was too great for Garry. Unfortunately he did not realise the true nature of the people he was dealing with. They were in it too deep to have this glory-hunting vicar wreck it. If you'll forgive another pun, they made sure he ended up too deep.'

'So wait a minute,' said Charlie, 'does that mean they were also behind the death of Roy Groves?' 'Actually no,' Arthur replied. 'Roy was no threat to them. He was a member of the trust, because he was someone on whom Edwin relied for financial advice. The old man probably thought that Roy would guard his interests after he had been persuaded by Ethel to structure his will as he did and to create the trust. It's not even certain that Roy knew about the illegitimate child. No, Roy was mixed up in a much bigger set of dealings and it seems he got his comeuppance from a quite unexpected source. Anyway, there we are. If between us we've pieced together a true picture of what's been going on, there's nothing we can do about it. As I've said many a time there's no evidence to prove any of it. In a few hours' time Ethel's one and only offspring will inherit a great amount of wealth. Although it's been achieved at a terrible cost, she might see it in a perverted way as justice being done. Come to think of it though, Charlie, unlike you, she may have put it all down to coincidence. I think the scheming may have come from her daughter-in-law. You know what they say about the woman behind the man. Now get along, I've kept you from fraternising with the vanquished. You'd better get some more of that good ale inside you before we have to go.' Arthur looked at his watch. 'And that's before too long.'

Another hour was not too long. Charlie with the rest of the Outcasts did some mingling whilst keeping a wary eye on Brian Stagden. The atmosphere was jolly. Michael Carter said of the result that they wouldn't let the Outcasts do that again in a hurry. Dean asked if the fixture next time could be arranged nearer June or July and Michael promised to see what could be done. 'We'll give you more priority than Nudgworth. That I can guarantee.' Simon and Sophie collected Syd and took their leave. Dean could see that the ladies were looking ready to go. He recognised his duty to get everyone ready for departure. Not unusually Charlie and David Pelham were the last to place their empty glasses on the bar counter. 'Let's hope,' said David, who was also last to climb on board the coach, 'it'll be less than twelve months before we come to Middle Daychurch again.' In the event it was less than fifty minutes.

There had been no opportunity in the party atmosphere of The Cow's Corner to complete the report which Arthur had begun in the changing-room. On the journey back this responsibility was delegated to Charlie using the coach's PA system. With only the occasional correction or prompt from Arthur Charlie got through the rest of the story. When he finished there was a collective groan. One or two began to raise questions, but these had not gone far when a phone rang at the front of the coach. 'Could you answer it for me?,' said Arthur handing the instrument to Charlie. It was pure luck that Charlie gave no identification. He simply said, 'Hello'. The lady at the other end asked if that was Mr Lambourn to which, reasonably in the circumstances, Charlie gave the answer 'no' and was about to dismiss the call as being of a nuisance nature when the voice said, 'Perhaps you're one of his associates. Are you Mr Smith or Mr Payne?' Charlie was two thirds of the way into his denial, but had got no further than saying, 'Nor am I Mr Smith,' when he felt a hand on his arm. Arthur gestured to Charlie to put the phone to his mouth. 'Mrs Foxwell,' said Arthur, 'it's very difficult for me to speak to you at the moment as I'm at the wheel of my car. If I hand the phone back to my partner, Mr Payne, who fortunately is with me, would you mind talking to him? I mustn't be caught breaking the law, must I?' Charlie took over. By the time the phone was close to his ear the proprietor of Sunnyrest Residential Care Home was into her stride. '. . .awkward time to ring, but I felt you needed to know seeing how important it was. Poor dear gentleman. He was my star resident. So kind, so gentle.' There was clearly more to come, but Charlie, trying to keep his voice as grave as seven pints of beer would allow, cut in. 'What has happened, Mrs er Foxwell?' 'Why, the resident Mr Lambourn came to see. I hardly know how to break it to you.' And then with an interesting indication of her priorities, she continued, 'I don't know what I'm going to say to his wife. I mean, she knew he was a bit off-colour, but this'. 'This what?' asked Charlie. 'I thought I'd already said, the lovely gentleman has succumbed to the virus. He died twenty minutes ago. Now I'm sure he would have wanted to share some of his good fortune with Sunnyrest where he was so happy. I think Mr Lambourn . . .' But at this point Charlie cut off her hopes. So Kenneth Stagden was dead. The other deaths had served no wicked purpose. Michael Carter was after all the winner – with just a few hours to spare.

The cheers which had greeted this news were silenced by Rashid Ali rushing forward and shouting to Arthur to stop. Arthur brought the coach to a halt in a convenient lay-by. 'What on earth's the matter?' he demanded. 'I'm sorry,' said Rash, 'but there was another detail in Edwin Carter's will which I didn't mention because I didn't think it relevant. If when the stipulated period ended, no-one not even Michael was alive the estate would revert to the trust which could dispose of it by unanimous decision. Currently there is only one trustee, this Mrs Daniels, Brian Stagden's grandmother. Arthur, if all you have told us is true, then Michael is now in extreme danger. We must warn him. Charlie immediately called Michael's home. Clarice answered. Michael had not yet come home. As far as she knew he was still at The Cow's Corner. 'Can you call him or call the pub? I don't want to sound too dramatic, but tell him on no account to leave there. He absolutely must wait till we arrive. And, Clarice, keep your doors locked and don't let anyone in whoever they are. I'll explain everything when I see you.' Arthur was already manoeuvring the coach to drive back the way they had come at the fastest speed he dared.

The landlord of The Cow's Corner was pleased with the day's takings. He had come to recognise that when the Outcasts were in the village consumption rose appreciably. On top of that his buffet bar continued to attract trade. However, what had surprised him this Saturday was that members of the home team, despite their defeat, had stayed on longer than usual. After the departure of the Outcasts the Middle Daychurch cricketers had seemed to hold a post-match seminar. The younger members of the Carter family, including those who had not been playing, had taken advantage to hang around and consume probably more than was wise. As their parents and elders were on hand the landlord was disposed to turn a blind eye.

When Charlie Colson came through the door the landlord wondered whether Christmas had come early. Although Charlie looked wistfully towards the pumps there was obviously something else on his mind. As soon as he spotted him he rushed over to Michael. 'Sorry to surprise you, but something urgent has come up.' 'Yes,' said Michael. 'Clarice called the pub. I'd left my mobile at home. I told her I was happy to stay here for an in-depth team talk. You know the kind of thing I mean.' He winked. 'Now what's this all about?' Without answering the question Charlie put his own. 'Is Brian around?' 'Carter or Stagden?' 'The latter.' 'No, funny you should ask. He got a phone call and rushed out with no explanation. He hasn't been back.' 'Right, I want you to come outside.' 'I didn't know you cared.' 'This is not funny, Michael. It's deadly serious and I mean deadly.' Charlie's demeanour seemed to convey something unusual and when David Pelham came into the bar wearing the same sense of urgency Michael complied.

Hurried farewells were said. Outside the trio marched to Arthur's coach. Michael noticed a light in the pavilion which puzzled him, but he was not given time to investigate. The coach took them to Michael's house. Clarice greeted them with the news that Brian Stagden had called asking if Michael could meet him in the pavilion. There was something very urgent he had to discuss with him without anyone else from the team being present. Arthur took over. In a few crisp sentences he explained why Michael should go nowhere near the pavilion and why he and his family should evacuate their house until tomorrow's deadline ('you know perfectly well what I mean, Michael') had passed. Arthur left nothing to the imagination and was pleased when Clarice overcame her husband's protestations. They were in the end persuaded to come to London with the Outcasts. Arthur knew where they could stay. In the morning it would be possible to review the whole situation and decide what more needed to be done.

Reflections

The next day was later referred to as Revelation Sunday. Arthur proposed that they should reassemble at the private hotel where Michael and his family had been installed. Symbolically the time was set for twelve noon. Not all the Outcasts made it. On the return to their own drop-off point in London some of those who thought their departure from The Cow's Corner had been excessively early reckoned that they could just make it through the door of The Sink and Plumber before last orders were called. Eight or nine Outcasts arriving at a late hour were enough to warm the heart of the landlord, but it had led to a few heads hurting in the morning. Yet they all believed they knew what there was to know.

It fell to Arthur assisted by Charlie to explain their theory to Michael. When he asked why they had not said any of this to him in the past Charlie said that it had seemed too sensitive. He left it to Arthur to admit that once they had got as far as learning the contents of Edwin's will Michael himself had featured in their suspicions. 'And you think,' said Michael 'that Brian might have killed me last night?' 'I'm not sure,' said Arthur. 'Everything up to that point had been made to look an accident. Remember the incident with the broken ski. I don't know why he tried to take you out then. His father was alive and well. It was unnecessary, but I think he may have got to the stage of being unable to stop himself. Last night with the unexpected death of his father you were very much in his way. My guess is that he would have kidnapped you and then decided on some way of disposing of you before noon today in another seeming accident. He and his mother between them were very inventive.'

'What's to be done? asked Michael. 'He can't just be left to get on with life. He can't touch the estate, but he might want personal revenge. Or,' as the thought struck him, 'he could go after Clarice or the kids.' 'There's just no evidence that's come to light. Nothing that would convince the police, let alone a jury. David found some letters hidden in the lavatory cistern back at the pavilion. They threatened to expose some wounding details about your Uncle Douglas, but I think that Brian placed them there well after Douglas' death. By then questions were being asked about the number of deaths in the Carter family. If the letters were found, as I am sure he intended, it would have added weight to the belief that Douglas had taken his own life. From all I know now I'm sure it wasn't suicide. I'm not sure how he did it, but I think Brian was your uncle's executioner.'

Arthur paused. 'There's one further point to consider, disturbing though it is. Once you've bought into this line of thinking there's no stopping the suspicion that all the deaths, excepting Philip's of course, were murders.' He paused again, this time for dramatic effect. 'Including Edwin's. The old man had a pretty robust constitution. Ironically his first-born, Kenneth, was not so well blessed. It created doubt in the mind of Brian and his mother – probably soon after they had congratulated themselves over the coup with Edwin's will. There was, of course, no serious risk that Kenneth would pre-decease his father, but maybe they needed insurance. The sooner that Edwin was out of the way the better. The countdown of years would then begin.' 'But it was diagnosed as heart attack when Grandpa Edwin died,' said Michael. 'Yes, but no-one knew whether his heart failure caused the accident or was a reaction when he realised he was going to crash. The car was never examined. Do you know what happened to it?' Arthur did not wait for answers. 'It was crushed at a garage not far away run by a certain very disgruntled Bill Pledger who Joseph sacked as the club umpire and with whom Brian Stagden had become very familiar. It's too late now for it to be checked, but the more I think about it the more likely that that is the explanation. It fits.'

'I ask again. Is there nothing that can be done?' Seeing Michael's distress, Arthur made an offer. 'I have a contact with someone who's very senior in the police. I'll run this whole story past him and see if he has any suggestions. But, if it's any comfort, I genuinely think that Brian Stagden will not strike again. He's covered his tracks so well to date, but he must know that I know what's happened even if I can prove nothing. He must also know that I will have spread my information to others. So, if anything else happens in Middle Daychurch, he will be the obvious suspect. That may not be a guarantee, but I hope it's some reassurance.' Michael did not seem entirely convinced, but could only say that he would make sure that Brian never played cricket alongside him again. 'Pity though, he was one of our best batters.'

The police eventually left 10 Cricketers Close, clueless as to who had killed Roy Groves and the whereabouts of Joyce Simpson. The gun from which the fatal shot was fired carried no fingerprints. The contents of the late man's briefcase yielded useful information regarding the fate of Frank Simpson and the criminal enterprise of which he had been part. They held a man under arrest for his involvement. It seemed that what was at issue between members of the gang was the whereabouts of the proceeds of a notorious diamond heist. The home and office of Roy Groves were raided to no avail. His wife seemed an entirely innocent party. Frank Simpson's will had been uncovered. It left the property in Cricketers Close to Shirley and the rest of his estate without detailed specification to his wife. That left a roof over Shirley's head, but not one which she felt the slightest desire to sleep under. She and Richard Love were now completely reconciled. He was determined to stand by her in every way as they pondered their future. Richard had been spared an embarrassing break-up with his lawyer girlfriend, Debbie. She and her sister were leaving the area to take up lucrative appointments elsewhere. Debbie was sorry. Richard was not. He had now discovered true happiness.

Charlie Colson had not expected to hear from Pete Simmonds, but the chef's voice over the phone betrayed real excitement. 'Thought you'd like to know.' He went on to report that the young chef who had walked out on them and seemingly some other restaurants, each time under a different name, had been arrested. Pete and his partner had been asked to identify the man. Not really sure why, Charlie felt a thrill run through him. 'When are you seeing him?' The answer was the next day. 'I'm going to email you a photograph of Brian Stagden. Please show it to this guy and ask him if he knows him. Watch his reaction.'

Twenty-four hours later Pete was even more excited. ''E's coughed,' he blurted down the phone. 'Went white, practically fainted and then it all poured out of 'im.' Charlie phoned Arthur, who in turn spoke to his police contact. 'Surely this makes a difference,' he argued. 'There's got to be a case for a search warrant now.' It transpired that even the local police had come to that conclusion.

There was one more Carter-related death in Middle Daychurch. Ethel Daniels died in her sleep. The cause of death in this case was never in doubt. Whether or not her son's passing may have affected her will to live inevitably lay in doubt. With her daughter-in-law and grandson in police custody it fell to Michael Carter to take charge. Whilst he made funeral arrangements Clarice began the patient task of sorting out Ethel's belongings. It was in the second week of her conscientious work that she came across an envelope bearing her husband's name. She left it to him to open it when they were both back home for supper.

The letter which Michael read proved to be a chilling testament. What emerged from it was Ethel's early approval for a plan put to her to persuade Edwin to draw up his will in a particular way. She had believed that this would allow her legitimised son to have his fair share of Edwin's estate without Edwin being aware of him. As the number of potential beneficiaries began to decline she had at first worried, but later she became alarmed. Her growing fears were expressed in such a way that they provided corroborating background to the prosecution which was mounted against Brian Stagden and his mother. Indeed it became clear that the acts of the son had been conceived and encouraged by the mother. There was insufficient evidence in respect of most of the deaths to sustain a murder conviction. The charge which Brian Stagden could not overcome was in respect of Garry Woodworth. The wet suit recovered from the house which he shared with his mother yielded vital evidence. A pubic hair from the hapless vicar had trapped in the zip of his assailant's wet suit as he had been pulled under the water.

Arthur suggested that a semi-celebratory gathering was called for in the wake of the unravelling of the Middle Daychurch mystery. He argued that Charlie deserved some tribute for his dogged belief that something very wrong had been occurring. Charlie had overcome the mockery and been proved right in the end even if not all his theories along the way had been upheld. The gathering was planned whilst Charlie was away on a recuperative holiday arranged for him by Liz and funded by her parents. The whole family had been on safari in Namibia and rightly (in Liz's view) cut off from the news.

Arthur had persuaded Michael Carter to join the party. Michael had insisted on putting a large sum of money into the pot. Charlie was keen to show off his photographs. 'We saw all the big five,' he reported with evident enthusiasm. 'Hope you didn't try to ride any, mate, like you did in Egalitières (*Unusually Cricket* 2010) and nearly killed yourself.' David Pelham pointed at a rhino. 'I should think that one could have finished the job.' 'Family photo?' Michael asked as a group of people were shown with glasses in their hands in the middle of the bush. 'I've met your in-laws,' said David, 'so who's the other lady in the picture?' 'She was just another passenger in our ranger's vehicle. An Australian lady, she said, but she sounded more English to me. She was very nice. A widow. I think she must have been well off. Obviously travelled a lot. Talked about Cyprus and Florida. Probably a bit too much, if I'm honest. Liz kept on encouraging her by saying she wouldn't mind going there.' Charlie flicked on to a shot of some lions remarking, 'That was a family group too.'

Charlie's praises were duly sung. Arthur's ingenuity was applauded. General satisfaction was felt. At a very late stage of the evening Charlie found himself propping up the bar next to Arthur. 'Do you know what?' he said. 'This mother of Brian Stagden. She must have been an evil witch. Who the hell was she? Where did she . . .?' At that point his fuddled brain ran out of words and his reaction was to reach for his pint. Not sure that Charlie was by that time in any condition to take it in, Arthur nevertheless supplied the information. 'Her name was Helen Morrison. She used to be in the hardware business.'

In the middle of the night Charlie woke from an alcohol-induced sleep and could not stop himself shivering as a memory haunted him. The whole story had not after all been told. And, as far as he was concerned, never could be.

Scorecards

First Match

Middle Daychurch Innings

Carter P.		b. Banks	4
Carter J.		b. Pelham	26
Carter D.		b. Banks	4
Carter G.	c. Rashid Ali	b. Banks	0
Bell		b. Banks	0
Norwell	c. Palmer	b. Thorogood	137
Carter M.	c. Birch	b. Colson	42
Carter A.	c. Rashid Ali	b. Thorogood	0
Carter T.	not out		0
Seymour		b. Colson	0
Love	absent		0
EXTRAS			7
TOTAL	(all out)		220

Bowling	*overs*	*maidens*	*runs*	*wickets*
Banks	4	0	42	4
Thorogood	6	3	21	2
Jenkins	7	0	48	0
Pelham	8	0	73	1
Colson	5.3	0	31	2

Outcasts Innings

Palmer	c&b.	Carter D.	47
Thorogood	c. Carter A.	b. Carter D.	41
Birch	c. Bell	b. Carter D.	18
Rashid Ali	run out		15
Colson		b. Carter D.	0
Jenkins	st. Carter J.	b. Carter D.	6
Pelham	LBW	Carter A.	16
Northwood	c. Norwell	b. Love	38
Newton		b. Love	11
Banks	not out		4
Jackson	c. Carter J.	b. Love	0
EXTRAS			6
TOTAL	(all out)		202

Bowling	overs	maidens	runs	wickets
Carter P.	6.2	1	37	0
Seymour	7.4	0	52	0
Carter D.	8	3	20	5
Carter A.	5	0	59	1
Carter T.	8	3	24	0
Love	1.3	0	4	3

Middle Daychurch won by 18 runs

Second Match

Outcasts Innings

Thorogood	c. Carter M.	b. Carter T.	11
Birch	c. Carter J.	b. Seymour	16
Faulds		b. Carter T.	0
Northwood	c. Stagden	b. Seymour	6
Jenkins	st. Carter J.	b. Carter A.	51
Burrill	st. Carter J.	b. Carter B.	54
Newton	LBW	Carter D.	20
Furness J.		b. Carter B.	0
Colson		b. Carter T.	29
Smith	LBW	Carter B.	24
Redman T.	not out		16
EXTRAS			23
TOTAL	(all out)		250

Bowling	overs	maidens	runs	wickets
Lingrove	7	2	39	0
Carter T.	8	0	32	3
Love	1	0	8	0
Seymour	2	0	15	2
Carter B.	3.3	0	56	3
Carter A.	8	0	58	1
Carter D.	8	2	21	1

Middle Daychurch Innings

Lingrove		b. Burrill	25
Carter J.	LBW	Burrill	8
Norwell	run out		52
Stagden	c&b.	Burrill	79
Carter M.	c. Newton	b. Burrill	43
Carter D.		b. Thorogood	4
Carter A.	not out		5
Seymour		b. Thorogood	1
Carter B.	not out		10
Carter T.	did not bat		
Love	absent hurt		
EXTRAS			24
TOTAL	(for 7 wickets)		251

Bowling	overs	maidens	runs	wickets
Thorogood	8	0	29	2
Jenkins	5	0	35	0
Burrill	8	0	66	4
Smith	6	0	60	0
Colson	2	0	26	0
Redman T.	3	0	26	0

Middle Daychurch won by 3 wickets

Middle Daychurch v. Nudgworth

Middle Daychurch Innings

Bell	retired hurt		0
Kirkham	run out		120
Norwell	run out		69
Lingrove		b. Pelham	12
Norrington		b. Bailey	20
Simmonds	LBW	Edrich	55
Seymour	st. Compton	b. Pelham	5
Carter D.	c. Wardle	b. Pelham	2
Carter A.	LBW	Edrich	8
Carter M.	not out		3
Love	LBW	Edrich	0
EXTRAS			30
TOTAL	(all out)		324

Bowling	overs	maidens	runs	wickets
Bailey	5	0	63	1
Pelham	8	1	38	3
Lock	6	0	59	0
Edrich	6.2	0	55	3
Kenyon	5	1	37	0
Brown	3	0	51	0

Nudgworth Innings

Simpson		b. Lingrove	0
Brown	c. Carter A.	b. Norrington	0
Kenyon		b. Lingrove	0
Hutton	c. Carter M.	b. Lingrove	7
Watson	c. Love	b. Carter D.	39
Wardle	c. Kirkham	b. Lingrove	0
Pelham	not out		27
Compton	LBW	Carter D.	6
Edrich		b. Carter A.	18
Lock	c. Norwell	b. Carter A.	10
Bailey		b. Carter D.	9
EXTRAS			7
TOTAL	(all out)		123

Bowling	overs	maidens	runs	wickets
Lingrove	5	2	6	4
Norrington	4	1	6	1
Carter D.	5.5	1	45	3
Carter A.	5	0	59	2

Middle Daychurch won by 201 runs

Fourth Match

Outcasts Innings

Palmer		b. Norrington	15
Thorogood	c. Seymour	b. Lingrove	8
Faulds	c. Seymour	b. Carter A.	51
Rashid Ali	LBW	Norrington	89
Burrill	c. Kirkham	b. Lingrove	65
Lederwood	c. Seymour	b. Norrington	3
Furness R.		b. Lingrove	38
Pelham	not out		7
Banks		b. Carter D.	12
Smith	not out		4
Redman N.	did not bat		
EXTRAS			4
TOTAL			296

Bowling	overs	maidens	runs	wickets
Lingrove	8	0	30	3
Norrington	8	0	40	3
Carter T.	8	1	58	0
Love	5	0	46	0
Carter D.	8	0	81	1
Carter A.	3	0	37	1

Fourth Match

Middle Daychurch Innings

Bell	c. Faulds	b. Banks	7
Kirkham		b. Burrill	46
Norwell	st. Rashid Ali	b. Furness R.	79
Stagden	c&b.	Furness R.	0
Love		b. Banks	52
Carter M.	c. Palmer	b. Smith	13
Carter D.		b. Furness R.	10
Seymour	c. Lederwood	b. Furness R.	0
Lingrove	LBW	Burrill	26
Carter T.	c. Thorogood	b. Banks	40
Norrington	not out		2
EXTRAS			13
TOTAL	(all out)		288

Bowling	*overs*	*maidens*	*runs*	*wickets*
Thorogood	6	1	27	0
Banks	5.4	2	26	3
Redman N.	5	0	26	0
Burrill	8	0	65	2
Furness R.	8	0	39	4
Pelham	3	0	36	0
Smith	4	0	57	1

Outcasts won by 8 runs

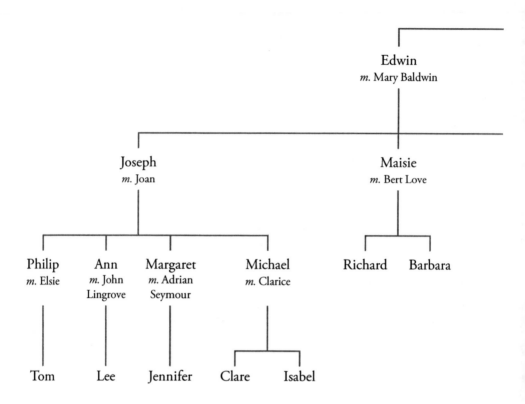

The Carter family

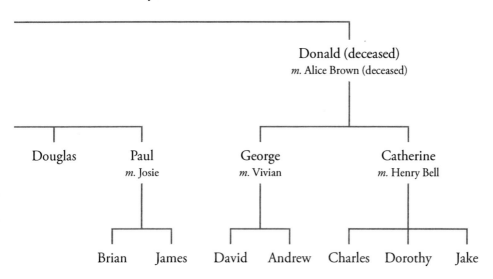

The author

ALAN HASELHURST was elected Member of Parliament for Saffron Walden in 1977 and served as Chairman of Ways and Means and Deputy Speaker of the House of Commons from 1997 to 2010. He was made a Privy Counsellor in 1999.

He is now Chairman of the House of Commons Administration Committee, Chairman of the UK Branch of the Commonwealth Parliamentary Association, and Chairman of the All Party Parliamentary Cricket Group.

He is a member (and now an Honorary Vice-President) of Essex County Cricket Club, serving on the Committee for 12 years until 2008. His other clubs are Yorkshire CCC (the county of his birth), Middlesex CCC, Rickling Green, Saffron Walden, Halstead, Langley, Audley End and Littlebury, as well as MCC. He is an honorary life member of Monton Sports Club in Greater Manchester. He is also a Lord's Taverner.

He still lives in a part of Essex which he is doing his best to keep rural.